Celebrating 40 Years of Play Research

Connecting Our Past, Present, and Future

PLAY & CULTURE STUDIES, VOLUME 13

Edited by
Michael M. Patte and John A. Sutterby

Hamilton Books

An Imprint of
Rowman & Littlefield
Lanham • Boulder • New York • Toronto • Plymouth, UK

Hamilton Books
4501 Forbes Boulevard, Suite 200, Lanham, Maryland 20706
Hamilton Books Acquisitions Department (301) 459-3366

Unit A, Whitacre Mews, 26-34 Stannary Street,
London SE11 4AB, United Kingdom

Library of Congress Control Number: 2016942719
ISBN: 978-0-7618-6816-3 (pbk : alk. paper)—ISBN: 978-0-7618-6817-0 (electronic)

Dedicated to

Sarah, Harrison, Oliver, Lillian, Rupert, JP, and Sylvester
for filling each day with playful exuberance
—M.M.P

Sandra, Andreu, and Sofia
—J.A.S.

Contents

List of Tables

List of Figures

Foreword

James E. Johnson

This lucky numbered volume celebrates the 40th anniversary of *The Association for the Study of Play* or TASP by publishing 10 chapters representing research on play in connection with many different topics, which is typical, but also with the intent of stimulating thinking about the past, present, and future of play studies. The authors and co-authors and the co-editors are to be commended for their contributions to this birthday party that marks with special recognition and praise the efforts of all those play scholars who have participated thus far in an important journey now clearly into the 21st century.

Since this organization's beginning there has been continued development of research activities and scholarship directed towards heightening awareness and understanding of play – leading to the emergence of a recognized new field and the apt designator Play Studies for the notable endeavors and accomplishments of our play pioneers, superheroes, and martyrs.

Play studies assumes that one can learn more about play by examining it carefully from many different angles than from just one vantage point. One learns and is informed by studying play through various lenses – biological, philosophical, sociological, and so forth. Play studies in principle also believes that the disciplines themselves not only complement each other for learning about play, but may also inform each other. However, for this to happen there has to be motivation to communicate across disciplinary lines aiming to creatively construct a wider and deeper concept map, cloud of understanding, or tree of knowledge about play in society.

The fact that there is interaction among members of the community of play scholars makes play studies as a field interdisciplinary and not just multidisciplinary. Indeed, cross fertilization of ideas has been a hallmark since the birth of the modern field of play studies, arguably with the beginnings of *The Association for the Anthropological Study of Play* (TAASP) in the early 1970s in Canada and the United States (Stevens, 2012).

Twenty-five people attended a planning meeting in May, 1974, at the Western Ontario campus to explore the possibility of creating a new organization devoted to promoting the study of homo sapiens at play. The first TAASP Newsletter begins:

> A sage once expressed the view that 'no man is an island'. If we substitute the term 'discipline' for 'man' we change only the wording of this old adage – the moral contained therein remains unaltered. In this day and age of the Global Village, the conscientious scholar cannot afford to hide behind the skirts of his mother discipline and ignore the possibility that others may share, and indeed be actively researching, areas of similar interest. (Salter, 1974, p.1)

TAASP was launched to foster research and scholarly interaction concerning play across the life span and included international members from the onset. The primary requirement for membership was interest in play study; members came from different areas and not just anthropology. Later TAASP was renamed *The Association for the Study of Play* (TASP).

TASP has met annually since 1974. Its purpose includes research, publications, symposia, conferences, workshops, social networking, and the production, integration, dissemination, and utilization of information from research findings about play. TASP has always been inclusive encouraging and appreciating ideas from members across all disciplines and fields of endeavor, novice and veteran scholars alike.

The acceptance of various tools of discipline inquiry, from soft to hard sciences, number crunchers to navel gazers, is another characteristic of play studies. The prevailing attitude is mutual respect for scholars interested in play studies, whether scholars are coming from social sciences, philosophy, humanities, biological sciences, humor studies, folk lore, comic studies, etc.

In addition to being multi- and inter- disciplinary, play studies can be a-disciplinary (this word was used by Brian Sutton-Smith, an inspirational leader and mover of TASP for many years). Play studies in its pure form is targeting play in itself. Emerging from and 'hovering above' all the different disciplinary foci on play comes a trans-disciplinary study, or play studies that is not like the study of play from any of the home disciplines of various scholars who have joined together to share in their pursuit of better understanding play. Although trained as a developmental psychologist and an expert in folklore, Brian Sutton-Smith has been unmatched in making play his glorious quest in academia until the time of his passing on March 7, 2015.

Those drawn to play studies do so for a variety of reasons. Perhaps many share an intrigue with daring to go a step further even if they are risking plunging into the depths of an abyss. It takes a certain amount of intellectual courage and 'true grit' to wade into areas of unpredictability, uncertainty, and multiple perspectives and enormous complexity. Play scholars seem to welcome this challenge. Perhaps they do because they are supported by like minded individuals with whom they not only share professional interests in play, but often have social and affective connections to go along with their shared commitments to better understand play.

All of us who have been involved in creating this anniversary Volume 13 of *Play & Culture Studies* are excited by our long past and never say die spirit when it comes to studying play, because play must be studied. We hope that this work contributes to our over-all developing field and to your own growth in understanding play. Enjoy the pages that follow but watch the cracks!

REFERENCES

Salter, M. (1974). Newsletter of The Association for the Anthropological Study of Play, Volume 1, Number 1.

Stevens, P. (2012). TA(A)SP: The formative years. *International Journal of Play, 1*(1), 96-102.

Acknowledgments

John and I are grateful to many people who helped make the thirteenth volume of *Play & Culture Studies* a reality. First, to the series editor James E. Johnson for his guidance and support throughout the editing process we own a debt of gratitude. Next, to Ashley Panko, a graduate student from Bloomsburg University for her technical support and dedication in putting the volume together. Finally, to our multidisciplinary colleagues who served as peer reviewers for the chapters in Volume 13 for their commitment and professionalism.

Andy Arleo, Universite de Nantes, France
Anna Beresin, University of the Arts, United States
Fraser Brown, Leeds Becket University, United Kingdom
JoAnne Cemore Brigden, Missouri State University, United States
Cindy Dell Clark, Rutgers University, Camden, United States
June Factor, University of Melbourne, Australia
Cleo Gougoulis, University of Patras, Greece
Myae Han, University of Delaware, United States
Olga Jarrett, Georgia State University, United States
James E. Johnson, The Pennsylvania State University, United States
David Kuschner, The University of Cincinnati, United States
Abby Loebenburg, Arizona State University, United States
Smita Mathur, James Madison University, United States
Ashley Panko, Bloomsburg University, United States
Nirmala Rao, University of Hong Kong, China
Jaipaul Roopnarine, Syracuse University, United States
Dorothy Singer, Yale University, United States
Peter K. Smith, Goldsmiths University of London, United Kingdom
Vejoya Viren, University of Texas, Brownsville, United States
David Whitebread, University of Cambridge, United Kingdom

Introduction

Michael M. Patte and John A. Sutterby

In his essay *TA(A)SP: The formative years*, Stevens (2012) details the beginnings of The Association for the Anthropological Study of Play, its theoretical rationale, its pioneering founders, and its seminal contributions to the study of play over the past forty years.

> Play, games, and sports are cultural products, and their rules and conduct reflect the wider values and sentiments of the cultures that produced them. Like all other cultural entities undergoing acculturation, when transmitted to other cultures they are shaped by the values of those cultures. In our increasingly multi-cultural world, therefore, any persons interested in play—coaches, supervisors, administrators, fans, as well as scholars, must recognize the cultural dimension. In 1973 a few North American scholars were sufficiently motivated by this recognition that they organized a new scholarly organization dedicated to examining and publicizing the cultural element in all forms of play. That early organization became The Association for the Anthropological Study of Play (TAASP); from 1987 to present, The Association for the Study of Play (TASP). (Stevens, 2012, p. 96)

Forty-two years since its founding TASP is recognized as the premier professional organization in academia throughout the world dedicated to interdisciplinary research and theory construction concerning play. During that time TASP has forged alliances with organizations advancing the study of play, organized yearly meetings to disseminate play research, and produced an impressive catalogue of research through a variety of publications (1974—present); edited collections including conference proceedings (1976-1987) and the Play & Culture Studies series (1998—present); and three peer-reviewed journals *Play and Culture* (1988-1992), *Journal of Play Theory &*

Research (1992-1997), and *The International Journal of Play* (2012—present).

Volume 13 of the Play & Culture Studies series titled *Celebrating 40 Years of Play Research: Connecting Our Past, Present, and Future* highlights contributions that reflect upon the rich forty-two-year history of TASP, that explore current interdisciplinary play research, and that advance future directions for play research. To this end, *Play and Culture, Volume 13* is organized into three sections: *Reflecting on Our Past, Exploring the Present, and Playing Into the Future.*

Section 1, *Reflecting on Our Past* focuses on the lessons learned from a group of ambitious scholars who organized a new association for examining the role of culture in all forms of play; reexamines a doctoral dissertation study on doll choice to assess racial identification and preference among black and white children in segregated and integrated kindergarten settings; and sheds light on a town's rich history as a central hub of toy production in the United Kingdom. In the first chapter, Phil Stevens Jr. reflects proudly as one of the founding members of TAASP on the cultural significance of the pioneering association for the study of play. Through a thoughtful analysis of the current play literature, Phil came to an uncomfortable conclusion, that contemporary scholars are unaware of TAASPs contributions to the understanding of play, that the great majority of its studies conducted from 1974 to the end of the last century lay buried and unacknowledged, and that these same scholars are expending time and energy replicating what has already been accomplished. Phil lays out five specific tasks for members of TASP and their students to rectify the current situation. In chapter two Olga Jarrett reexamines her dissertation doll choice research as a means to examine current issues surrounding school desegregation and cross racial collaboration and understanding in the United States. She reflects on the challenges of conducting such a study in contemporary school today due to the changing dynamics of early childhood education including few play materials and didactic, scripted curricular approaches. Vicki Thomas' chapter offers a historical account of changes in the commercial manufacture of toys in Northampton, England. The account covers how toy companies have evolved in the products they produce and how they have adapted to historical events like the second World War and the eventual consolidation of toy companies into larger and larger corporations.

Section 2, *Exploring the Present* provides a glimpse into the bourgeoning field of intergenerational play; explores the questions 'what is gendered play?' and 'what influence do toys have in children's gendered play?'; examines the role of cognition in solving popular puzzles; and introduces a number of issues related to geriatric play across the lifespan. In chapter four Cohen and Waite-Stupiansky examine the intergenerational play of pre-service teachers and older adults through the collection of play histories. The interactions between the college students and older adults serves several purposes. First, it helps the younger generation understand the play activities of the older generation. Second, it helps the college students examine how play has changed over time in terms of play settings and play materials. In the fifth chapter Heikkila seeks to understand the role of toys in children's gendered play. In her study, gendered play is understood to be a play situation where gender explicitly or implicitly matters through the use of language and through the way in which a play situation is carried out by the children taking part in the play. Alward's chapter examines the role of cognition in relation to individual paper and pencil puzzles generally found in newspapers. Drawing on the work of Piaget and the idea of the development of conservation in human cognition, he explores the rules that constrain what types of answers are appropriate in solving these puzzles. In chapter seven Nell and Drew highlight issues of geriatric play and how people continue to be meaningful players throughout the lifespan. They argue that play is an important quality of life factor as it impacts both mental and physical health and call upon the seminal work of Erik Erikson and the idea of 'transcendance', a return of play and joy for adults in their later stages of life.

Section 3, *Playing Into the Future* offers the unique and insightful perspective of the self proclaimed 'Empress of Play' Ann Marie Guilmette on those who have lead The Association for the Study of Play; makes the case for promoting an international dialogue and cutting edge approaches for researching play and culture; and implores play scholars to examining the topic with a wide ranging curiosity. In the eighth chapter, Ann Marie Guilmette reflects upon her 40-year relationship with TASP's most prominent players. Her essay eludes to timeless traditions, great debates, hilarious roasts, provocative keynotes, and bawdy presidential addresses. Using Chinese astrology as an intellectual overlay, she celebrates the foundational contributions of the men and women responsible for establishing, sustaining, and leading TASP into the 21st century. In chapter nine, Al-Mansour, Sevimli-Celik, and Johnson argue for a deepening examination of play and culture through a range of innovative research approaches (drawing tasks, participatory photography, participatory observation, video conferencing). The authors share the results of a transcultural study of play project focusing on mothers from the countries of Turkey and Saudi Arabia. In the volume's final chapter titled *Playing Into the Future*, Henricks calls on play scholars to invoke the spirit of play in its scholarly formulations. He argues that discipline specialization has worked against the study of play and believes that the advancement of play studies depends on the integration of various disciplines. Finally, Henricks implores the play study community to recognize and integrate both modernist and postmodernist approaches.

Readers of *Play and Culture Studies, Volume 13* will be enriched through exploring play's rich past, considering current trends in the study of play, and imagining play's limitless future.

REFERENCES

Stevens, P. (2012). TA(A)SP: The formative years. *International Journal of Play, 1*(1), 96-102.

Section I: Reflecting on Our Past

Chapter One

Forty Years at Play

What Have We Achieved?

Phillips Stevens, Jr.

KEYNOTE ADDRESS DELIVERED AT THE 40TH ANNIVERSARY
MEETING OF THE ASSOCIATION FOR THE STUDY OF PLAY
ROCHESTER, NY, APRIL 25, 2014

In the first decade of our existence we made great contributions to the under-standing of play, from all available angles. Forty years later, a comprehen-sive overview reveals that contemporary scholars seem unaware of our con-tributions, and have spent considerable time and energy repeating much of what we did. Great insight is now being offered by the rapidly expanding field of neuroscience, and much of our earlier conclusions about the impor-tant of play at all stages of human and most animal development are being confirmed. TASP was pioneering then, and we are today a unique organiza-tion, representing all fields, and we should make a concerted effort to resur-rect and broadly disseminate our important contributions.

Forty years ago we could not have imagined this event. It is a great honor for me to be here, and a truly unexpected fulfillment of a young scholar's ambition in 1974. I will spare the reader the reminiscences and thanks ex-pressed in my oral remarks, which I have here relegated to a footnote. [1]

It is fortuitous that TASP's fortieth annual conference was held jointly with the New York Folklore Society, whose journal I edited in the 1980s. Before I get to a review of our accomplishments, I want to offer a few reflections on the folkloric significance of the number forty, drawing from some observations I made in 1985 when we published the Fortieth Anniver-sary Issue of the journal (Stevens, 1985). In popular culture, popular senti-ment, the age of forty marks a significant milestone in life and in achieve-

3

ment. It too frequently means "over the hill," or the point where one begins to yearn for a selectively remembered past, or the age one might assert not yet to have reached—like Jack Benny (who died in the year of our founding).

In Biblical lore forty commonly means a considerable quantity or "a long time" (as compared to, say, three or seven, "a short time"). It rained on Noah for 40 days; Jesus was in the "wilderness" for 40 days. 40 days—1½ lunar months—were time enough for the complete overhauling or transformation of a human system or institution or personal way of life; and in 40 years—the duration of the Israelites' journey under Moses to the Promised Land, an entire generation would be replaced. My edition of the Oxford Concordance to the New Revised Standard Version has 92 entries—to forty, forty days, forty nights, and forty years! Of course there are many others. 40 acres and a mule. 40 winks . . .[2]

So, forty, especially forty years, is culturally significant; and we all should be proud.

But, as I will emphasize here, we should look back, into our early history. I have written about the heady time of our founding, and the remarkable people who shaped us, in the first issue of the *International Journal of Play* (Stevens, 2012). I hope you will read that short article; it contains some unique observations on our first five years, including the origin of our skeleton-and-orangutan logo—which I'm really pleased to see still in use!—and some important insights into the nature of our subject matter, which are essential background to what I will say here.

It's important that we keep in mind that TA(A)SP was the pioneer organization; it was and is unique; and not only is it still here, it seems quite healthy. Forty years later is an appropriate time for an assessment; and, fortuitously, our anniversary comes at an important—even, perhaps, pivotal—time for the study of play.

TAASP was founded with the rationale, as I said in my IJP article, that

> forms of play, games, and sports are cultural products, and their rules and conduct reflect the wider values and sentiments of the cultures that produced them. Like all other cultural things undergoing acculturation, when transmitted to other cultures they are shaped by the values of those cultures. In our increasingly multi-cultural world, therefore, any persons interested in play—coaches, supervisors, administrators, fans, as well as scholars, must recognize the cultural dimension. (p. 96)

The concept of culture, the focus and the unifying concept of the broad discipline of anthropology, needs some explication. It should be conceptualized as operating simultaneously on three levels. The first job of any scientific investigation is description. For us, this is the ethnographic, the level of straightforward reporting based on standard social science methods of data collection: observation, interviewing, and participation. No comparison, no analysis; but detailed description of the phenomena under study, in all their aspects and manifestations, in all conditions of their operation, including all potentially influential factors. The result is, in fact, the description of a cultural system, and it may be a lengthy process.

The ultimate aim of science is explanation. Situational explanations based in function may be possible at the ethnographic level, but explanation of phenomena is more meaningful at the ethnological level, the level of cross-cultural comparison of systemic ethnographic data, the level at which we can see correlations and patterns and begin to make general statements about humanity. From this level we can identify beliefs, behaviors and products that seem culturally universal—such as play—and hence possibly inherently human. That then brings us down to the biological level, which was recognized as essential to explanation over a century ago but which could not be investigated meaningfully until the development of the incredible methodologies of the brain sciences of today. It is here that the most important insights into the condition of being human are being made. Advances in neuroscience, especially some with direct relevance to our subject matter, are dizzyingly rapid today—in this paper I will refer to some that occurred during the months just before and after my Keynote Address!

In our early years, ethnology was sufficiently advanced that we could offer logical statements about the human condition. We built on the work of several giants in play studies, including alphabetically Stewart Culin, Roger Caillois, Karl Groos, Johan Huizinga, Iona and Peter Opie, John Roberts—I could go on with various others; but I must include Brian Sutton-Smith who was at once ancestral and vitally contemporary. We generally relied on Huizinga's classic definition of play, which play scholars then practically committed to memory:

> . . . a free activity standing quite consciously outside "ordinary" life as being "not serious", but at the same time absorbing the player intensely and utterly. It is an activity connected with no material interest, and no profit can be gained by it. It proceeds within its own proper boundaries of time and space according to fixed rules and in an orderly manner . . . (1955, p. 13)

In the first decade of our existence we analyzed this definition exhaustively, dissected it, wrote treatises on different elements within it, debated its apparent contradictions (e.g. "rules"), justified parts and modified parts of it. We recognized that play is universal in people and higher animals, and we looked at the play phenomenon in people cross-culturally and, I can say confidently, from all theoretical angles.

Now, 40 years later, where are we? And where is play scholarship generally? The invitation to talk to you obliged me to recognize and try to fill some huge gaps in my knowledge.

I had quit my intensive study of our subject in the early 1980s, though I made a few later contributions (Stevens, 1988, 1991, 1992). I have continued an interest in humor as play since my dissertation fieldwork in Bachama, Northeastern Nigeria in 1969-71 (Stevens, 1973) and later work in the same area, and have always hoped to publish a collection of Bachama trickster tales. So I have followed Don Nielson's work in humor, and just this year I found a new work with an intriguing title: *The Trickster Brain* (Williams, 2012).[3] But in the 1980s I went in other directions. From time to time a considerate President of TASP invited me back to a panel discussion by Past Presidents, at each of which I was flattered to have been included but had very little to say. So in mid-2013 when Michael Patte invited me to this role, I had some work to do! I went back and perused the magnificent archive of *Play and Culture Studies*, and I looked at the old Newsletters that are online at the TASP website, plus all the early issues in my own archives which should be available at your website by now. I reviewed all early volumes of our annual Proceedings, published by Leisure Press, and the complete set of our journal *Play & Culture* which I have saved. And I found myself mightily impressed by the work we have done, the insights we have published on this topic, this phenomenon of such critical importance to the development of apparently all complex life forms.

And then I reviewed some recent studies of play by some widely cited scholars including Burghardt (2005), Pellegrini and Smith (2005), Smith (2009), Pellegrini (2009, 2011), Bateson and Martin (2013), and some others. I relied heavily on their subject headings and indexes, and although I tried to be very careful I realize both that I might have missed some critical material, and that my selection might not be widely considered as fairly representative.

But even if there are some exceptions which I missed, I came to some uncomfortable conclusions—the great majority of what we did from 1974 to the end of the last century is buried, unacknowledged—and a lot of it is being done again, by contemporary scholars apparently unaware of the replication.[4] Play is being defined and re-defined; Huizinga is rarely cited. I was reminded of an observation by Clifford Geertz in his classic and oft re-printed paper, "Religion as a Cultural System," first published in 1966. Bemoaning what he saw as anthropologists' repeated declaration of well-established accepted theoretical conclusions about religion, he said,

> In art, the solemn reduplication of the achievements of accepted masters is called academicism, and I think this is the proper name for our malady also (Geertz, 1966, p. 2).

Now, to be sure, other disciplines similarly complain about reinventing the wheel; and this may be an enduring, endemic problem in the humanities and social sciences today. But it's unfortunate, wasteful of time and resources, and obviously detrimental to progress.

In my review, particularly startling is the fact that play scholars today still seem uncertain of what it is they are talking about, and see a need to begin their studies with a new definition. Consider, for example, Peter K. Smith's 2009 *Children and Play* (Wiley-Blackwell); and I think it's fair to say it's representative. He spends 6 pages (4-10) discussing various forms of play and "playful behavior," then there is a three-page section titled "Things that are Probably Not Play: Exploration, Stereotypic Behavior, Work, Rule-Governed Games."

"Things that are probably not play" . . . 35 years later. His entire book has one page titled "anthropological perspectives," but no discussion of the work of TAASP, or our rationale for why there should be an anthropological perspective, and only one of our publications is cited—see below. He mentions TASP on p. 217, simply as one of two societies dedicated to the study of play, the other being the International Toy Research Association. He does cite works of some of our early contributors, like Helen Schwartzman's 1978 study of children's play, *Transformations*, and David Lancy's "Play in Species Adaptation" in the 1980 Annual Review of Anthropology, and a couple of other anthropologists, including Fredericka Oakley's paper on play deprivation in infant macaques which was presented at our 2nd annual meeting in Detroit, and published in our first volume of Proceedings (Lancy & Tindall, 1976)—but it's likely he was referring to that article because the name of Oakley's more famous mentor, Peter C. Reynolds (who was not there for the presentation) was on the paper. To his great credit, in his recommendations for future research he mentions the work of Jaak Panksepp, of whom more later.

I made similar observations as I perused other recent studies by well-regarded scholars. Anthony Pellegrini's widely-cited 2009 work, *The Role of Play in Human Development*, cites no TASP studies at all, and does not even mention Huizinga. These are really unfortunate omissions, because the 21st century has seen a great revival of study of play in animals but there have been only a few studies of play among people. One other major one is Pellegrini's (2011) *Oxford Handbook of the Development of Play*, an edited collection of original writings by no fewer than forty (another instance of that important number!) modern scholars; but its focus is principally children and, again, neither TASP nor any of its publications are mentioned anywhere therein. The most recent general work I consulted is Patrick Bateson and Paul Martin's 2013 study, *Play, Playfulness, Creativity and Innovation* (Cambridge). In their preface they state:

> The different meanings given to the term 'play' have created much confusion and have contributed to the view that play is enigmatic and almost beyond the

boundaries of science. The categorization of play as any behaviour that is not 'serious' has tended to trivialize an activity that is likely to have important beneficial outcomes, both in humans and other species. (p. ix)

In his review of this book Pellegrini (2014) speaks of a long unproductive period in play studies (referred to also by several other modern scholars), "perhaps," he says, "due to (rightful) skepticism regarding some of the over-blown claims for play" and cites some names from the 1980s but doesn't specify the "over-blown claims." He praises some new directions which "have embedded their discussions in evolutionary biology," but I reviewed some of the works he cites and found them lacking in most of the ways that I critiqued Smith. Pellegrini had edited a festschrift for Brian Sutton-Smith in 1995, boldly titled *The Future of Play Theory*. Brian and some of the contributors were productive TA(A)SP members and officers (Garry Chick, John Loy, F.F. McMahon, Bernard Mergen, Helen Schwartzman), and in their individual papers some of them mention the association; but our contributions to the field receive no acknowledgement at all. And, given the title and the year of publication, I was disappointed to see no mention of a role for neuroscience.

Gordon Burghardt's comprehensive and exemplary 2005 study of play among animals also does not cite our early work, but he proposes a five-point definition of play which incorporates many aspects we liked, and adds some new ones, and which has been widely cited by other scholars.[5] Bateson and Martin recognize "neural correlates of play" (2013, p. 25) and include neuro-biological investigation among their "suggestions for future research" (pp. 127-8). Burghardt also sees promise in neuroscience, as we will consider in a later section. But first, let's look at one of the most basic foci of scientific explanation.

FUNCTIONS OF PLAY

In a 1977 TAASP essay justifying an anthropological approach to play, Brian paraphrased a 1972 statement by Margaret Mead:

> . . . that from any worthwhile scientific point of view, anthropologists had never really studied the subject. There were a few records here and there . . . and many accounts in the Human Relations Area Files, but in general these records did not tell you how this play was functioning in the lives of the players. (Sutton-Smith, 1977a, p. 222)

Brian stresses the lack of cross-cultural studies of *functions* of play. The methodology of science utilizes two principal facets of a phenomenon as guides to procedure: correlation and function. Science cautions that both are true but situational; alone their explanatory value is limited, but they may be useful guides to subsequent directions. In the first decade of our existence we identified a great number of socio-psycho-cultural functions of play, and we explored each one in great depth. Consider some of them. You will recognize them. Some are in titles of our proceedings, or in our essays in our journals, or in our Newsletters. The grammatical articles and prepositions like "as" or "in" or "of" or "and" may vary, sometimes in important, sometimes unimportant ways:

Play as/and exploration
Play and/as socialization
Play and/as enculturation
Play as performance
Play and cognition; play as cognitive function
Play and/as paradox
Play as/and creativity
Play and intimacy
Play and inter-ethnic communication
Play and humor
Speech play—play and/in language
Play in species adaptation (seen already; Lancy, 1980)

And play and health, stressed by Burghardt (2005) and Panksepp and Biven (2012), and emphasized again in this conference (Dell Clark & Patte, 2014).

And "play as adaptive potentiation"—recognize that? Right, Brian Sutton-Smith, the title of a short essay he marked as a "footnote to his 1976 Keynote Address," but one that he had used before. Brian is responsible for other combinations, identification of other functions of play—such as 1974 "play as novelty training."

And more. We laid out a multitude of functions of play. I don't want to dwell longer on this, but function is an important topic identified by many contemporary researchers, especially the two I consider the most insightful and important: Burghardt 2005 and Panksepp and Biven 2012. And none of our early work on the functions of play is cited by today's scholars.

We talked for long about the definition problem, as I indicated earlier. Following Gregory Bateson's insightful essays, 1972 (1955) "A Theory of Play and Fantasy," and 1956 "The Message 'This is Play,'" we reconsidered Huizinga's notion of "voluntariness" and "purpose." We reconsidered the presumption of a sharp dichotomy between play and work; see, for example, Helen Schwartzman's special section of five papers in Michael Salter's 1978 edited collection of our third Annual Proceedings. When I was President of TAASP the Society for the Anthropology of Work was forming, and I approached them with the proposal to discuss a theoretical collaboration—but it quickly became evident that they were not interested in work as a human state, but rather the social and political organization of work. In my 1978 Presidential Address (Stevens, 1980) I followed up on Schwartzman's themes and offered consideration of Mihaly Csikszentmihalyi's (1974) concept of "flow" as a way to conceptualize Huizinga's observation that play "absorbs the player intensely and utterly," and hence as a way to re-consider the play-work dichotomy. Contemporary scholars (e.g. Brown 2009, p. 63ff.) have come to similar conclusions about what we have called a "play element in work" without citing us.

In my 1978 address I said that among our failings was not heeding Bateson's warnings about mixing logical-type levels, about confusing members of classes with the classes themselves. "What we have been doing," I said, "has been to confuse the play act with the experiencing of the act" (1980, p. 322; italics original). This accords with anthropology's distinction between an etic perspective on culture, categorizing things according to the researcher's own classificatory scheme; and an emic perspective, that of the actor. And, Bateson and Schwartzman and I, all in different contexts, had suggested that a problem with trying to identify play as a unit of study, which was a problem then and is identified as a problem today by scholars I have cited, is that play is not bounded, not easily separable by the observer; it rather is a state, on a cognitive, conceptual, and behavioral continuum. I am confident that neuroscientists like Panksepp, Biven, and Siviy will bear this out, and that this will form the basis for a new and generally accepted definition of play.

THE MOST FRUITFUL DIRECTIONS FROM HERE

Promising new directions are set by Steve Siviy, as he indicated in his keynote address at this conference (Siviy, 2014), and his mentor, Jaak Panksepp.[6] In preparation for this paper I found Panksepp's 2012 work, *The Archaeology of Mind*, with psychotherapist Lucy Biven, to be especially valuable. Chapter 10 is titled "PLAYful Dreamlike Circuits of the Brain: The Ancestral Sources of Joy and Laughter." A central theme in this chapter is fun. Fun! I'll get back to this later. In a section titled "The neurochemistry of play" Panksepp shows that laughter promotes opioid release in the brain which produces the same kind of response that generates the transcendent state in the altered states known in anthropology as shamanic ecstasy and possession trance (which we can note was discovered in the 1980s; see, e.g., Prince 1982; and see the 2014 work by Berk and colleagues cited below). This chapter should be required reading for all students of play. But Panksepp, too, ignores most earlier research, including all of ours, and feels a need to freshly define his subject. He falls back on a sentiment exasperatingly common among today's researchers: "It is hard to define play, but you know it when you see it" (p. 352). He goes on to justify his contention that play is fundamentally a neurological phenomenon, that it is based in a core brain system, and that it is essential for normal growth and development . . .

> . . . a play-deprived child probably has a higher than normal probability of not only being diagnosed with ADHD but also of becoming reclusive and a potential menace to society as an adult (2012, p. 386).

Here he cites Stuart Brown 1998, a work cited by most students of play among animals. He mention's Harry Harlow's mid-1950s work on social deprivation among monkeys, but he does not mention Stephen Suomi and Harlow's 1971 study, "Monkeys at Play" in the *Natural History* supplement (*Natural History*, 1971), which stated essentially the same thing about play deprivation in human children. This was not a TASP product; but its lead paper is by Edward Norbeck, who delivered the first TAASP keynote address in 1976; Sutton-Smith is there too (1971); and in the 1970s we obtained 100 extra copies from *Natural History* and distributed it widely among our membership. But in Panksepp's conclusion, most frustrating to me is this:

> Until recently, most neuroscientists and psychotherapists have tended to ignore the possibility that all young mammals, including our children, have a fundamental urge to PLAY—to engage in joyful competitive interaction. Perhaps "play" was seen as childish and therefore unimportant (2012, p. 386).

Let's back way up. In my essay, "Laying the Groundwork for an Anthropology of Play" (1977), which I had intended be regarded as a prelude to Brian's earlier "Towards an Anthropology of Play" (1977), I addressed these very issues. Neuroscience then was rudimentary, but we saw the same issues and came to the same conclusions. Early in that essay I said,

> Play is an integral aspect of human social behavior. Play, moreover, is a phenomenon at least as old as the emergence of the phylogenetic Class Mammalia, from which the genus Homo is a very recent offshoot . . . there exists a fundamental fact with which anthropologists must reckon: both animals and people play from birth to death. Moreover, there is solid evidence that play is not only an integral aspect of the mammalian way of life, but that it is necessary and vital to "normal" development of both the organism itself, and of its maturation as a social being. We social scientists, particularly we anthropologists, have come very late to the serious recognition of what is a vitally important behavioral phenomenon. (1977, pp. 238-239)

There may be weak support for my second sentence, above; in the first clause I might have inserted the word "surely" or less boldly, "probably". But note that 38 years ago I declared that our recognition of this dimension of play was "late." A later section of my essay is titled "Toward a Biological Perspective" (pp. 242ff.), and one of my proudest items from that period of my career is a letter from neuroscientist Michael Persinger of Laurentian University, praising that essay. I will return to this topic later.

PLAY AS AN "ALTERED STATE"

Near the beginning of this paper I said that the 40th anniversary of TASP "comes at an important—even, perhaps, pivotal—time for the study of play." Several of the scholars I have cited cite various work by Stuart Brown, M.D. (e.g. 1998, 2009[7]). I found an online TED talk, "Serious Play," he delivered in May 2008[8], in which he declares that play is an "altered state."

On April 2 this year I happened to hear a conversation on NPR's *On Point* with Edward Slingerland, author of *Trying Not To Try: The Art and Science of Spontaneity* (Slingerland, 2014). Slingerland, a scholar of Asian studies, had been inspired by the Chinese concept of *wu-wei.* He begins his discussion with the concept of "being in the zone," and cites comments by musicians, actors, and athletes, especially an article in Sports Illustrated, February 2, 2005, which quotes several basketball players about how their best play occurred in such a state. On the NPR program was Mihaly Csikszentmihalyi, who said that what Slingerland was talking about, was flow! (40 years, we might note, after his introduction of the concept. It was met with skepticism, even rejection then; today it is part of the vocabulary of psychology.) And we recognize it as the essence of the play experience.

I will relate just a few more serendipitous examples of my suggestion that this is a pivotal time for the study of play[8].

In all the functions we identified, and more, there is one which almost all scholars then and now recognize, but which most[9] pass right over, "play is fun."

"Play is fun." We take it for granted, and we move on to the next, more erudite, apparently more promising. But several current research trends indicate that "fun" is a fundamental and probably essential element of the normal, healthy development of perhaps all living things. And if we make "fun" a subset of "play," we're right on. Again by coincidence, 2014 saw the publication of a social history of fun by historian John Beckman (2014). We can examine this concept at all my three levels of culture simultaneously.

I happened to see an article in *The Week* magazine for March 14, 2014, titled "Do atoms play?" by David Graeber, condensed from a longer version in *The Baffler* No. 24, 2014. The online promotional blurb says "Hey, it's our play issue, in which David Graeber hopscotches over the robotic universe of contemporary science and winds up inventing a new law of reality. Barbara Ehrenreich calls for a science that can explain why fun is fun." The article speculates about the universality of play among animals, even insects. [10] And just a month later, April 14, I learned of an NPR follow-up by Alva Noë, "Could Playfulness be Embedded in the Universe?" [11]

Variations on the aphorism, "laughter [or humor] is the best medicine" have been expressed from biblical times (*Proverbs* 17:22), through the *Reader's Digest*. Laughter usually signifies fun (acknowledging and deferring what Panksepp calls "dark laughter . . . in response to seeing others hurt, humiliated, or embarrassed . . . "; 2012, p. 370) and both Panksepp and Siviy have presented extensive evidence that sounds which can only be labeled laughter are features of animal play. There has been some exciting new research on this phenomenon—also in the first half of 2014!—that has great significance for understanding play as a state of consciousness, and its functions in organismic development and operation. Lee Berk and his colleagues at Loma Linda University Medical Center (Berk et. al. 2014a & b; Bains et.al., 2014) reported to the meeting of the Federation of American Societies of Experimental Biology in April, that joyful laughter very quickly generates gamma brain wave patterns similar to those generated by meditation. All regions of the brain become involved, and dopamine, which fuels the reward circuitry of the brain, flows freely, creating an intensely pleasurable effect. A news report of May 2 says,

> It's the brain wave pattern associated with cognitive "flow," with being "in the zone," with the highest state of cognitive processing . . . Meditation, with its well-established benefit, may not be for everyone, Berk said. But humor is certainly within reach for all, and in the interest of our health, he said, we should dose ourselves regularly. (Healy, 2014)

And my wife showed me an article in the July 2014 issue of *Real Simple* magazine (Wadyka, 2014) summarizing several clinical studies of the past decade that verify positive neuro-physiological functions of laughter, for immune function, pain tolerance, cardiovascular health, and memory retention [12] —the latter referring to one of Lee Berk's studies.

Play is fun, fun is pleasurable, enjoyable, carefree—healthy. Play is healthy. Playful fun, fun-filled play has a serious important developmental function, innumerable clinical studies show it—happy people are healthier than unhappy people, and this statement has been verified for people at all stages of life, from infancy through old age. Play—fun—is therapeutic, refreshing, invigorating, good for us. I am certain that neuroscience will soon show that play has some sorts of clear restorative functions with important evolutionary value.

In conclusion, I'd like to set five tasks for TASP members and their students.

1. First, and immediate. How could play scholarship have been so careless? Why has our work been so blatantly ignored by recent and contemporary scholars? These are not just rhetorical questions—I think their answers will be helpful to the remedy—and a remedy really is essential. One of you, or a committee of you—being mindful, of course, of problems with "committees" (remember the definition of camel! [13]), should go back through our history and compile the definitive volume on where the study of play really stands today.

2. All of academia is fragmented; let's acknowledge that, and work at better cross-disciplinary communication. Get our stuff out there, into the academic organizations, libraries, databanks, clearinghouses, indexed digital archives. Remember, TASP is really the only organization that stands astride the whole field, and can be the central clearinghouse for play data.

3. The definition problem. Far too much time and energy have been spent on this. I have recommended Burghardt's (2005, pp. 70-82). Let us agree to agree with Huizinga 60 years ago and the neuroscientists of today that play is a cognitive state on a continuum of consciousness, which the player of any age can freely move into and out of and back into again. But lest any think that we're ruling out sports and games that are governed by rules, let us return again to Huizinga's sub-title: "the play element in culture" (my italics [14]). The cultural context of play is essential to our investigations.

4. Play is fun. Fun is a tremendously, incalculably important element of play. Explore that. The cognitive and physiological functions of happiness. People like Gordon Burghardt, Steve Siviy and Jaak Panksepp will guide you. [15]

5. And one thing more. Remember another *Reader's Digest* column, "My Most Unforgettable Character"—I have several in my life, and one is Alyce Cheska. She died on October 6, 2012, at the age of 91. A remarkable woman, one of a few to whom we owe the existence of this organization. Her archives are housed at the University of Illinois at Urbana-Champaign. Here's a project for a young play scholar—an essay on her life and contributions to our field of study.

NOTES

1. Two of our founding giants, Allan Tindall and Alyce Cheska, have passed on – Allan in 1976; his arm-twisting brought me into this field of study, and I dedicated our second volume of Proceedings to his memory (Stevens, 1977); and Alyce in 2012; I will say more about her later. Others are still quite active. Co-founder Kendall Blanchard is here! From Americus, GA, Jimmy Carter country, just to be with us. Ann Marie Guilmette joined the association a year or two after our founding; she is a neighbor of mine, in Ft. Erie, Ontario, and I'm glad to see she is on the program. I contacted some others from the early years: our first president Michael Salter,

and Helen Schwartzmann, David Lancy, and Claire Farrer all send us their regrets and best wishes. I am sorry that Brian Sutton-Smith can't be with us, his inexhaustible energy and good cheer stimulated us over the years. It is fortuitous that the New York Folklore Society is meeting with us; I was the Editor of their journal, *New York Folklore*, for six years in the 1980s, the later years with Ellen McHale, who is on our program. I extend my deep gratitude to Michael Patte, who invited me to deliver this address, and who made available many TASP publications from the last two decades. Thanks also to Marcia Nell, who made various adjustments to the Program to accommodate me. Thanks again to Michael for his invitation to revise my talk for publication, and for his flexibility in scheduling. The written version has benefited greatly from last-minute and cordial in-put from Lee Berk and Gordon Burghardt.

2. At this point in my talk, I said, "I hope not. I protested to Michael Patte that a serious talk should not be scheduled right after lunch!"

3. And I was attracted by its subtitle, *Neuroscience, Evolution, and Narrative*. But I was quickly disappointed; it is almost immediately clear that the author's intended scope is far beyond his expertise.

4. This year Anthony Pellegrini (2014, p. 92) spoke of "the earlier period of research, the 1970's and 1980s, [which] saw an out-pouring of research and theory…" That statement should refer to us! But he cites only researchers in child psychology.

5. Burghardt's "five criteria" are discussed at length in Chapter 3 of his great work. Elsewhere (Graham & Burghardt, 2010, p. 394) he summarized them:

> Briefly, these criteria state that play is (1) incompletely functional in the context in which it appears; (2) spontaneous, pleasurable, rewarding, or voluntary; (3) differs from other more serious behaviors in form (e.g., exaggerated) or timing (e.g., occurring early in life before the more serious version is needed); (4) is repeated, but not in abnormal and unvarying stereotypic form (e.g., rocking or pacing); and (5) is initiated in the absence of severe stress.

6. An early draft of the TASP 2014 conference program listed Panksepp as delivering Saturday's keynote address. I found it particularly exciting, and supportive of my themes, to have mine flanked by two papers from current neuroscience. Alas, Panksepp couldn't attend.

7. Brown's 2009 work is a personal memoir in conversational tone; I cite it here as an overview of his multi-faceted career.

8. In their overview of 100 years of studies of animal play, Graham and Burghardt (2010, p. 411) also suggest that, with the potential of neurobiology, "we may be on the brink of a new phase of play research;" and in a 2014 survey of play's evolutionary history among animals Burghardt notes, "With the rapid development of neuroscience it seems likely that experimental studies of the function of play in laboratory model animals will increase rapidly" (p. 95). I should mention here the 2009 work by Sergio and Vivien Pellis, *The Playful Brain: Venturing to the Limits of Neuroscience* because it is cited by so many contemporary students of animal play; but I must say that its provocative title is misleading: it is very narrowly focused on rats, with comparative reference to a few other animals, and it doesn't go near the "limits" of neuroscience (and, ho hum, it doesn't mention TASP or any of our earlier studies).

9. There are exceptions. Robert Fagen (1992), for example, spoke extensively of the restorative value of fun. This important article appeared in Volume 5 of our journal, *Play and Culture*, which was by then well established in academia.

10. The author and a companion casually observe the apparently playful antics of an inchworm, and refer to studies of ants and other insects. Gordon Burghardt referred me to his 2012 study of spiders (Pruitt, Burghardt, & Riechert, 2012)

11. Visited at: http://www.npr.org/blogs/13.7/2014/04/13/302189232/could-playfulness-be-embedded-in-the-universe

12. The others were: immune function: referring to a 2003 study by Mary Payne Bennet and others, in *Alternative Therapies in Health and Medicine*; pain tolerance: a 2011 study in *Proceedings of the Royal Society B; Biological Sciences*, by Robin Dunbar; cardiovascular health: referring to uncited "recent studies" by Michael Miller, MD, of Center for Preventive Cardiology, University of Maryland Medical Center, Baltimore.

13. "A camel is a horse designed by a committee."

14. Huizinga had originally subtitled his work "the play element *of* culture," postulating that play is fundamental to culture itself, and in his 1938 Foreword, reprinted in English translations (1955, vii) he reports that he vehemently held to this position.

15. In September 2015 Gordon Burghardt referred me to the January 2015 issue of *Current Biology*; the 25th Anniversary issue of that important journal, with a special section devoted to "the biology of fun"! (http://www.cell.com/current-biology/issue?pii=S0960-9822%2814%29 X0025-4).

REFERENCES

Bains, G., Berk, L., Daher, N., Lohman, E., Petrofsky, J., Schwab, E., & Deshpande, P. (2014). Effectiveness of humor on short-term memory function and cortisol levels in age matched elderly and diabetic subjects vs. control group. *FASEB J.* 28(684), 4.

Bateson, G. (1956). The message, "This is play." In Bertram Schaffner, ed., *Group Processes: Transactions of the Second Conference* (pp.145-242). New York: JosiahMacy, Jr. Foundation.

Bateson, G. (1972). A theory of play and fantasy. (orig. 1955). In Bateson, *Steps to an Ecology of Mind: Collected Essays in Anthropology, Psychiatry, Evolution and Epistemology* (pp. 177-193). San Francisco: Chandler Publishing Co.

Bateson, G. (1978). Play and Paradigm. Keynote Address, 3rd Annual Meeting of TAASP, San Diego, CA, April 1977. In Salter, Michael, ed., *Play: Anthropological Perspectives* (pp. 7-16). Proceedings of the 3rd Annual Meeting of TAASP. West Point, NY: Leisure Press.

Bateson, P., & Martin, P. (2013). *Play, Playfulness, Creativity and Innovation*. Cambridge: University Press.

Beckman, J. (2014). *American Fun: Four Centuries of Joyous Revolt*. New York: Pantheon Books.

Berk, L., Alphonso, C., Thakker, N., & Nelson, B. (2014a). Eustress humor associated laughter compared to stress differentially modulates EEG power spectral density across frequency bins 1-40Hz. *FASEB J.* 28(684), 10.

Berk, L., Alphonso, C., Thakker, N., and Nelson, B., (2014b). Humor similar to meditation enhances EEG power spectral density of gamma wave band activity (31-40Hz) and synchrony. *FASEB J.* 28(684), 5.

Brown, S. (1998). Play as an organizing principle: Clinical evidence and personal observations. In M. Bekoff and J.A. Byers, eds., *Animal Play: Evolutionary, Comparative, and Ecological Perspectives* (pp. 243-259). Cambridge U.P.

Brown, S., with Vaughan, C. (2009). *Play: How It Shapes the Brain, Opens the Imagination, and Invigorates the Soul*. New York: Avery.

Burghardt, G. M. (2005). *The Genesis of Animal Play: Testing the Limits*. Cambridge, MA: MIT Press.

Burghardt, G. M. (2014). A brief glimpse at the long evolutionary history of play. *Animal Behavior and Cognition* 1(2), 90-98.

Clark, C. D., & Patte, M. (2014). Play as a healing act: Creative excursions, imaginativereframings, and the transformative power of bisociation. Paper presented at TASP, April.

Csikszentmihalyi, M. (1974). *Flow: Studies of Enjoyment*. Chicago: PHS Research.

Fagen, R. (1992). Play, fun, and communication of well-being. *Play & Culture* 5(1), February, 40-58.

Geertz, C. (1966). Religion as a cultural system. In Michael Banton, ed., *Anthropological Approaches to the Study of Religion* (pp. 1-46). London: Tavistock.

Graber, D. (2014, March 14). Do atoms play? *The Week*, 40-41.

Graham, K. L., & Burghardt, G. M. (2010). Current perspectives on the biological study of play: Signs of progress. *Quarterly Review of Biology* 85(5), December, 393-418.

Healy, M. (2014). Laughing found to elicit physical, mental benefits of meditation. (*Los Angeles Times*) In *The Buffalo News*, Friday, May 2, p. A9.

Huizinga, J. (1955). *Homo Ludens: A Study of the Play Element in Culture*. Boston: Beacon Press (orig. Dutch 1938; English trans.: Routledge & Kegan Paul 1949).

Lancy, D. F. (1980). Play in species adaptation. In Bernard J. Siegel, Alan R. Beals, & Stephen A Tyler, eds., *Annual Review of Anthropology* (pp. 471-495). Alto, CA: Annual Reviews, Inc.

Lancy, D. F., & Tindall, B. A., eds. (1976). *The Anthropological Study of Play: Problems and Prospects*. Proceedings of the First Annual Meeting of the Association for the Anthropological Study of Play. Cornwall, NY: Leisure Press.

Natural History. (1971). *Play*. Supplement, December.

Norbeck, E. (1971). Many at play. *Play. Natural History* supplement, December, 48-53.

Oakley, F. B., & Reynolds, P. C. (1976). Responses to social play deprivation in two species of macaque. Paper presented at the first annual meeting of TAASP, Detroit, April.

Panksepp, J., & Biven, L. (2012). *The Archaeology of Mind*. New York: W.W. Norton.

Pellegrini, A. D., ed. (1995). *The Future of Play Theory: A Multidisciplinary Inquiry into the Contributions of Brian Sutton-Smith*. Albany, NY: SUNY Press.

Pellegrini, A. D. (2009). *The Role of Play in Human Development*. New York: Oxford University Press.

Pellegrini, A. D., ed. (2011). *Oxford Handbook of the Development of Play*. New York: Oxford University Press.

Pellegrini, A. D. (2014). Review of Bateson, Patrick, & Paul Martin, *Play, Playfulness, Creativity and Innovation* (Cambridge U.P. 2013). *International Journal of Play* 3(1), 92-94.

Pellegrini, A. D., & Smith, P. K., eds. (2005). *The Nature of Play: Great Apes and Humans*. New York: Guilford Press.

Pellis, S., & Pellis, V. (2010). *The playful brain: Venturing to the limits of neuroscience*. London: Oneworld Publications.

Prince, R. (1982). The endorphins: A review for psychological anthropologists. *Ethos* 10(4), Winter, 303-316.

Pruitt, J. N., Burghardt, G. M., & Riechert, S. E. (2012). Non-conceptive sexual behavior in spiders: A form of play associated with body condition, personality type, and male intrasexual selection. *Ethology* 118, 33-40.

Salter, M. (1978). *Play: Anthropological perspectives*. New York: Leisure Press.

Schwartzman, H. B. (1978). *Transformations: The Anthropology of Children's Play*. New York: Plenum Press.

Slingerland, E. (2014). *Trying not to try: The art and science of spontaneity*. New York: Crown Publishers.

Smith, P. K. (2009). *Children and play: Understanding children's worlds*. Malden, MA: Wiley-Blackwell.

Stevens, P., Jr. (1973). *The Bachama and their Neighbors: Non-Kin Joking Relationships in Adamawa, Northeastern Nigeria*. Ph.D. dissertation, Department of Anthropology, Northwestern University. An Arbor: University Microfilms, #74-7828.

Stevens, P., Jr., ed. (1977a). *Studies in the Anthropology of Play: Papers in Memory of B. Allan Tindall*. Proceedings of the 2nd Annual Meeting of TAASP, Atlanta, March-April. West Point, NY: Leisure Press.

Stevens, P., Jr. (1977b). Laying the groundwork for an anthropology of play. In Stevens, ed., *Studies* (pp. 237-249).

Stevens, P., Jr. (1980). Play and work: A false dichotomy? In Helen B. Schwartzman, ed., *Play and Culture*. Proceedings of the 4th annual meeting of TAASP. West Point, NY: The Leisure Press, pp. 316-324.

Stevens, P., Jr., ed. (1985). *New York Folklore*, 11, 1-4, 40th Anniversary Edition.

Stevens, P., Jr. (1988). Table tennis and sorcery in West Africa. *Play & Culture* I(2), Summer, 138-145.

Stevens, P., Jr. (1991). Play and Liminality in Rites of Passage: From Elder to Ancestor in West Africa. *Play & Culture*, special issue in honor of Brian Sutton Smith. Garry Chick, ed. 4(3), 237-257.

Stevens, P., Jr. (1992). On "depth" in play, culture, and ethnographic description. *Play & Culture* 5(3), 252-257.

Stevens, P., Jr. (2012). TA(A)SP: The formative years. *International Journal of Play* 1(1), March, 96-102.

Suomi, S. J., & Harlow, H. F. (1971). Monkeys at play. *Play. Natural History* supplement, December, 72-76.

Sutton-Smith, B. (1971). Children at play. *Play. Natural History* supplement, December, 54-59.

Sutton Smith, B. (1974). Play as novelty training. *In One Child Indivisible.* Proceedings of the Conference of NAEYC, 227-58.

Sutton-Smith, B. (1977a). Towards an anthropology of play. In Stevens, P., ed., *Studies*, 222-232.

Sutton-Smith, B. (1977b). Play as adaptive potentiation. (orig. in *Sportswissenschaft* 5, 1975, 103-118). In Stevens, ed., *Studies*, 232-237.

Siviy, S. (2014). How the brain uses play to help prepare for life. Keynote address given at TASP 40th anniversary conference, April 24.

Wadyka, S. (2014). You just gotta laugh. *Real Simple*, July, 144-151.

Williams, D. (2012). *The Trickster Brain*: Neuroscience, Evolution, and Narrative. Lanham, MD: Lexington Books.

Chapter Two

Doll Studies as Racial Assessments

*A Historical Look at Racial Attitudes
and School Desegregation*

Olga Jarrett

For nearly 75 years, forced-choice doll studies have been used to assess the racial self-identification and preferences of young black and white children. The Clark and Clark doll study paradigm that found that black children rejected black dolls and identified themselves as white influenced the Brown v. Board of Education, Topeka, KS (1954) decision that segregated schools were inherently unequal. This paper reports on doll choice research including the Jarrett's dissertation study (1980) using a free choice doll play story-telling scenario to assess racial identification and preference among black and white kindergarteners in segregated and integrated settings. White children chose more own-race dolls to initiate their stories but many white children in integrated settings chose black dolls as friends. Black children appeared to choose color of dolls randomly in both segregated and integrated settings. This paper reviews trends since 1980, both in terms of doll studies and in terms of desegregation/re-segregation.

I joined The Anthropological Association for the Study of Play (TAASP) while a doctoral student in the mid-1970's, having learned about the association from Dr. Barry Klein, student of Dr. Joe Frost and my first academic advisor. At that point, the organization was only a few years old. By the time of my first conference attendance of The Association for the Study of Play (TASP) in 1998, I was engaged in several areas of play research leading to publications on playfulness in science and the effect of recess on classroom behavior. But one major study has never been published, my dissertation, completed in 1980. I was reworking it for submission to a journal when our youngest son was born 5½ weeks prematurely, providing me with a very reasonable excuse to postpone writing. Now, after a mere 30-year postponement, the theme of this volume, "reflecting on our past, exploring the present, and playing into the future" prompts a revisit to my dissertation that used a doll study technique to explore the topic: *Assessment of Racial Preferences and Racial Identification of Black and White Kindergarten Children in Mono-racial and Bi-racial Settings* (Jarrett, 1980). A re-examination of the dissertation offers an opportunity to look at the historical context in which the research was conducted, share a doll play methodology that could be useful to current researchers, and examine the current issues surrounding school desegregation and cross-racial collaboration and understanding in the U.S. In presenting this dissertation research, I thank my dissertation advisor, Dr. Lorene C. (Quay) Pilcher, whose superb mentorship influenced and still influences the quality of my work.

BACKGROUND

Historically, doll studies have played an important role in the assessment of racial identity and attitudes in America. Dr. Mamie Phipps Clark designed the first doll study for her master's thesis at Howard University in 1939. Using choice of black or white dolls to study racial self-identity and preference of African American children, she found that the majority of the black children preferred the white dolls and rejected the black dolls. This research, *The development of consciousness of self in Negro pre-school children* (APA, n.d.), was published with her husband, Dr. Kenneth B. Clark in 1939. Using both segregated and integrated populations of black children ages three to seven, the Clarks then conducted numerous studies using the following experimental situation. Children were presented with four dolls dressed in diapers. Two dolls were brown with black hair and two were white with yellow hair. The children were then asked the following questions in order (Clark & Clark, 1947):

1. Give me the doll that you like to play with.
2. Give me the doll that is a nice doll.
3. Give me the doll that looks bad.
4. Give me the doll that is a nice color.
5. Give me the doll that looks like a white child.
6. Give me the doll that looks like a colored child.
7. Give me the doll that looks like a Negro child.
8. Give me the doll that looks like you.

Though some of the children played with the dolls during the assessment, this was not primarily a playful situation. Some of the children who were talkative and relaxed at the beginning of the experiment became upset when required to self-identify. "Indeed, two children ran out of the testing room, inconsolable, convulsed in tears" (Clark & Clark, 1947, p. 178). Across these studies, the Clarks found the majority of children age five and up preferred the white dolls and labeled the black dolls as bad. Some also identified themselves as white and in a subsequent coloring activity, colored themselves much lighter that they actually were. Some of the children may have chosen white dolls because few black baby dolls were available at that time. Collectors of African American dolls (Hix, 2013; Irons, 2013) note that early black dolls were mammy dolls, topsy-turvy dolls (can be turned inside out to switch doll colors), and homemade rag dolls, dolls quite different from the ones employed by the Clarks. However, the emotional reactions of many of the children suggest that something deeper and more sinister was occurring. Clark and Clark concluded that racial segregation damaged children's self-perceptions, and their research provided important testimony against segregated schools in the cases leading up to Brown v. Board of Education, Topeka, Kansas. Footnoting the Clark and Clark research, Chief Justice Earl Warren wrote:

> To separate [blacks] from others of similar age and qualifications solely because of their race generates a feeling of inferiority as to their status in the community that may affect their hearts and minds in a way unlikely ever to be undone... Segregation of white and colored children in public schools has a detrimental effect upon the colored children. The impact is greater when it has the sanction of the law; for the policy of separating the races is usually interpreted as denoting the inferiority of the negro group. A sense of inferiority affects the motivation of a child to learn. Segregation with the sanction of law, therefore, has a tendency to [retard] the educational and mental development of negro children and to deprive them of some of the benefits they would receive in a racial[ly] integrated school system. (FindLaw for legal professionals, 347 U.S. 483 [1954])

Brown v. Board of Education has special significance in psychology, since this was the "first time that psychological research was cited in a Supreme Court decision" and because social science data were so important in the case (Benjamin, Lundy, & Crouse, 2002, p. 38). Nearly 20 years later, when TAASP was formed, school desegregation, which was to proceed "with all deliberate speed," was just being reluctantly launched in many communities. Desegregation in Atlanta, where my dissertation study was conducted, had taken place in steps since 1961 in response to court rulings under the case of Calhoun v. Cook filed by the NAACP against the Atlanta School Board in 1958. In 1961, a grade-a-year plan was implemented that allowed black children to transfer to white schools if they wished and that year nine black students transferred to previously all white schools (Georgia Advisory Committee to the U.S. Commission on Civil Rights, 2007). In 1965, all grades were desegregated, enabling black children to transfer to white schools, space permitting. Five years later, free transportation was offered to black children wishing to attend white majority schools. Still, the vestiges of a dual school system remained. Only 39% of the schools could be considered desegregated, with 10% or more minority students. In response to another court order, a compromise agreement was reached in 1973 (Research Atlanta, 1973). In this agreement, a black superintendent, Dr. Alonzo A. Crim, and other black administrators were hired, school racial quotas were set for the hiring of teachers, schools were paired and rezoned, and the recruitment of black transfer students was increased. This plan increased the number of bi-racial schools, desegregating all of the white schools but leaving over 60% of the schools black segregated. Due to white flight, between 1968 and 1980 Atlanta lost more white students than did any other city in the nation, and by 1986 the public school population was 93% black (APS timeline, n.d.).

DISSERTATION METHODS AND FINDINGS (JARRETT, 1980)

The major purpose of the research was to compare the effects of segregated and integrated settings on the racial attitudes of black and white kindergarten children. Another purpose was to better understand the meaning of racial preference and self-identification by relating these variables to other measures and eliminating some of the methodological problems of previous research. Previous findings with young black children have been interpreted to mean that white-choice behavior reflected negative own-race feeling and poor self-esteem but with young white children research has been interpreted to mean that white-choice reflected either a good self-image or prejudice toward blacks. A doll play scenario was developed to separate own-race and other-race attitudes.

Setting

The dissertation research was conducted with 96 kindergarten children in an all white suburban school, an all black parochial school, and three bi-racial public schools in metropolitan Atlanta. All schools served both middle and lower income families. The sample was evenly divided by race, sex, and setting and the demographics of the schools also reflected the demographics of the neighborhoods. The three bi-racial schools served 58%, 62%, and 75% black children with 76%, 71%, and 80% of all the children, respectively, receiving free and reduced-price lunch.

Doll Play Story-Telling Procedure

Clark and Clark's methodology appeared to have some concerning issues. The forced choice requirements did not allow the children to like both black and white dolls. This confounded using the methodology to examine both same-race preference and other-race acceptance. Also, it was not playful. My adaptations stemmed from my childhood dollhouse play, my interest in miniatures, and my involvement in the civil rights movement. For the dissertation, I created a scenario that permitted children to use dolls in a semi-structured story telling situation and enabled them to employ all black dolls, all white dolls, or dolls of both colors. This approach is based on the assumption underlying play therapy: that the child expresses his feelings about significant people through socio-dramatic play with dolls representing those people (see Axline, 1948).

I prepared four dollhouse size families (two white and two black) because no suitable commercial dollhouse dolls could be found. I purchased four identical white bendable "Brown Family" dolls from Sears and painted two families two shades of brown. I then consulted with African American racial identity researcher, Dr. Margaret Beale Spencer, who at that time was a professor at Emory University. She noted what I should have noticed: my paint job made the black dolls less attractive than the white dolls, and I also needed to paint the white dolls. My final doll families were as follows: Two families were painted brown, one a dark brown, the other a medium brown. The hair of the adult dolls was painted black but the boy and girl dolls were given textured hair made from black furry fabric. The two white doll families were painted with white flesh-colored paint. The white adult dolls had brown painted hair. One white boy and one white girl were given brown hair cut from a doll wig; the other boy and girl received similar blond hair. The dolls were re-dressed in more durable and attractive clothes so that pairs of black and white dolls were dressed exactly alike. Four black and four white raters agreed that the doll families were equally attractive. Figures 2.1 and 2.2 show the dolls and the procedures.

In the assessment situation, the experimenter, working with children individually, asked each child to choose a doll family with a boy and a girl to live in a cardboard screen "house." The dolls chosen were coded according to how many own-race dolls were selected. The score, called *racial preference*, could range from 0 (no own-race dolls) to 4 (all own-race dolls). The child was then shown a box of dollhouse furniture and encouraged to arrange the furniture in the house.

Figure 2.1.　Dollhouse families.

Figure 2.2.　Child arranging dolls and constructing a story.

After the child had arranged the furniture, he/she was invited to choose two dolls, a best friend and a next best friend, to visit and play in the house. These choices were coded and yielded three *friendship choice* scores. The first two scores, *best friend choice* and *next best friend choice* were obtained by assigning a 0 or 1 to each doll chosen, with 0 representing an other-race choice and 1 representing an own-race choice. The third score was *total friendship choice*, a sum of own-race scores on *best friend choice* and *next best friend choice*. A total friendship choice score of 0 represented no own-race choices; a score of 1 represented one doll chosen from each race; and a score of 2 represented two dolls chosen from the child's own race.

I then encouraged the child to tell a story about what happened next. For motivational purposes, the story was taped, and at least part of the story was played back for the child to hear. Most children participated enthusiastically, choosing dolls and arranging furniture. Almost all made up a story, sometimes lasting 15–20 minutes. For those interested, the instructions and scoring procedures are found in the Appendix.

Finally, each child was asked which doll he/she would be in the story and which doll looked the most like him/her, yielding 0 to 2 own-race choices in racial self-identification. It was assumed that racial preference and racial identification scores reflected degree of own-race acceptance. It is also assumed that friendship choice scores reflected degree of acceptance of other races. Enough dolls were available for the subject to choose all own-race or all other-race dolls, if desired. In order to evaluate reliability of the doll choice procedure, 26 children (eight from the black mono-racial group and six from each other group) were retested a month later with the storytelling procedure. A comparison between initial doll choice and retest doll choice showed that 75% of the children were consistent in choice of doll they would be in the story (88.9% of all white children, 88.9% of black children in the bi-racial setting, and 25% of the black mono-racial setting children. Similarly, 88.5% of the children were consistent in choice of the doll that looked like them (100% of the white children, 83.3% of the black children in the bi-racial setting, and 75% of the black children in the all black setting).

A socio-metric examination by Asher, Singleton, Tinsely, and Hymer (1979) of the child's choice of friends he/she liked to play with was employed in the two most evenly bi-racial classrooms and allowed a comparison between color of doll choice and race of friend choice. A self concept measure (Brown, 1966) showed almost perfect scores for both races with little variability for either race. Therefore, these will not be discussed in detail.

RESULTS

As a measure of racial self esteem, children were asked Who would you be in the story (*would be*)? and Which doll looks most like you (*look like*)? Table 2.1, shows how black and white children in mono-racial and bi-racial settings answered this question.

The variable, *racial identification,* was created by adding the *would be* and *look like* scores. In order to ascertain whether the children differed in self-identification by race and setting, a MANOVA was computed with black/white and mono-racial/bi-racial as the independent variables and own racial preference, racial identification, and self concept as the dependent variables. The results were significant for race, $F(3, 99)= 10.639. p < .001$. There were no main effect differences for setting and no interactions. Subsequent 2 (race) x 2 (setting) ANOVAs indicated that white children chose

significantly more own-race dolls than did black children on racial preference, $F(1, 92) = 20.70, p < .001$ and on racial identification, $F(I, 92)= 25.11$,
$p <.001$. Table 2.2 shows the means and standard deviations for the three
dependent variables.

Table 2.1.   Choice of dolls representing racial identification

	Doll the child would be in story		Doll that looks like the child	
	Other race doll	Same race doll	Other race doll	Same race doll
White				
Mono-racial	3	21	1	23
Bi-racial	3	21	2	22
Black				
Mono-racial	13	11	8	16
Bi-racial	12	12	7	17

Table 2.2.   Means and standard deviations for own-race racial preferences (0-4), racial identification (0-2), and self concept score (out of 14 total)

	Racial preferences		Racial identification		Self concept	
	Mean	Sd	Mean	Sd	Mean	Sd
White						
monoracial	3.25	1.33	1.83	.48	13.00	1.02
biracial	3.21	1.18	1.78	.51	12.96	1.49
Black						
monoracial	1.67	1.71	1.08	.78	13.08	1.10
biracial	2.08	1.56	1.21	.78	13.08	1.35

A third analysis examined choice of doll friends by race and setting using
chi-square. The black children chose dolls similarly, with 19 children in the
all black setting and 21 children in the bi-racial setting choosing at least one
black doll and 5 children in the all black setting and 3 children in the bi-racial
setting choosing two white dolls as friends. However, the white children
differed according to setting, $X^2(1)= 4.15$, $p < .05$. Table 2.3 shows doll
choice of the white children.

To assess the validity of the choice of dolls' friends as an indicator of
cross-racial friendship, a correlation between choice of at least one other-race
doll and choice of other-race best friends was computed using socio-metric
data from the two most racially balanced classrooms (55% and 58% black).
This analysis showed a significant correlation between choice of dolls and
choice of friends, $r = .52$, $p < .01$. However, this relationship occurred be-

Table 2.3.   Doll choice by white children according to setting

	All white dolls chosen	At least one black doll chosen
Mono-racial setting	14 (58.3%)	10 (41.7%)
Bi-racial setting	7 (29.2%)	17 (70.8%)

cause of the correlation within the white sample (r = .62) rather than the black sample (r = .34).

DISCUSSION

An examination of the means of children's choice of dollhouse figures to live in the house (*racial preference*) and on choice of dolls they would be in the story and that look the most like them (*racial identification*) suggests that white children showed white preference whereas black children chose almost randomly. Specifically, 64.5% of the white children chose all-white doll families to initiate their stories while only 27.1% of the black children initiated their stories with all-black doll families. However, an additional 39.6% of the black children used one or more black dolls in mixed-race families, making a total of 66.7% of the black children who started their stories with some black dolls. Lower rates of racial self-identification and self-choice among black children could be the result of lower self-esteem, as interpreted earlier by the Clarks, or it could reflect unfamiliarity with black dollhouse families and the occurrence of more bi-racial families among the black sample than the white sample. [A pilot study I conducted in a diverse private school in the 1990's suggested that at least some children chose dolls to reflect their own families including two daddy dolls and two mommy dolls in gay and lesbian families and a parent of each race in biracial families.] Further research might also note whether doll choice reflects two parent or single parent households. In the dissertation study, all of the children chose both a father and a mother doll, probably representing the ideal family.

Doll Play Story-telling Procedure

This methodology appears to be a useful technique for assessing the racial attitudes of white children, given high test-retest consistency and the significant correlation between peer choice and doll friend choice. The black children in the bi-racial setting also exhibited high test-retest consistency in the procedures designed to measure own-race attitudes. However, it cannot be assumed that self-acceptance and other-acceptance factors were adequately separated for these children. Test-retest consistency was low for the black children in the mono-racial setting. On the second administration, 37.5% of these children started their stories with different race dolls, 25% identified themselves as a different race, and 75% switched the race of doll they wished to be in the story. There was no directionality to the change. This inconsistency raises doubts about the reliability of this procedure for this population. Perhaps, as suggested by Banks (1976), many black children choose black and white dolls at random.

For both black and white children, the doll play story-telling procedure was a pleasant, low pressure, low anxiety experience. It did not introduce racial stereotypes and was acceptable to school administrators. Children of both sexes and both races delighted in the opportunity to play with the dolls, arrange the furniture, and talk into the tape recorder. Though the semi-structured aspect of the procedure meant that choice, an important aspect of the definition of play (Klugman & Fasoli, 1995), was somewhat limited, most children clearly were playing as they told their stories. Many children had to be coaxed into ending their stories; some asked for an opportunity to "tell another story." Children not in the sample repeatedly asked for the opportunity to play with the dolls and tell a story. In a similar study comparing kindergarten and first-grade children (Jarrett & Quay, 1984) the methodology was equally popular with first-graders. The doll play story-telling procedure might also be applicable for the intermediate grades, since older children in a pilot study indicated that they enjoyed the experience. This procedure could be incorporated into the school language arts program at early childhood or intermediate levels, combining data collection with practice in oral communication.

CONCLUSION

Possibly, the most important finding of the study concerns the effect of desegregation on the white children's choice of friends. White children in segregated classrooms showed a definite white bias while most white children in bi-racial classrooms chose friend dolls in the doll study and actual classroom friends of both races.

UPDATE 2014

Play Trends

The years since 1980 and 2014 have seen some negative trends. In 1980, kindergartens were places where children played with dolls, dollhouses, blocks, puppets, and dress-ups. A doll play study was not an oddity in such classrooms. However, today, many kindergartens have no play materials (Miller & Almon, 2009; Almon & Miller, 2011). They use books and worksheets to teach academics that used to be taught in first grade. A former kindergarten teacher, now a recent Ph.D. graduate, recalls the day a truck arrived at her school; loaded up all the blocks, play housekeeping furniture, dolls, dollhouses, and puppets; and hauled them off to a school warehouse, leaving her only with curriculum materials for teaching state kindergarten reading and math standards. If permission could be obtained to do such a study today, children might be less familiar with dollhouse people of either race, in spite of the increased commercial availability of dollhouse families representing several races (products.lakeshorelearning.com). In school, children play together less in other ways too. Now, many children do not have recess (Jarrett, 2013) and there are nine Atlanta Public Schools without playgrounds (Fortner, Faust-Berryman, & Keehn, 2014).

Effects of Desegregation

According to the Harvard Civil Rights Project, integrated classrooms have promoted gains in three areas: "enhanced learning by all students, higher educational and occupational aspirations particularly among minority students, and evidence of positive social interaction among members of different racial and ethnic backgrounds" (Kurlaender & Yun, 2002, cited in Gallagher, 2007, p. 15). According to Kirp (2012), black students who attended integrated schools did better in many ways than those who remained in segregated schools. They were more likely to graduate from high school and college and later earned 25% more than those in segregated schools. The author suggested that these advantages were due to a higher investment from society in these integrated schools and that the students were held to higher expectations. Research on the Charlotte-Mechlenburg schools found that "the more time both black and white students spent in desegregated elementary schools, the better is their academic achievement (measured by standardized tests) and the higher are their secondary track placements" (Mickelson, 2002, p. 7). These benefits could be explained by "better material and human resources" but also by the beneficial effects of "classroom diversity on thinking" (p. 7).

However, some research is mixed on whether desegregation has promoted better outcomes for black children. According to John (2014), school integration has not meant school equity, as some black children have been tracked into remedial classes. Research comparing teacher expectations and referrals by race found that teachers had more positive expectations for Asian and white students than for Latino and black students, making referrals that reflected these expectations (Tenenbaum & Ruck, 2007). Another study comparing white and nonwhite teacher attitudes toward black and white children indicates that white teachers evaluate black children more negatively than they evaluate white children, especially in schools where over 40% of the children are black (McGrady & Reynolds, 2013).

For the black community, the current concern seems to be school quality rather than integration. Although lack of school resources and the humiliation of being denied entrance to neighborhood schools were important reasons for school desegregation, research by Walker (1996) indicates that black schools before desegregation had certain advantages, including highly committed, well educated, and caring black teachers. Many excellent black teachers lost their jobs during desegregation. Many predominantly black schools are currently plagued by lack of resources and a revolving door of inexperienced teachers. Also, schools are being called upon to solve academic problems that have their origins in racism, poverty, and lack of resources rather than education *per se*. My own work involves preparation of the very best teachers for high poverty schools serving black and immigrant children, teachers who are committed to staying in these schools rather than using them as stepping stones for "better positions." But does that mean that school integration is no longer important?

Re-segregation

Another trend is the abandonment of desegregation by the Supreme Court. The case of Milliken v. Bradley, 1974 (FindLaw, 418 U.S. 717) struck down busing as a necessary way to desegregate Detroit area schools. By the new millennium, federal policy focused not on desegregation but on narrowing the achievement gap in largely segregated schools (Kirp, 2012) through No Child Left Behind (2001) and later through Race to the Top (2009). According to Kirp, (2012), offering "the sobering lesson that closing underperforming public schools, setting high expectations for students, getting tough with teachers, and opening a raft of charter schools isn't the answer." The cases of Meredith v. Jefferson County Board of Education and Parents Involved in Community Schools v. Seattle School District No. 1 [2007] further limited the use of race as a way to integrate schools (Greenhouse, 2007), effectively dismantling further integration attempts (Bigg, 2007). As of 2007, Atlanta Public Schools (Georgia Advisory Committee Commission on Civil Rights, 2007) was one of 35 school districts in Georgia that had *unitary status*, meaning that it was no longer under court order to desegregate. Currently, there are fewer classrooms in the Atlanta Public Schools that are truly biracial than there were in 1980. During the 2010–2011 school year, the school population identified as 79% black, 1% Asian, 6% Hispanic, 12% white, and 1% multiracial (Governor's Office of Student Achievement, 2010–2011). Out of the 65 elementary schools, 41 enroll at least 95% black or multiracial students and 38 have no white students. Nine schools enroll at least 40% white students with three of these enrolling at least 75% white students. Only one school is as racially balanced as the bi-racial schools studied in the dissertation. Research on suburban schools (Frankenberg & Orfield, 2012) gives many examples of white flight to the suburbs, followed by blacks and Latinos looking for better housing and better schools. Encouraged by "racial steering of prospective home buyers," white families then move further and further from the city, promoting resegregation of schools (Orfield, 2012, p. 229).

A recent "equity audit" of Atlanta Public Schools conducted by a Georgia State University research team (Fortner, Faust-Berryman, & Keehn, 2014) shows that schools serving higher percentages of white students have more experienced teachers than schools in the black majority sections of the city. Six of the nine schools without playgrounds serve only black children, three have some Hispanic children (10% - 39%), and none have any white children (Governor's Office of Student Achievement, 2010–2011). My own research in a neighboring county, shows a disparity in playground quality between virtually all black or all Hispanic schools and schools with higher white populations (Jarrett, 2014).

Peace educators in Northern Ireland and Israel see school integration as one way to counter hostile community divisions between Catholics and Protestants and between Jews and Arabs (Hughes & Donnelly, 2007). Although currently only 6% of the schools in Northern Ireland and only four schools in Israel are truly integrated, research suggests that integration is possible and promotes collaboration. Gallagher (2007) expresses concern that, in contrast, American schools are becoming more segregated following a period of retrenchment that has undone much of the desegregation in the 20 years following Brown v. Board of Education. The following examples from my own experience show just how separate some black and white communities are. A black retired Atlanta teacher and school administrator, on assuming a faculty teaching position at our university, confessed that she had never before taught a white person. When I (white female) visited an all-black kindergarten class, I told the children they could ask me questions. Their first question was: "Why do you hate black people?" A recent conversation with a white parent revealed that he assumed that the mostly black middle school his son would be assigned to was a bad school. Societies with little communication between races have the seeds for misunderstanding or worse.

Recent Doll Studies

Most research on racial self-acceptance continues to employ forced-choice of dolls or drawings of children differing in skin color (Clark, 1992; Gopaul-McNicol, 1992; Powell-Hopson & Hopson, 1992; Burnett & Sisson, 1995; Jordon & Hernandez-Reif, 2009; Byrd, 2012), and the findings tend to be similar to Clark and Clark (1947; 1950). These findings could be explained, at least partially, by the recognition even by young children, of "white privilege" and the advantages of being white in America (McIntosh, 1989).

A CNN pilot demonstration study designed by Margaret Beale Spencer (CNN, 2010) used drawings with five different skin shades rather than dolls. This study found the following: When asked about positive characteristics (smart, nice), white children showed white bias and when asked about negative characteristics (looks bad, dumb, mean) showed bias against dark skin. When asked about both positive and negative characteristics, black children chose skin colors close to the mean, rather similar to the medium brown choice shown in research with black adults (Coard, Breland, & Raskin, 2001). Though an article on the study claimed that the CNN research showed "white and black children biased toward lighter skin" (CNN U.S., 2010), Spencer noted that "white youngsters are even more stereotypic in their responses concerning attitudes, beliefs…, and preferences than the African-American children." The findings of this study could actually suggest that black children exhibit less bias than white children.

Final Thoughts

Gary Orfield (2012, p. 217), professor of education, law, political science, and urban planning at UCLA, states the following about re-segregated schooling:

> Segregation has never succeeded in producing equal schools or truly viable communities on any scale. In the context of American society, separate is unequal because of the imbalance of power and resources of many kinds across the racial lines and the deeply rooted attitudes that blame the victims of segregation for the inequalities they face. If we do not achieve integration where it is possible, we will be deepening the divisions in our society and undermining the future of many communities, just as the stakes are rising very dramatically. We now face the dual challenges of massive demographic transition and intense world competition, both of which demand that we educate all our people and prepare our youth to live and work successfully in extremely diverse communities.

Improving test scores, required by No Child Left Behind (2001) and Race to the Top (2009) is not sufficient to "prepare our youth to live and work successfully in extremely diverse communities" (Orfield, 2012). According to Kirp (2012), "if we're serious about improving educational opportunities, we need to revisit the abandoned policy of school integration."

Play and the Applicability of Doll Play Story-telling Paradigm

No Child Left Behind and Race to the Top use test scores to evaluate both schools and teachers, often increasing time for "test prep" and decreasing time for play and hands-on projects. Healthy school experiences include not only adequate resources, competent and committed teachers, and a diverse student body but also opportunities to have fun together. Dramatic play and block play in kindergarten encourage perspective taking and collaboration. Recess, supervised by caring, observant adults, provides opportunities for children of different ethnicities to play together in positive ways. Projects in science and social studies are not only challenging and fun; they require collaboration, often across gender and racial lines. The doll play story-telling scenario (1980) proved to be a non-stressful way to assess own-race identity and cross-racial relationships, both of which are important in a diverse society. It was fun for both black and white children. We recommend this methodology for further research examining the effects of integration, especially with white students.

REFERENCES

Almon, J. & Miller, E. (2011). The crisis in early education: A research-based case for more play and less pressure. Retrieved from www.allianceforchildhood.org

American Psychological Association (APA) (n.d.). Featured psychologists: Mamie Phipps Clark Ph.D. and Kenneth Clark, Ph.D. Retrieved from www.apa.org/pi/oema/resources/ethnicity-health/psychologists/clark.aspx

Atlanta Public Schools (APS) Timeline (n.d.). Retrieved from www.mindspring.com/~sartor/gradyhs/APS_chronology.htm

Asher, S. R., Singleton, L. C., Tinsley, B. R., & Hymel, S. (1979). A reliable sociometric measure for preschool children. *Developmental psychology, 15,* 443–444.

Axline, V. M. (1948). Play therapy and race conflict in young children. *Journal of Abnormal and Social Psychology, 43,* 300–310.

Banks, W. C. (1976). White preference in blacks: A paradigm in search of a phenomenon. *Psychological Bulletin, 83,* 1179–1186.

Benjamin, J., Lundy, T., & Crouse, E. M. (2002). The case of Kenneth B. Clark. *American Psychologist, 57*(1), 38–50.

Bigg, M. (2007, August 29). Report: Segregation in U.S. schools is increasing. *Washington Post.* Retrieved from *http://www.washingtonpost.com/wp-dyn/content/article/2007/08/29/AR2007082902111 pf.html*

Brown, B. (1966). The assessment of self-concept among four-year-old Negro and white children: A comparative study using the Brown-IDS self-concept referents test. Bethesda, MD: EIRC Document Reproduction Service, ED036378.

Brown v. Board of Education, Topeka, KS (1954). Retrieved from http://caselaw.findlaw.com/us-supreme-court/347/483.html

Burnett, M. N. & Sisson, K. (1995). Doll studies revisited: A question of validity. *Journal of Black Psychology, 21*(1), 19–29.

Byrd, C. M. (2012). The measurement of racial/ethnic identity in children: A critical review. *The Journal of Black Psychology, 38*(1), 3–31.

Clark, K. B. & Clark, M. P. (1950). Emotional factors in racial identification and preference in Negro children. *The Journal of Negro Education, 19*(3), 341–350. Retrieved from http://www.jstor.org/stable/2966491

Clark, K. B. & Clark, M. P. (1947). Racial identification and preference in Negro children. Retrieved from i2.cdn.turner.com/cnn/s010/images/05/13/doll.study.1947.pdf

Clark, K. B. & Clark, M. K. (1939). The development of consciousness of self and the emergence of racial identification in Negro preschool children. First published in *Journal of*

Social Psychology, S.P.S.S.J. Bulletin, 10, 591–599. Retrieved from http://psychclassics.yorku.ca/Clark/Self-cons/

Clark, M. L. (1992). Racial group concept and self-esteem in black children. In A. K. H. Burlew, W. C. Banks, H. P. McAdoo, & D. A. Azibo (Eds.), *African American psychology: Theory, research, and practice* (pp. 159–172). Newbury Park, CA: Sage Publications.

CNN (2010). CNN Pilot Demonstration. Retrieved from i2.cdn.turner.com/cnn/2010/images/05/13/expanded_results-methods-cnn.pdf

CNN U.S. (2010. Study: White and black children biased toward lighter skin. Retrieved from www.cnn.com/2010/us/05/13/doll.study/

Coard, S. I., Breland, A. M., & Raskin, P. (2001). Perceptions of and preferences for skin color, black racial identity, and self-esteem among African Americans. *Journal of Applied Social Psychology, 31*(11), 2256–2274.

FindLaw for Legal Professionals, 347 U.S. 483 (1954). Retrieved from http://caselaw.lp.findlaw.com/scripts/getcase.pl?court=US&vol=347&invol=483

FindLaw for Legal Professionals, 418 U.S. 717 (1974). Retrieved from http://caselaw.lp.findlaw.com/scripts/getcase.pl?navby=case&court=us&vol=418&invol=717

Fortner, C. K., Faust-Berryman, A., & Keehn, G. T. (2014). Atlanta Public Schools equity audit report. Retrieved from http://s3.documentcloud.org/documents/1201231/aps-equity-audit-report-final.pdf

Frankenberg, E. & Orfield, G. (Eds.) (2012). *The resegregation of suburban schools: A hidden crisis in American education.* Cambridge, MA: Harvard Education Press.

Gallagher, T. (2007). Desegregation and resegregation: The legacy of Brown versus Board of Education, 1954. In Z. Bekerman & C. McGlynn (Eds.), *Addressing ethnic conflict through peace education : International perspectives* (pp. 9–19). New York: Palgrave MacMillan.

Georgia Advisory Committee to the United States Commission on Civil Rights (2007). Desegregation of Public School Districts in Georgia: 35 public school districts have unitary status, 74 districts remain under court jurisdiction. Retrieved from http://www.usccr.gov/pubs/GA-DESG-FULL.pdf

Gopaul-McNicol, S. A. (1992). Racial identification and racial reference of black preshool children in New York and Trinidad. In A. K. H. Burlew, W. C. Banks, H. P. McAdoo, & D. A. Azibo (Eds.), *African American psychology: Theory, research, and practice* (pp. 190–194). Newbury Park, CA: Sage Publications.

Governor's Office of Student Achievement. 2010–2011 Report Card: All schools, state of Georgia (n.d.) Retrieved from http://reportcard2011.gaosa.org/%28S%2813p1bvafmnniq5wgntv2ymfe%29%29/k12/demographics.aspX?ID=761:ALL&TestKey=EnR&Test-Type=demographics

Greenhouse, L. (2007, June 29). Justices limit the use of race in school plans for integration. *The New York Times.* Retrieved from http://www.nytimes.com/2007/06/29/washington/29scotus.html?_r=0&pagewanted=print

Hix, L. (2013, February 21). Black is beautiful: Why black dolls matter. Retrieved from http://www.huffingtonpost.com/2013/02/22/black-is-beautiful-why-bl_n_2743600.html

Hughes, J., & Donnelly, C. (2007). Is the policy sufficient? An exploration of integrated education in Northern Ireland and bilingual/binational education in Israel. In Z. Bekerman & C. McGlynn (Eds.), *Addressing ethnic conflict through peace education: International perspectives* (pp. 121–133). New York: Palgrave MacMillan.

Irons, M. E. (2013, June 23). Doll museum depicts the African-American experience. *The Boston Globe.* Retrieved from www.bostonglobe.com/business/2013/.../story.html

Jarrett, O. S. (1980). *Assessment of racial preferences and racial identification of black and white kindergarten children in mono-racial and bi-racial settings.* (Unpublished doctoral dissertation}. Georgia State University, Atlanta, GA.

Jarrett, O. S. (2013). A research-based case for recess. US Play Coalition in collaboration with the Alliance for Childhood and the American Association for the Child's Right to Play. Retrieved from http://usplaycoalition.clemson.edu/blogs.php?id=17

Jarrett, O. S. (2014). Recess deprivation and play space inequalities: Issues of social justice. Paper presented at the annual conference of the American Educational Research Association, Philadelphia.

Jarrett, O. S. & Quay, L. C. (1984). Cross-racial acceptance and best friend choice: A study of kindergarteners and first graders in racially balanced classrooms. *Urban Education, 19*(3), 215–225.

John, A. (2014, May 15). Even well-integrated schools treat black students differently. *New Republic.* Retrieved from http://www.newrepublic.com/article/117775/brown-v-board-60-years-later-racial-divide-students-teachers

Jordon, P., & Hernandez-Reif, M. (2009). Reexamination of young children's racial attitudes and skin tone preferences. *Journal of Black Psychology, 35*(3), 388–403.

Kirp, D. L. (2012, May 19). Making schools work. *The New York Times.* Retrieved from http://nytimes.com/2012/05/20/opinion/sunday/integration-worked-why-have-we-rejected-it.html ?_r=0

Klugman, E., & Fasoli, L. (1995). Taking the high road toward a definition of play. In E. Klugman (Ed.). *Play, Policy, and Practice.* St. Paul, MN: Redleaf Press.

McGrady, P. B., & Reynolds, J. R. (2013). Racial mismatch in the classroom: Beyond black-white differences. *Sociology of Education, 86*(3), 3–17.

McIntosh, P. (1989). White privilege: Unpacking the invisible knapsack. *Peace and Freedom, 49* (July/August), 10–12.

Mickelson, R. A. (2002). The academic consequences of desegregation and segregation: Evidence from the Charlotte-Mecklenburg Schools. Presented at the Conference on the Resegregation of Southern Schools, University of North Carolina at Chapel Hill. Retrieved from http://civilrightsproject.ucla.edu/research/k-12-education/integration-and-diversity/the-academic-consequences-of-desegregation-and-segregation-evidence-from-the-charlotte-mecklenburg-schools/mickelson-academic-consequences-desegregation.pdf

Miller, E., & Almon, J. (2009). Crisis in the kindergarten: Why children need to play in school. Retrieved from www.allianceforchildhood.org

Orfield, G. (2012). Conclusion: Going forward. In E. Frankenberg & G. Orfield, (Eds.), *The resegregation of suburban schools: A hidden crisis in American education* (pp. 215–237). Cambridge, MA: Harvard Education Press.

Powell-Hopson, D., & Hopson, D. S. (1992). Implications of doll color preferences among black preschool children and white preschool children. In A. K. H. Burlew, W. C. Banks, H. P.

McAdoo, & D. A. Azibo (Eds.), *African American psychology: Theory, research, and practice* (pp. 183–189). Newbury Park, CA: Sage Publications.

Research Atlanta (1973). Analysis of Atlanta compromise school desegregation plan. Retrieved from http://digitalcollections.library.gsu.edu/cdm/ref/collection/researchATL/id/3888

Tenenbaum, H. R., & Ruck, M. D. (2007). Are teachers' expectations different for racial minority than for European American students? A meta-analysis. *Journal of Educational Psychology, 99*(2), 253–273. Retrieved from http://psycnet.apa.org/journals/edu/99/2/253/

Walker, V. S. (1996). *Their highest potential: An African American school community in the segregated south.* Chapel Hill: University of North Carolina Press.

APPENDIX

Doll Play Story-Telling Procedure and Coding

Materials: Cardboard screen, dollhouse furniture, blocks, car, and four dollhouse families, two white and two black. Each family set has a father, mother, boy, and girl.

Setting: Examiner and child sit together at a table or on the floor away from other children.

Script: I would like you tell me a story. This house (show screen) is where the story starts. Can you pretend this is a house? In this house lives a family with two children, a boy and a girl. Here are some dolls. You decide what family to put in the house. (The child may need to be reminded that there are a boy and a girl).

Table 2.4.   Check dolls used

	Same race	Other race
father		
mother		
boy		
girl		

You can put some furniture in the house. I have a lot of furniture here. Use the things you wish. You can use blocks to make furniture I don't have, if you wish. (Allow a few minutes for arranging furniture.)

The mother tells the little boy/girl (depending on the sex of the child) that he/she can have some friends over to play. So he/she invites his/her best friend. Which doll do you want to be the best friend? Then she says another friend can come too. So he/she invites his/her next best friend. Which doll do you want to be the next best friend?

Table 2.5.   Sex Choice

	Same race	Other race
First choice		
Same sex		
Other sex		
Second choice		
Same sex		
Other sex		

What do you want to happen next? I'm going to put on the tape recorder and you can tell me a story about these people. Then you can listen to some of the tape and hear yourself talk. You may use more dolls in your story, if you wish. (If the child doesn't talk, encourage him/her and ask questions.)

Record the story and note other dolls used and the roles they play. When the story is finished and the child has listened to some of the tape, the child is asked:

If you could be any doll in your story, which one would it be?

Table 2.6. Would be

Same race	Other race
Same sex adult	
Other sex adult	
Same sex child	
Other sex child	

Which doll looks the most like you?

Table 2.7. Look like

Same race	Other race
Same sex adult	
Other sex adult	
Same sex child	
Other sex child	

Chapter Three

Playing in Northampton

Connecting Past, Present and Future

Vicki Thomas

Play generates creativity was the central argument of an exhibition held at the University of Northampton, England in 2013. Play was shown to be beneficial for everyone, whatever their age or capabilities. In the past the town and surrounding region was a hub for toy producers in the United Kingdom, with firms like Bassett-Lowke, Mettoy, and Rosebud Dolls innovating with new materials and processes. Today the area remains at the center of toy and playground design and distribution, with organizations like John Crane, Toymaster, DKL Marketing, MGA Entertainment, Miracle Design and Play, and Sue Ryder—all based in the region. Industry play linked projects with undergraduate product designers have generated creativity. They have also stimulated exhibitions and collaborations with the School of Education and Northamptonshire County Council and conversations have started with policy makers at the UK Government level and with UNICEF about the creative benefits of play in the future.

The "All Play" Exhibition "ALL Work and No PLAY Makes You a Dull DESIGNer" (Thomas, 2013) was broad in scope but focused on design. It had six themed areas. 'Toy stories' about the benefits of manufacturing toys in Northamptonshire; 'Early Benefits' showcasing the design work, behind Abbatt, Galt and Page, producing educational toys for children; 'Caring Connections' demonstrating how play and toy making can be therapeutic and raise money for good causes; 'Design Futures' highlighting how play can have design benefits at University level and encourage innovative design; 'Global Well-Being' looking at the design challenges of working in the global toy trade; and 'Creative Communities' highlighting how interiors are being designed to allow for play at work in order to increase creativity in

39

business and also to show how spaces are being set aside where the people of all ages can play with toys and games. Play, the exhibition, demonstrated that play is beneficial for everyone, whatever their age or capabilities. This paper is just about the toy stories and global connections and how Northampton-shire became an area for innovative toy design.

METHODOLOGY

Play is understood as a cultural (Sutton-Smith, 1986) and social process, similar to the one described by Mauss' gift exchange theory (Mauss, 1954); it occurs in all cultures and societies. Huizinga's (1938) older definition of ludic play is important as it stresses that play involves the whole community and is not just for children. His notion of providing a place for play is also central to this study.

For academics teaching product design at an undergraduate level, design is often presented as process, rather than a drawing, pattern, or plan. Design is often described as a problem solving activity. In the United Kingdom design is considered a creative industry (Smith, 1998). It is seen to generate intellectual property that can be licensed worldwide. Art and Design Schools are involved with enabling students to be creative, to come up with 'fresh' ideas (Hegarty, 2014) and ways of seeing (Berger, 1995). Sir John Hegarty (2014) defines creativity as "the expression of self". Graduates have to be confident of their abilities and skills. Through our work we have observed that play is beneficial to teaching creative design (Schaber, Turner, & Betts, 2007; Schaber & Turner, 2008; Schaber, Thomas & R. Turner, KTP Final Report, 2010).

> If confidence is one key to success, enjoying your work is another. Even more than confidence, the sense of excitement that accompanies being creative will spur you on. Just think of it as playing—you can do anything you want, go anywhere you like. (Hegarty, 2014, p.15)

Today we are living in a connected world, a networked one. The notion of a network (Law & Hassard, 1999) in Bruno Latour's (2005) Actor-network Theory is important as it argues that objects are actors and can effect change. It is evidenced in this paper that materials, processes, and specific toys have influenced a network of toy design businesses in the region. Geographical spatial approaches (Atkins & Bowler, 2001) are also being adopted in order to understand and improve design at a local level. Location, understanding where the designed object or creative person is in a network or space, is considered important. The movement of people to and from other areas of toy manufacture and distribution is also significant, so theories that look at the role of diaspora in social change and knowledge exchange need consideration (Braziel & Mannur, 2003; Thomas, 2010). Play, it is argued here, is a creative process, developing a sense of self (Hegarty, 2014) and a notion of one's place or role (Sutton-Smith, 2001). It is not only valuable to a child's development (Moyles, 2010) but remains important throughout life. Play encourages design and making things to play with. Like Mauss's (1954) gift exchange process, it can generate trade, business, and enterprise (Piperoplou-los, 2012; Thomas, 1985) and involve a whole community and exchanges between communities and cultures (Sutton-Smith, 1986; Thomas, 2012).

The idea of an exhibition was initially proposed in 2010 as part of a Knowledge Transfer Partnership (KTP) with a toy distributor, John Crane Toys, based in Northampton (R.Turner, KTP Final Report, 2012). Jonathan Thorpe, the Managing Director, suggested that the project's academic part-ners should research and record the history and extent of the local toy trade. He highlighted how many toy traders, like John Crane Toys and DKL Ltd., were still based in the area. The Product Design Department at the University of Northampton has led a number of partnerships (Schaber & Thomas, 2008; R. Turner, KTP Final Reports, 2009; 2010; 2013). These are graduate 'ap-prenticeship' schemes backed by government grants, which allow firms to build partnerships with universities. Knowledge and expertise is transferred both ways with the Associate (a post-graduate) working as a conduit embed-ding knowledge and expertise in the organizations. Three of the KTPs were about the design of toys and playthings: doll houses for Sue Ryder (R.Turner, KTP Final Reports, 2009), wooden toys for John Crane Ltd. (R.Turner, KTP Final Report, 2012), and air hockey games for BCE (Distribution) Ltd. (R.Turner, KTP Final Report, 2010).

This chapter is the outcome of Jonathan Thorpe's request. It does not attempt to look at all the creative benefits covered by the exhibition but rather draws on the research and publications linked to the KTPs. The task of organizing and curating the "All Play" Exhibition was a research exercise in itself (Thomas, 2013) as it provided an opportunity to go back to the KTPs providing case studies for this paper. Fifty-two firms and organizations in-volved in designing for play were also contacted. Oral history interviews (Victoria &Albert Museum, 2014) capturing first hand accounts from the makers involved in toy manufacturing in the UK as well as additional contri-butions members of the public who were involved as consumers, employees, and suppliers were collected by Northampton Borough Council in collabora-tion with staff from the University of Northampton. Some organizations and individuals contributed information that was edited for the display and cata-logue and they are credited as "players" (Thomas, 2013). Original toys, catalogues, and designs were studied. The artifacts were lent by designers, manufacturers, and toy collectors. There were also visits to collections in museums; including Coventry, Wellingborough, 78 Derngate, Jeyes in Earls Barton, and the Mabel Lucie Attwell Museum. The exhibition was first held in a Northampton town center mall, at the Collective Collaboration Gallery in June 2013 (Thomas, 2013) in order to invite a wider community contribution to the research.

In the second venue on Avenue Campus, two play spaces were set out. The Avenue Gallery became a giant playhouse and the corridor outside the gallery turned into a play street (Thomas, 2013). The exhibition was not advertised directly to families and local school groups, as there were health safety concerns, due to the lack of adult supervision. The audiences were primarily undergraduates, staff from other faculties such as trainee teachers, local companies, and invited guests. It was open to all, but not targeted at children and families. There was a summer exhibition "Batteries not Included" at the Museum of Northampton focusing on the local history of toys planned specifically to appeal to family visitors.

The KTP projects and related reports and publications (R. Turner, KTP Final Reports, 2009; 2010; 2012; Schaber et. al., 2007; Schaber et. al., 2008; Schaber, et. al, 2010) inform this paper as case studies. Trade contacts and evidence were drawn from participant observation undertaken away from the University and through the accounts designers working in the trade (Thomas, 2013). The Museum of Childhood, part of the Victoria & Albert Museum was undertaking a parallel study recording oral histories of key individuals working in the British toy manufacturing industry. These studies have informed this study as well (V&A, 2014). The Museum's researchers were limited in the amount of data they could collect and so they were interested in working with a University to gather information about local firms. University staff undertook eight interviews and additional ones by local museum volunteers, using a similar oral history format to the V&A (2014) study. These oral histories are to be archived at the Guildhall Museum, Northampton, and will be available to researchers once new facilities are complete.

This chapter is primarily a design history of the local toy trade in the twentieth century and it asks why Northampton continues to be a hub of the toy trade today. Trade is an important description as it covers a network of exchanges and commercial relationships, not just manufacturing. The chapter indicates what we may be able to learn from this history about the possible future for the trade at the local level.

As indicated by some of the terms defined above, the chapter draws on a variety of theoretical approaches, from sociology, social anthropology, history, psychology, educational theory, geography, design management, studies of diaspora, and play theories. The evidence is also drawn from a study of the toys produced and the verbal accounts of those involved in trade past and present.

CONNECTING THE PAST

Northamptonshire is a county in the East Midlands in the center of the England. Birmingham to the northwest was center of the batch production of small metal goods referred to as the "toy trades" in the 18th and 19th centuries (Thomas, 1985). Northampton's manufacturing specialism during the 19th century was leather and particularly shoe production but the town also has a history of specialist engineering. This industrial heritage is reflected in the toy trade. Wenham Bassett-Lowke, backed by his father, a local boiler manu-facturer, started an innovative model engineering company (Bassett-Lowke, 1999; Fuller,1984; Vale, 2013). Before the First World War he was import-ing and adapting German model train engines and selling them to wealthy individuals who had the money and land to invest in miniature trains. These were toy and playthings for adults. Nuremburg was the European centre of toy production of all kinds, He went there regularly to import engines and components, but he also used other sub-contractors in the town like Winter-ingham's (Precision Tools) Ltd. (Fuller, 1984).

Bassett-Lowke was a model maker, an entrepreneur, design promoter, and local council member. He bought the newest products such as bathroom fittings from the United States, commissioned modern designers like Charles Rennie Mackintosh and Peter Behrens; and working for the local Corporation he inspired modern buildings such as the public swimming baths. He re-corded local industrial production, community history, and play activities on film (Bassett-Lowke, 1992). He was searching out innovative design and this was reflected in his work and life. He was a key actor in the network that linked German engineering and toy production to the town. The film showed the town using aerial photography and started with a detailed description of its location. It was produced to attract industry and investment in the town, specifically showing it was a good place to work and play. He also had retail outlets in London, Manchester, and Edinburgh and promoted his products extensively with posters and graphics (Fuller, 1984).

Owners of ships and trains used Bassett-Lowke to promote their compa-nies. They were display and demonstration pieces used by governments. Hornby in Liverpool established a lead on Bassett-Lowke's company in de-veloping toy train sets for children, but as far as model engineering was concerned they had set the quality standard for the U.K. Later, Bassett-Lowke went on to produce the Trix range that competed on scale with Horn-by (Fuller, 1984; Vale, 2013).

When toy producers with Northamptonshire trading partners in Germany needed to evacuate from the Nazi regime in the late 1930s, they looked to friends and family in England. W. F. Graham is today a local children's book publisher, but their founders were toy traders with family in Germany and England. Because of the family's British connections, they were interred during WWI in Germany. So as soon as a second war seemed likely, they evacuated to England (W. Graham, Personal Communication, May 8, 2014). Philip Ullmann, who owned Tipp & Co, a toy factory in Nuremburg, was aided in 1933 by retailers Marks and Spencer to leave Germany. This is evidence of a Jewish and German diaspora having an effect on the toy trade locally. Bassett-Lowke gave Mr. Ullmann and his partner Arthur Katz space in his premises to set up their new company, Mettoy (V. & A., 2014). They started out producing vehicles made from tin plate. Toy production stopped and war production took over. In 1944 a new factory was set up in Fforest-fach, Swansea, to aid wartime production (Fforestfach, 2012). It was this site that was to become the factory for production of die cast toys and the Corgi brand (A. Fuller, Personal Communication, May 23, 2014; Taff, 2006). Much of the design and development remained in Northampton (A. Fuller, Personal Communication, May 23, 2014; Taff, 2006, Cleemput, 2010). The Taff (2006) account is written based on experience working in Swansea, and illustrates the network of specialist knowledge required to produce the toy vehicles.

The post-war decades were the peak of toy production in Northampton-shire and in Great Britain as a whole. A fuller economic history of UK industry has been researched and published in a series of studies by Kenneth Brown (1998; 2011). British manufacturing firms across the country were converting back from wartime production. The War destroyed much of the toy industry in Germany, and it took sometime for production to start in the Far East. This provided a window of opportunity for Northampton entrepren-eurs to design, manufacture, and sell toys worldwide. Tipp & Co had sur-vived under Nazi owners producing models for the Third Reich, and the Ullman family went back to Germany to reclaim their business (Victoria & Albert Museum, 2013). But much of the toy trade was destroyed (W. Gra-ham, Personal Communication, 8 May, 2014) and Nuremburg needed time to rebuild.

Back in Great Britain, Mettoy started to diversify, exploring plastics pro-duction in Northampton. This would lead them to be the major United King-dom producer of plastic footballs, as well as a new toy called the space hopper.

Wholesale traders in London were looking to find new suppliers. The oral history account (J. Orme, Personal Communication, April 1, 2014) and me-moires of John Orme (Autobiography, n.d.), a specialist toolmaker based in Rushden, indicate that London based Jewish businessmen initiated product development. Initially they funded expensive tolling for injection-molded plastics. One of the first plastic products developed for their company was Christal Ware. They also started producing the bucket alongside with other plastic nursery items such as baby baths. This was going to change the seaside experience for the next generation of children. Plastics were lighter and considered safer and more hygienic. Once the tooling was paid for the products were affordable.

Just after WWII, Eric Smith opened a doll factory in Raunds, with compensation money provided by the government due to the bombing that destroyed his family's London factory. This became Rosebud Dolls (British Pathé, 1968). Orme made the plastic injection tools for their doll production (J. Orme, Autobiography, n.d.). Rosebud had started producing dolls using composites. This was a step change in itself and an advance from cloth, wooden, or porcelain dolls. Plastic dolls were revolutionary in that they allowed new forms of play, were less likely to break, could be washed more easily, and were considered safe, hygienic and affordable. Dolls' hair could be added by machine, washed, and dressed. This in turn led to later technical advances in dolls (British Pathé, 1968) including: walking talking dolls, like the one immortalized in song by Cliff Richard (Bart, 1959), as well as drinking, crying, and diaper wetting baby dolls. Rosebud produced Beatles Dolls using the standard tooling relying on the clothes designers and distinctive hairstyles to make them recognisable (Hillier, 1965). These toys were designed to have mass popular appeal.

John Orme had trained as an apprentice toolmaker in the aircraft industry from the age of 14 (J. Orme, Autobiography, n.d.). After the war he moved to Northamptonshire to take up a post with a firm supplying equipment to the tanning industry. Although his background and training were based in the local industries, he was to leave his mark as an innovator in tool making for the plastics industry. His role in developing tools for rotary molding plastics drove new product innovation forward.

> One day I had a visit from a man who owned a large rubber company in London. He asked if I could make a machine to produce playballs and footballs from P.V.C. Plasto. I knew this could be done, and that the ball would be cheaper and more attractive with bright colors and patterns. So we designed a machine and made the essential moulds which met his requirements. When this became known, I was inundated with orders for machines from toy making companies, plastic moulders and Sports Equipment firms. At this time I had carried out some toolmaking work for I.C.I., the biggest firm in Britain. As they supplied the P.V.C. Plastol for this new development, they gave me every possible co-operation. (J. Orme, Autobiography, n.d.)

Orme was a key actor and change maker in the history of the local toy manufacturing industry. The rotary moulding machines are still named after his firm and the products such as road cones, plastic petrol tanks, and the space hopper were significant designs that relied on his innovative design. He was a creative designer and loved the innovation process.

Orme thus not only supplied Rosebud Dolls, but the tooling for the space hopper and footballs that became the staple production by Mettoy in North-

ampton in the 1960s and 1970s. Orme went on to sell the tooling globally
and his son said that his father "felt he exported soccer to Africa" (J. Orme,
Personal Communication, April 1, 2014) as his machines mass-produced
footballs at a price that made them readily available. The Orme rotary machines are central to the history of toy production in Northamptonshire.
There was a network of firms all exploiting his innovations. In Actor-network terms, these machines were actors changing the design history of the
toy trade and John Orme (Personal communication, April 1, 2014) would
argue also increasing participation in sport worldwide.

Bassett-Lowke, Mettoy, and Rosebud were the major companies in
Northamptonshire. Other firms like Avon Cosmetics used the same technology to produce children's collectible bath toys. Small manufactures such as
Tresco based in Earls Barton (J. Osborne, Personal Communication, April
25, 2013) were producing novelties like the toy divers that were shown at the
Victoria & Albert Museum in 1946—proving that "Britain Can Make it".
Burbank was a soft toy company also based in Wellingborough (MACE,
1977), which produced teddies and plush toys. Some toys were made using
new synthetic plush and rubber moulded faces. Burbank took on licensed
properties such as Disney characters and film properties such as Dr. Doolittle
(Media Archive of Central England, 1977).

Neither Rosebud nor Burbank was with the first toy firms to take on
licenses. Chad Valley in Birmingham had produced licensed dolls for Mabel
Lucie Attwell (Henty, 1999; Thomas, 2013) about the time of WWI and
Bonzo the Dog (Babb, 1988) in the 1920s. In Leicester Alfred Pallet had
started to explore plastic in 1919 starting Caselloid Ltd. Like the first companies to use rubber and gutta percha, the precursors to plastic technology, fire
was always a danger (Thomas, 1985). In 1925 Pallet produced an innovative
celluloid doll, Diddums, modeled in clay by Mabel Lucie Attwell (Henty,
1999). They supplied Woolworths and Marks and Spencer. The company
changed names and premises to develop into Palitoy Playthings and a trade-
mark was taken out in 1937. So Northampton was not the first in plastic toy
production but the innovators were all in the same Midlands region. By 1980
Rosebud, Mettoy, and Palitoy had been bought by Mattel and were producing plastic toys such as Barbie, Action Man, and the Star Wars spacecraft in
the U.K. (Media Archive of Central England, 1982; V&A, 2013).

The Americans were coming and the creator of Barbie in 1959, Ruth
Handler, bought out Rosebud for 'a million' according to local accounts (J.
Osborne, Personal Communication April 25, 2013). Burbank went the same
way. Giving Mattel a base to sell into Europe and the common market in the
1970s. The oil crisis came just as the first sets of entrepreneurs were retiring
(Brown, 2011). Ex-employees, that were trained at local technical college (V.
& A., 2013) now The University of Northampton, often started new toy
companies. A group of employees was formed to start Blossom (Dolls), as

they could not buy the Rosebud name from Mattel. To compete with Bur-bank they bought a small soft toy company Be Be and started Panther Sports to supply footballs and sports equipment. Plastics technology and rotary moulded production were central to their activities (A. Laughton, Personal Communication, September 10, 2013).

Be Be Dolls had been established by Frank and Ernest Popper in about 1948. They had fled from Czechoslovakia in the 1930s. After setting up a toy firm in London they moved the business to Ringstead, in East Northampton-shire. Although, the firm had the word dolls in the company name they specialized in teddy bears and soft toys. The firm was sold to Blossom when the Poppers retired. The new owners started to add rubber faces to some of the toys like monkeys.

By the 1980s all the companies struggled with the cost of raw materials, with cheap production in the Far East and the revival of production in Ger-many. Volume manufacture started to shift elsewhere. The first set of entre-preneurs were retired and skilled staff who continued to design toys but worked in new company structures with production shifting abroad.

Another factor to be considered is that the products that these Northamp-ton firms produced were not considered "good" design by the government-backed Design Council (Brown, 1998). The Abbatt family had campaigned for what we would now call "educational" toys since the 1930 (V. & A., 2013; Thomas, 2013). Their toys were based on education and psychological approaches to child development. The Abbatt story runs alongside the work of designers like Ken Garland who designed for them and later for Galt in the 1960s-1970s (Garland, 2012). Their work was a world away from the whole-sale volume business of the Northampton trade. Wood was favored and when that became too expensive they used cardboard (Garland, 2012).

Northampton was well placed to die stamp cards for games and puzzles. Specialist toolmakers could be used to produce the die stamps and cutters for stamping leather and card. There is some evidence that some Northampton tooling and packaging firms diversified from supplying the leather trade with stamping tools and shoe boxes to produce games and puzzles (J. Osborne, Personal Communication, April 25, 2013) and toy boxes which were general-ly subcontracted locally by the toy companies (A. Fuller, Personal Communi-cation, May 23 2014). Here again it was tooling and production skills that made a difference.

Hilary Page (1953) was a designer and innovator that had a foot in both camps. He studied European traditional toys like stacking dolls and read the new child psychology to design his Kiddicraft toys ranges. But unlike the Abbatt family, he embraced plastics for nursery toys. He developed plastic building blocks and invested in their tooling. Unfortunately for him, the Lego owners came to the U.K. to buy tools. They wanted to diversify and produce plastic toys. It is said that they approached the same toolmakers that Page had

Chapter 3

used. Page had only patented his designs as his intellectual property in the U.K. They were able to make changes and a launch their own version on the continent. Orme's business (J. Orme, Autobiography, n.d.) illustrates the huge investment that was needed for tooling and also the importance of international patent protection, neither came cheap. In Page's case he was making design innovation and the investment in tooling himself without the backing of a large trader like Chritstal Ware. In the post war decades, the government backed the export of machine tools and in doing so also aided the demise of its homegrown toy industry.

In the past toy manufacturing came to the region because of its skilled workforce in metal and leather production. A historical study for Dunlop of rubber innovation in the 19th Century has shown that it was leather producers that were forefront of experimentation and exploitation of new materials and technology (V. Thomas, Archive Report, 1983). The machine tools used for processing the rubber were kept secret rather than patented. The role of toolmakers is significant and also how they commercialized their intellectual property. A network of trade and business connections with German toy producer and Jewish enterprises in London and Nuremburg were key to providing local support for these firms to flourish. Rotary plastics molding machines and tools produced by Orme link many of these firms. When oil prices rose and plastics production shifted to the Far East many of these firms could no longer compete and the emphasis shifted to design and product development (A. Fuller, Personal Communication, May 23, 2014). In export promotional terms, led by organisations like the Design Council, these toys were not considered high quality. But the machines were the creative designs and the expertise and knowledge was exported successfully. John Orme saw the potential of new technology in the transistor (J. Orme, Personal Communication, April 1, 2014) and Mettoy in the computer (Victoria & Albert Museum, 2013) but they were too late and not well placed to compete with US, China, and Japan on the next wave of innovation.

CONNECTING THE PRESENT

Today manufacturing may have disappeared and brands merged into larger specialist groups. Yet the area remains a center for toys and playthings through design and distribution, with organizations like John Crane, Toymaster, DKL Marketing, MGA Entertainment, Miracle Design and Play, and Sue Ryder with their head offices and national toy distribution offices based in the region. The University of Northampton grew from an art and engineering college serving local industry to a center of the toy distribution hub (Victoria & Albert Museum, 2013). The current Maidwell building at Avenue Campus was purpose built to train engineers and artists to design for the local industry. Its new purpose built campus is featured in Bassett-Lowke's film of 1930s (Bassett-Lowke, 1992) covering the history of the town, its geographical connections, and its people at work and play. The art students are featured dressed for a theatrical performance or pageant. The Mettoy archive notes that their design staff attended the engineering classes at the college, as it was then, on a day release basis (Victoria & Albert Museum, 2013).

The KTP projects brought a new generation of toy traders to the campus and the Product design department's studios (Schaber, Turner, & Betts, 2007; Schaber & Turner, 2008; Schaber, Thomas & Turner, 2010). The students relaxed and played. They brought in their old toys such as Transformers and relived play experiences by creating marble runs (Garland, 2012). They were asked to design for a younger generation, so they considered the future and what they thought to be "right" and "good". They looked at the psychology of play and educational toys. Are the materials safe? Are they sustainable? They seemed to go beyond just researching the developmental benefits of play for children. Sue Ryder (R. Turner, KTP Final Report, 2009) is a charity wanting to create exclusive designs for their retail outlets. They wanted different products. So intellectual property had to be considered. Students and the associate had to appreciate and design for global ethical production. They also had to understand the products were there to raise funds for the therapeutic work of the charity. The consumer for the fantasy castles and stools that resulted from the KTP were often sold to the over 50 age group. The designs had to be beneficial on a number of levels.

Playground design should not be overlooked in developing an understanding of play related business in the region currently. Miracle Play and Design is a company originating in the United States of America, employing two graduates for the Product Design course. The play equipment they design fits with the landscape and indicates new emphasis on what is considered good design for play. Wicksteed Park is a theme park in the region but also has a linked playground equipment company. The product design department only this year has been involved with designing themed bins for the park—typical of the rotary produced products still produced today using Orme's technology.

Ravensden (M. Pape, Personal Communication, March 15, 2014) is a toy and gift company based in Rushden. They are a family firm of specialist traders and they supply primarily animal themed toys and gifts. Barry and Susan Pape started as suppliers of live animals to theme parks and developed into supplying the parks with income generating merchandise. They have long established relationships with suppliers of soft toys in South Korea and Indonesia and export the products they have designed to other similar attractions worldwide.

Travis Designs Ltd. and GSC Ltd. are children's costume companies based in the region. Both produce role-play outfits for the toy trade and educational markets. They also compete to supply the Disney theme parks and other visitor attractions. Designing for licensed merchandised continues to be an important part of the regional industry. It started with Diddums (Henty, 1999) and Bonzo (Babb & Owen, 1988) through to Disney, Star Wars (Media Archive of Central England, 1982) and James Bond (Taff, 2006) franchises to promotional merchandise. Fleming's (1996) book dealing with toys as popular culture explores the whole rise of toy merchandise and their links to popular culture in far more detail than is possible here.

Adrienne Fuller (Personal Communication May 23, 2014) in her account of product development in the collector's die cast commented how important television programing is from Morse (Central Independent Television, 1987) to Only Fools and Horses (British Broadcasting Corporation, 1981). Toys and play are now vital to marketing campaigns. Ravensden have produced soft toys as marketing incentives; toy monkeys for Barclay Card and plush meerkats for Compare the Market.com.

Licensed merchandise links the toy trade into a much larger global network of business. It affects creativity, Jim and William Osborne (W. Osborne, Personal Communication, April 25, 2013); local toy retailers argue that this has lead to "lazy design". The same products are just redesigned for the next film or craze. Not true innovation but often just surface changes occur. But successful licensed ranges can earn huge sums for the manufactures and make industry-changing sum for the property owners. Star Wars merchandise is estimated to have made $66 billion and changed the funding of films (Fleming, 1996). Osborne Toy & Sports (W. Osborne, Personal Communication, April 25, 2013) sell to the model train enthusiast, but also sell large quantities of models following in the footsteps of Airfix—being plastic—but now part of fantasy worlds created by Games Workshop—Warhammer. Oxford Miniatures, producers (A. Fuller, Personal Communication, May 23, 2014) of die cast road vehicles, are suppliers to the adult modeling enthusiast producing the cars to the same scale as the train set. Playing by creating and organizing miniature worlds continues a long tradition that pre-dates Bassett-Lowke (Fuller, 1984; Fleming, 1996; Sutton-Smith, 2001).

DKL and John Crane are also importers and toy distributors. In contrast, they do not rely on licensing. DKL is a family firm founded in March, 1989, by the Hawaleschka family. DKL's name originates from family names Dorte, Kai, Lise and Kai Hawaleschka (Managing Director). They have been in toys for most of their lives having an interest sparked by relatives who owned toy factories in Sweden and Denmark (Thomas, 2013). They supply educational and craft toys primarily. Like Mettoy they gave space to John Crane Toys (Turner, 2012) when they set up in the early 1990s. They are a second-generation toy trade family choosing to be based in Northampton.

Today John Crane Toys' own ranges are along the lines of those backed by Abbatt and Galt in the 1960s. They want to design quality products in the U.K. to meet the demands of educational and retail buyers such as the John Lewis Partnership, but also develop new products to sell through newer on-line channels. They heard about The University of Northampton's work in the toy field, so live design projects with students resulted and led to the KTP (R. Turner, KTP Final Report, 2012).

Independent toyshops through Toymaster can buy both DKL and John Crane's products. Traditional town center toyshops are currently under threat by the supermarkets diversifying from food and the Internet. Toymaster is a buying group based in Northampton allowing small shops to come together to buy in volume and thus compete on price. Toymaster is a key actor in the local network although they do not design or produce toys. All these companies benefit by Northampton's geographical location, local road networks and the collaborative business network or cluster that still exists in the region (Piperopoulos, 2012).

MGA Entertainment is one of several distribution companies based in the new town of Milton Keynes just south on Northampton. Although an American company, its roots are firmly fixed within the regional history. Andy Laughton is sales director and son of Don (A. Laughton, Personal Communication, September 10, 2013) who originally trained as a chemist at Rosebud Dolls. When the company was sold to Mattel, he was one of members of staff that went on to start Blossom.

Don Laughton (A. Laughton. Personal Communication, September 10, 2013) developed a styling head doll that exploited the plastics doll technology and started to work with German suppliers of similar products, Zapf Dolls. Today MGA distribute Zapf Dolls and also Little Tikes outdoor play equipment. This was rotary molded locally for many years using Orme machines and local expertise. Blossom, Panther, and Be Be were later bought by Chettles, an animal products company, producing lines such as animal based glues and by-products linked to the leather trades. The links to the traditional local leather industry are still in evidence. Galt was bought out by the U.S. owners of Elmer's Glue, coincidentally, originally an animal by-product too (Thomas, 2013).

Sue Ryder's (R. Turner, KTP Final Report, 2009) roots are different but relate to different beneficial aspects of play. Sue Ryder is a charity providing care homes for those living with a disability. They own a string of retail outlets raising funds through toy sales. Their KTP with the University of Northampton generated an estimated $1,275,000 from toy sales during the partnership for their therapeutic work (R. Turner, KTP Final Report, 2009). By the "All Play" Exhibition in 2013 this income was $1,500,000. A section of the "All Play" Exhibition looked at the design of toys for disability and for therapeutic play environments (Thomas, 2013). Like Bassett-Lowke products, Sue Ryder doll houses are bought by adults for themselves or bought to give to their grandchildren. Jonathan Thorpe (R. Turner, KTP Final Report, 2012) argues that John Crane toys are not purchased because of children's television or pester power but by an older over-fifty generation. There is an exchange of knowledge and experience between the generations through play and shared hobby activity.

The Sue Ryder case study also shows how toys are being sold to fundraise for charities and organizations. Design work is being done to generate income for all sorts of good causes. In the exhibition we included examples of work done in hospitals, toy libraries, and pet charities (RSPCA) as well as for UNICEF (Thomas, 2013) and Sue Ryder (R. Turner, KTP Final Report, 2009). Good toy designs today have to be "good" on more levels. DLK has designed a green doll house that won the Slow Toy Movement Award. The Slow Toy Movement was initiated by Thierry Bourret, of Asorbi Toys who is trying to set new standards (Thomas, 2013). John Crane Toys, like all the manufacturers, have to meet improving European toy safety standards. The materials such as wood, like foodstuffs, increasingly have to be traceable to where the trees are grown. Local soft toy wholesalers Best Years have been distributing knitted soft toys from Northampton for twenty years. They have to meet all the safety standards but also stress that their toys are 'fairly traded'. Recycled toys are being sold to adults and others are being made from recycled materials, like plastics, but testing is strict. Some argue (R. Turner, KTP Final Report, 2012) that the safety standards are so high that they have now become restrictive. Few children are now hurt and that with risk removed so has some of the play benefits (Boesveld, 2014). Toys now have to be green and need to be seen as green. Batteries are not included or required. Being a good toy designer is a complex creative requirement.

Today, the toy trade is still in the Northamptonshire. The geographical advantages remain. The regional skills remain in engineering, leather, and plastics tooling. Connections to the global toy business have remained strong. Products are designed and distributed in the region but they are now made in India, China, South Korea, and Eastern Europe. The U.K. retail markets for toys are changing. Toymaster based in Northampton is assisting with the survival of the independent toyshop. Toys are now being designed and distributed directly by retailers, be it Sue Ryder, John Lewis, Disney, or the major supermarkets or leisure companies. The product design team at the university through its KTPs and exhibitions has a role to play. They have an ongoing role to play in encouraging students to create innovative toy designs and by working in partnership with the local toy trade.

CONNECTING THE FUTURE

The "All Play" Exhibition in October 2013 coincided with a gathering of teachers for a conference featuring a guest speaker from UNICEF. The exhibition included a time line from Plato to today, showing how play had grown in importance in educational pedagogy. There was an assumption made by the curators that all accepted the educational benefits of play. But the conference delegates and the UNICEF speaker stressed that these ideas, central to educational toys and play, are being challenged by current U.K. government policy with play being devalued in the curriculum. Other countries in the Far East were being cited as examples, where play is considered a distraction.

The UNICEF speaker also argued that the importance of play is often been undermined or devalued in disaster or emergency situations. The charity had gone to great efforts to include playthings, toys, and school materials to be stockpiled ready when a response was needed. The educational and therapeutic benefits of play, so actively encouraged at the end of the twentieth century, are also being challenged. In contrast the WeKIDS Educational Organization, based in Taiwan is looking to import Northampton educational expertise, in teaching through play. They want to design and produce toys and playthings for nurseries all over China, as they are learning the benefits of play to children's education.

A visit to the "All Play" Exhibition encouraged the local Borough Council Museum staff to record the local industry and extend a planned toy exhibition, "Batteries not Included" to reflect its role as 'Toy Town'. Fifty percent of the display area was dedicated to the local toy trade and the rest reflected on community's memories of play. The long-term plan is to build up the play and toy archive and have a permanent toy trade display.

Collaborations with the School of Education are going to develop into an exhibition proposal on the development of educational toys in school and at home, exploring their continued importance in the U.K. and also researching what knowledge is being exchanged with China. The 3-D department is also being asked to collaborate with universities in Beijing, helping to educate their designers so that they can work in the new global market.

The final part of the "All Play" Exhibition looked at play interiors being created in commercial premises such as Pixar and Google. Play was seen as important in the work place. Enlightened factory owners favored sports clubs in the nineteenth century. Northamptonshire firms like Bassett-Lowke (1992) valued sport too. Now it seems to be play as you work. The 3-D department educates interior designer and architects. The design of playful spaces is seen as important not just for creative business, schools, and hospitals but also when we retire—play in the third age (Thomas, 2013). Creating a space for play is starting to be valued by all.

The future is likely to see further growth of computer and screen-based technologies. The products may not be manufactured in the U.K. Much of the design, development, and software has links with creative companies based in the U.K. and in the East Midlands. A computer games design course is now a key part of the 3-D Department. We are working with local intellectual property owners Trumpington. They are owners of three children's TV shows, from 1970s - 80s, and are seeking help to adapt their content for applications. Games, books, films, television, theme parks, and marketing campaigns are all integrated on a global level. Toys are designed in a connected playful world.

What is the future of the Northampton trade? The key is networking and connectivity. It is important to have research about the local history in order to understand the legacy on toy design and distribution globally.

CONCLUSIONS

The Northamptonshire toy trade is based on its location of major communication routes. It is one of a collection of Midland towns that developed as specialist production centers during the industrial revolution. Northampton specialism was in leather and shoe making. Tool making and specialist engineering made it possible for firms to adapt and exploit new plastic materials. The role of tool makers like John Orme were important in attracting firms to the area, but his rotary plastic machine tools made toys like plastic dolls and footballs available worldwide.

WWII closed the major toy production area in Germany and even took production away from Northampton when Mettoy moved its die-cast toy production to Swansea. Pre-war connections through trade and family brought German and Jewish entrepreneurs from Germany and London to the region. For the decade or so after WWII Britain led the world in toy production. Other countries bought new machinery as they rebuilt after the War. Innovators in the U.S. brought in new forms of toys such as Barbie and they continued to exploit valuable intellectual property generated by books, film, and then television. Whilst British toy design saw designers, like Ken Garland, focus on educational toys and quality batch production, firms like Mattel invested in Northampton's successful volume toy producers. This move opened the European market to them. A decade later with rising petrol prices internationally and quality plastic production opening in the Far East, particularly in Hong Kong, production shifted away. For Mettoy's Corgi Brand

> The Company had recognized that the market for die cast cars was changing, new electronic based products were the craze, the new age range that now bought die-cast had contracted. The company embarked on the introduction of

radio-controlled products, which was disastrous as most of them didn't work correctly and the battery life was very poor. (Taff, 2006 p.28)

Mettoy continued to innovate and saw their future in computing. They launched the Dragon 32, but technology was changing too swiftly for them to compete. In 1983 Mettoy closed and production ceased in Swansea and Northampton.

By the 1980s the area was a location for design, development, and distribution. Many original entrepreneurs had retired, so there has been some urgency in recording their accounts of the industry. In several instances family members are still involved and employees trained by the first generation are still part of the toy trade network. The staffs trained at Mettoy have continued to work together. Now Oxford Miniatures are selling vehicles to adult train enthusiasts at a scale to match their vintage toy trains (A. Fuller, Personal Communication, May 23, 2014). Adults continue to play and require toy design.

The toys produced in Northampton have always appealed to the adult purchaser. From expensive toy trains for their own use, through innovative cheap fun plastics for their children, to educational toys having an extra perceived value. Today the focus is on global wellbeing. This means that toys have to meet a whole new set of criteria to be considered worthwhile. The local firms based in Northampton have set out to meet those challenges.

Technologies are changing and the Internet and screen technologies are altering the focus of the trade once again. The Northampton firms have not always been successful in adopting new technology. They could not compete with the Far East on the transistor or computer. But they do not face the new challenges alone. Toys are now part of a much wider global culture and market place filled with publishers, film companies, computer games companies, television, social networking, and the Internet. The University in Northampton is preparing to support and encourage creativity as there is a new shift in skills and the global trade requires expertise.

Toy trading and playing in Northampton continues to connect the town as it did in the past. Its legacy of design, innovation, and distribution remain an important strength and vital to its ability to be player in the global trade.

REFERENCES

Atkins, P., & Bowler, I. (2001). *Food in Society: Economy, Culture, Geography*. London, England: Arnold Headline.

Babb, P., & Owen, G. (1988). *Bonzo the Life and work of George Study*. Shepton Beauchamp, England: Richard Dennis.

Bart, L. (1959). *Living Doll* [Recorded by Cliff Richard] [Single]. London, England: Columbia Records.

Bassett-Lowke, J., & Milner, J. (1999). *Wenman Joseph Bassett-Lowke (1877–1953)*. Chester, England: Rail Romances.

Bassett-Lowke, W. (1992*). Northampton official film presented by the New Industries Commit-tee of the Corporation: Re-edit of original film made in 1932.* Northampton, England: Northampton Corporation.

Berger, J. (1995*). Ways of Seeing.* London, England: Pelican.

Betts, S., Schaber, F., & Turner, R. (2007*). From Ivory Tower to Fantasy Castle: A Design-Case Study of Industrial Collaboration.* Paper presented at International Conference on Engineering Education, Coimbra, Portugal.

Boesveld, S. (2014). *When one New Zealand School tossed its playground rules and let stu-dents risk injury the results surprised.* Retrieved April, 22, 2014, from http://news.nationalpost.com/2014/03/21/when-one-new-zealand-school-tossed-its-playground-rules-and-let student-risk-injury-the-results-surprised/

Braziel, J. E., & Mannur, A. (2003). *Theorizing Diaspora.* Oxford, UK: Blackwell Publishing.

British Pathé Ltd. (1968). *Rosebud Toys* [Television News]. January 25, 1968. London, Eng-land: British Pathé.

Brown, K. (1998). Design in the British toy industry since 1945. *Journal of Design History,* 11(4) 323–333.

Brown, K. (2011). *The British Toy Industry.* Oxford, U.K.: Shire Publications.

Butt, R. (Executive Producer). (1981). *Only Fools and Horses* [Television Series] London: British Broadcasting Corporation.

Childs, T. (Executive Producer). (1987). *Inspector Morse.* [Television Series]. Oxford: Central Independent Television.

Cleemput, M. (2010). *The New Great Book of Corgi 1956–2010.* London: New Cavendish.

Fforestfach (2012). *Work-Mettoy -The forest history.* Retrieved April, 24, 2012 from http://www.fforestfachhistory.com/mettoy.html.

Fleming, D. (1996). *Powerplay -Toys as Popular Culture.* Manchester, England: Manchester University Press.

Fuller, R. (1984). *The Bassett Lowke Story.* London, England: New Cavendish Books

Garland, K. (2012). *Galy Tots the graphic work of Ken Garland and associates for James Galt & Company from 1961–1981.* London, England: Pudkin Books.

Hegarty, J. (2014). *Hegarty on creativity: There are no rules.* London, England: Thames & Hudson.

Henty, J. (1999). *The Collectable World of Mabel Lucie Attwell.* Shepton Beauchamp, Eng-land: Richard Dennis.

Hillier, M. (1965). *Pageant of Toys.* London, England: Elek Books.

Huizinga, J. (1938). *Homo Ludens.* London, England: Routledge.

Latour, B. (2005). *Reassembling the Social: An Introduction to Actor-Network Theory.* Oxford: Oxford University Press.

Law, J., & Hassard, J. (1999). *Actor Network Theory and After.* Oxford U.K.: Blackwell Publishers/The Sociological Review.

Mauss, M. (1954). *The Gift Forms and Functions of Exchange in Archaic Societies.* London, England: Routledge & Kegan Paul.

Media Archive of Central England (1977). *Teddy Bears,* [Television News] March 2, 1977, Lincoln, England: Anglia Television.

Media Archive of Central England (1982). *Star Wars,* [Television News]. October 28, 1982, Lincoln, England: Central News.

Moyles, J. (2010). *The Excellence of Play.* Maidenhead, England: Open University/McGraw Hill.

Page, H. (1953). *Playtime in the First Five Years.* London, England: George Allen Unwin Ltd.

Piperopoulos, P. (2012). *Entrepreneurship, innovation, and business clusters.* Fareham, Eng-land: Gower.

Schaber, F., & Turner, R.L. (2008, April). *Enhancing student learning in design: Research and inquiry skills through live projects.* Paper presented at 4th Centre for Learning & Teaching in Art & Design Conference, New York.

Schaber, F. (2008, September). *Last works: Networks of design, business, and technology in the shoe and leather industry.* Paper presented at Networks of Design Conference. Falmouth, England.

Schaber, F., & Thomas, V. (2008). Knowledge Transfer: Industry, Academia, and the Global Gift Market. *Design Management Journal*, 4(1), doi:10.1111/j.19487177.2008.tb00015.x

Schaber, F., Thomas, V., & Turner, R. (2010). Designing toys, gifts and games: Learning through knowledge transfer partnerships (pp. 482–498). In *Handbook of Research on Trends in Product Development: Technological & Organizational Perspectives*, A. Silva & R. Simoes (Eds.). Hershey, Pennsylvania: IGI Global.

Smith, C. (1998). *Creative Britain*. London: Faber & Faber.

Sutton-Smith, B. (1986). *Toys as Culture*. New York: Gardner Press.

Sutton-Smith, B. (2001). *The Ambiguity of Play*. Harvard: Harvard University Press.

Taff. (2006). *A Journey Through Time*. Swansea, Wales: Benjamin-Smith Ltd.

Thomas, V. (2013). Playing at the crossroads. In *Institute for Small Business and Entrepreneurship Conference Proceedings*. Cardiff, Wales: ISBE 9781900862264.

Thomas, V. (2012, September). *All Work and No Play make Jack a Dull Designer*. Paper presented at The Material Culture of Sport, Design History Society Annual Conference: Brighton, England.

Thomas, V. (2009). Roots, routes and recipes: The family tree contextualising design in F. Hackney, J. Glynne, J., V.Minton, (Eds.). *Networks of Design: Proceedings of the 2008 Annual International Conference of the Design History Society*. (pp. 365–374) Bacon Raton: Universal Publishers.

Thomas, V. (1985). *Gifts: The designer's role in the commercialization of gift exchange* . Presented at Art Historians' Conference: London.

Thomas, V., & Schaber, F. (Eds.) (2013). *ALL work and no PLAY makes you a dull DESIGNer Exhibition Catalogue*. Northampton: Northampton Design Research Group.

Vale, B. & Vale, R. (2013). *Architecture on the Carpet—The Curious Tale of Construction Toys and the Genesis of Modern Buildings*. London, England: Thames & Hudson.

Victoria & Albert Museum (2014). *British Toy Making Project*. Retrieved April 25, 2014 from http://www.museumofchildhood.org.uk/collections/british-toy-making-project.

Section II: Exploring the Present

Chapter Four

Play for All Ages

An Exploration of Intergenerational Play

Lynn E. Cohen and Sandra Waite-Stupiansky

The purpose of this study was to determine how play has changed over the generations and find patterns and trends in childhood play from generation to generation. Continuity theories of reminiscence framed intergenerational play memories. The overall method was qualitative with a descriptive design. The investigation was an assignment in a play course in which over 70 college students conducted interviews with someone 25 years older than themselves. The results indicated that an important place for play was outside within participants' neighborhoods. The toys of choice were dolls and figurines, balls, bikes, and board or card games. The most popular play material reported was natural or homemade items such as sticks, dirt, or structures made out of cardboard. Results reported from technology interview questions indicated differences between elders and university students' use of technology play. Providing the opportunity to bridge older and younger generations highlights the importance of tapping into the potentialities of using play in interdisciplinary programs to understand play theory and research across the life span.

The United States will experience many demographic changes in the 21st century and trends indicate that there will be a changing age structure driven by increased longevity. *Healthy People 2020's* (United States Department of Health and Human Services, 2010) vision is to create a society in which all people live long, healthy lives and includes healthy development and behaviors across all life stages. Bengtson (2001) claims multigenerational relationships will be more important in the 21st century for 3 reasons: (a) demographic changes of population aging, (b) the importance of grandparents fulfilling family functions, and (c) the strength of intergenerational solidarity over time. The guiding questions for this chapter are how play will be affected by

61

these changing demographics and how can future early childhood educators be part of the change?

Play is universal and can provide mutually beneficial relationships between younger and older generations. Shared play experiences across the life span can improve cognitive development, social development, physical development, and healthy emotional development (Davis, Larkin, & Graves, 2002). Intergenerational play takes place as soon as an infant is born. A parent playing peek-a-boo or reading a board book to a newborn helps infants learn about their world. Much research has been conducted on intergenerational play (Davis, et al., 2002) and intergenerational use of technology games (Chua, Jung, Lwin, Theng, 2013; Siyahhan, Barab, & Downton, 2010). Another area of research related to the benefits for both older adults and children are intergenerational programs (George & Singer, 2011; Hayes, 2003). Intergenerational programs foster the understanding that play and learning is a lifelong process.

This chapter includes a description of a study designed to help participants understand an integrated sense of play theory and research across the life span. As teacher educators teaching a play course to undergraduate and graduate students, we conceptualized a project to start investigating play across generations. The primary goal was to engage students in conversations with older adults to reminisce about their own play experiences (Merriam, 1995). A second goal was for students to apply developmental theories (e.g., Erikson, 1963) to the understanding of multigenerational relationships. The last goal was for students to develop interviewing skills, then to conceptualize and critique changes in play across the generations. The overall method is qualitative with a descriptive design. The investigation is an assignment in a play course in which college students interview someone 25 years older than themselves. There is limited research related to play memories (Sanburg, 2001) that frames the research using reminiscence theory (Butler, 1963; Parker, 1995), so we embarked on a pilot study to look in that direction.

The chapter begins with examining theories of reminiscence to frame our study on intergenerational play memories. A review of literature related to intergenerational programs and play and technology follows. The programs in this review describe play interventions and experiences implemented with cross age participants. Next, the methodology of the study and results are described. The chapter ends with implications and a call for future research related to intergenerational play theory.

The guiding questions pursued were:

1. What are the patterns and trends from members of past generations as they give their personal recollections of their childhood play?
2. How has play changed over the generations?

REMINISCENCE: A CONTINUITY THEORY APPROACH

Reminiscence is sometimes defined as the recalling and re-experiencing of one's life events. It is the process of recollecting memories of oneself in the past. One way to make memories more meaningful is to ask questions to help recall meaningful memories or life events. Early writings by Erikson (1963) and Butler (1963) have influenced most subsequent work in this area. Two of Erikson's (1963) life stages, generativity versus stagnation and ego integrity versus despair, are related to theories of reminiscence. Generativity versus stagnation is a reflection of a person's life. Generativity includes contributions to society, productivity, and providing guidance to the next generation. Adults are reflecting on memories of accomplishments and disappointments. Erikson's (1963) last stage of the life cycle, ego integrity versus despair, posits that with approaching death, the older person feels a need to review and evaluate his or her own life.

Butler's (1963) view of reminiscence became prominent with his article on life review and reminiscence, "The Life Review: An Interpretation of Reminiscence in the Aged." Butler (1963) proposed that as one approaches death, one engages in a life review and defines life review as "a universal mental process characterized by progressive return to consciousness of past experience, and particularly, the resurgence of unresolved conflicts" (p. 66). Butler (1963) further argued that in order to adapt to old age, an individual must review the experiences of life, revive them, and reintegrate them; the life review is conceived as "possible response to the biological and psychological fact of death" (p. 66). Reminiscence is a normal process that emerges from a desire to enjoy, grow, cope, or change.

Researchers (Lo Gerfo, 1980; Wong, 1995) have discussed types of reminiscence which take place. Three specific types are as follows: (a) information, (b) evaluation, and (c) obsessive (Lo Gerfo, 1980). Informative reminiscence is "focused on the factual material reviewed instead of on its relevance to a re-evaluation of the personality or life history" (Lo Gerfo, 1980, p. 40). It is about retelling, reliving, and sharing memories of the past. Informative reminiscence was used in this study when college students asked older adults to share their memories of play. Recalling memories is a source of mastery and gratification in old age.

Evaluative reminiscence is based on Butler's (1963) work on the life review process. For Butler (1963) the life review included reminiscing from the past from an evaluative perspective. It involves recalling memories throughout one's life in an attempt to come to terms with old guilt, conflicts, and defeats, and to find meaning in one's accomplishments.

Obsessive reminiscence is characterized by unpleasant past events and can be associated with poor mental health (Wong, 1995). It is accompanied by feelings of guilt, shame, resentment, and despair on an unpleasant past. It also may occur upon the death of a loved one, close relative, or friend. Methods of psychodrama help reminiscers to discuss their feelings and work through issues to find new outlets to relieve anxieties.

The literature on reminiscence theory is beyond the scope of this chapter. Instead, Parker's (1995) continuity theory approach to reminiscence is used to examine the play memories of older adults. Parker states, "there must be a recall of what has come before and the role of reminiscence is a valuable mechanism for creating a sense of continuity with older adults" (Parker, 1995, p. 521).

Older adults in this study shared their play memories and past events with college students to help provide continuity between play from one generation to other generations. Based on continuity theory the purpose was to examine, describe, and increase the understanding of intergenerational play by sharing the play memories between two generations. Before discussing the current study, a review of intergenerational programs focusing on play is in order.

PLAY: INTERGENERATIONAL PROGRAMS

Intergenerational programming can be defined as a "way to bridge the generation gap by engaging younger and older generations in structured activities" (Belgrave, 2009, p. 9). Intergenerational programs unite people of different ages and provide opportunities for individuals, families, and communities to enjoy and benefit from the richness of a culturally and generationally diverse society. They give children positive role models and break down barriers created by fear and uncertainty. Intergenerational programs give older adults needed feelings of accomplishment, worth, and joy. They offer both groups a medium through which they can share their talents and experiences (Generations United, 2007).

Intergenerational play creates a context for social interaction and learning for both younger and older generations. Pairing younger generations with older adults in play situations that are active and interactive have benefits that can result in positive outcomes for all ages. The play can include art, music, cooking, or puppet play. Most intergenerational programs that involve one or more play activities have specific outcomes that are geared towards the younger and the older generations. Two specific outcomes are to enhance cross-age interactions and to improve cross-age attitudes. Additional goals may be based on the age and functioning level of the generations. For older adults, wellness may be a goal of improved psychosocial well-being as they engage in cross-aged interactions during intergenerational programs. Children may improve their attitudes toward older adults or even teach them new technology skills. College students may have a goal to work with geriatric populations (Belgrave, 2009).

The Foster Grandparent Program was introduced in 1963 as a component of the war on poverty. The purpose was to provide opportunities for low-income persons aged 60 and over to support children with special needs while reducing isolation and poverty among elders. Since 1963, intergenerational programs have grown exponentially in the United States and include people of multiple ages and address many social concerns (Generations United, 2007). Intergenerational programs benefit older adults when they play with younger generations. Older adults learn to navigate a technological society, engage in physical activity, and acquire more concentration. Younger generations acquire positive social emotional attitudes about diversity and disabilities. Below is a description of several intergenerational research studies in which participants engaged in intergenerational play activities.

Preschoolers and Older Adults

Intergenerational studies (Heyden & Daly, 2008; Hayes, 2003; Holmes, 2009) were conducted in facilities that combine two generations (preschoolers and older adults) in the same facility. A childcare center located in the same building or in close proximity was found to be a major logistical advantage (Holmes, 2009) allowing for spontaneous interactions between generations and allowing for a more naturalistic approach to cross-age play and interactions. Two studies (Heyden, 2007; Heyden & Daly, 2008) described an accordion book art project for children and older adults. The purpose was to help "participants engage in inter-and-intra-generational discussion to see how they are alike and different" (Heyden & Daly, 2008, p. 82). In this intergenerational site the young children have been at the facility since "infancy, spending time with elders and persons with disabilities" (Heyden & Daly, 2008, p. 85) so the goal was to build upon the attitudes of participants through a shared play activity. The findings concluded that a better understanding between ages can be maintained through dialogic playful interactions.

Similarly, Hayes (2003) examined the following intergenerational play activities: (a) music and singing, (b) cooking, (c) gross motor activities (i.e., indoor basketball and bowling), and (d) art and craft activities. Results from both studies indicated that the most meaningful encounters between generations occurred during non-structured open ended play activities. The sing-a-long activities engaged the children, but not the older adults. Older adults worked as partners with children and appeared happier when engaged in cooking activities. Additionally, older adults with dementia appeared to have increased concentration when they participated in art and cooking activities. An interesting finding speculated by Hayes (2003) was that older adults with dementia that were spectators and "were not involved directly in an activity still derived some benefit from being within an intergenerational environment" (p. 124).

Playful intergenerational activities in programs can also change the way children portray older adults. Holmes (2009) interviewed preschoolers individually before and after participating in a cross age program. A key interview question, "What do old people do?" generated positive and realistic perceptions of older adults at the conclusion of the study (Holmes, 2009, p. 117). Responses prior to participation included, "they bought presents and gave hugs or older people are poor, ill, or just hung around" (p. 119). After participation in an intergenerational program, responses were more positive and included "they love to sing or they make good play dough cakes." The findings provide evidence that intergenerational programs can promote positive attitudes toward older adults.

Unlike the research of Heyden and Daly (2008), Hayes (2003), and Holmes (2009), Rosebrook (2002) conducted an empirical study to examine social playful interactions between older adults and preschoolers. The study included 200 preschool children assigned to one intergenerational (experimental group) and two non-intergenerational (control group) preschool centers. Children in the experimental group had been playing and interacting with senior adults for 12 months prior to administration of the assessments for the study. The preschool children in the experimental group achieved higher developmental scores on the Personal/Social component of the Learning Accomplishment Profile than preschool children in the control group. The researchers determined that these results support the assertion that generationally enriched environments do enhance the person/social development of preschool children. One can easily understand the use of cross-age playful activities in research using preschool participants. Play is ubiquitous and elementary-age children have hobbies, interests, and talents to share with older adults in intergenerational programs.

Elementary Students and Older Adults

Belgrave (2011) and Biggs and Knox (2014) examined cross age interactions and cross age attitudes with elementary-age children. Whereas, Belgrave's (2011) empirical research examined the effect of music, Biggs and Knox's case study (2014) examined essays written by Girl Scouts after conducting service learning activities in an assisted living facility. Belgrave (2011) employed singing, structured conversations, instrument playing, and moving to music activities to engage child and older adult participants. Favorite Girl Scout activities included,

> . . . reading to the seniors, celebrating and decorating for holidays and birthdays, playing games together, making arts and crafts, baking cookies, having a

tea party and an ice cream social, doing skits and play for the residents, singing together, planting flowers and gardening, giving manicures, watching television and movies together, walking together, and playing with the residents' pets. (p. 62)

Data analysis of Belgrave's (2011) cross age interventions revealed the interventions "structured conversations" and "moving to music" were more effective in eliciting interaction behaviors than the interventions "singing" and "instrument playing." Results of bi-weekly post-session questionnaires revealed a significant improvement in adults' and children's attitudes after their participation in the intergenerational program. Briggs and Knox's (2014) conclusions were similar. Eighteen essays mentioned social interactional play and activities. In a focus group, one girl stated, "The elderly join our troop and do our activities with us. When I first came here, no one really came out of their little private areas. Once they realized that we would be here twice a month, they started coming out and being near our meetings" (p. 63). Two older adults were former troop leaders when they were younger and "talked about how things are different these days" (p.63). Eleven essays reflected positive attitudes about seniors, growing older, and living in nursing homes. Clearly, benefits for elementary-age students and older adults include increased opportunities for relationship building, learning and mentoring play activities, social interaction, and personal changes.

George and Singer (2011) used a randomized experimental design to evaluate the effects of an intergenerational volunteer program to enhance the quality of life with older adults with dementia. The intervention group participated in hour-long structured volunteer session with a kindergarten class and a sixth grade class in alternating weeks during a 5-month interval. The kindergarten children engaged in singing and small group reading and writing activities and the 6th graders participated in intergenerational life-history reminiscence sessions. The control group received 12 hours of seminars on aging. Results indicated a significant decrease in stress for the older adults in the intervention group that participated in cross-age activities with children. This is an important finding for future use of intergenerational programs that involve playful interactions between young and older adults with dementia.

College Students and Older Adults

Some higher education programs offer service learning programs to bridge course work and real-world experiences to expose students more fully to social, educational, and community issues. The Educational Council (2013) defines service learning as "a teaching and learning strategy that integrates meaningful community service with instruction and reflection to enrich the learning experience, teach civic responsibility, and strengthen communities" (www.edcouncilk.org/servicelearning).

Studies (Lokon, Kinney, & Kunkel, 2012; Penick, Fallshore, & Spencer, 2014) describe intergenerational service learning to supplement college course work and enhance community-university relations. The overall purpose of both investigations was to assess college students' attitudes toward older adults after participating in cross-age interactions. Although the researchers' investigation had similar goals, there were differences in instructional techniques, participants, and methodologies.

The goal of the Penick et al.'s (2014) study was for college students to have weekly discussions with older adults using discussion prompts. The questions were guided by Erikson's theories and "encouraged reminiscence to support ego integrity, while similar and often identical questions for young adults explored identity and relationships" (Penick et al., 2014, p. 31). Using a different instructional technique, Lokon et al.'s (2012) service learning research involved elders with art-making and creative play. Another difference between the two college age studies was Lokon et al. (2012) investigated the impacts of intergenerational programming involving college students and elders with dementia in an intervention called *Opening Minds through Art*. Penick et al.'s (2014) study was an investigation with an established program entitled, *Meaningful Connections*; the older adult participant recruitment was from senior centers and assisted living facilities with no reported health issues. Also, pre–and post–test data were gathered using two measures: (a) Aging Semantic Differential Scale and (b) Community Service Attitudes Scale in Penick et al.'s (2014) investigation compared to a qualitative analysis of 300 journals written by college students in Lokon et al.'s study.

Given the differences between the intergenerational college service learning programs, the reported outcomes were very similar. The findings (Penick et al., 2014; Lokon et al., 2012) provided evidence that both programs positively impacted college students' attitudes toward older adults, with and without dementia. Lokon et al. (2012) noted further research is needed to analyze the impact of an intergenerational art program from the perspective of the older adults.

INTERGENERATIONAL PLAY AND TECHNOLOGY

Technology is pervasive in our society which includes computerized gift registries, banking, and email. While some older adults may try to avoid the technology boom and "bank with live tellers and write letters in long hand" (Azar, 2002, p. 28), many older adults are utilizing the internet, social media, and cell phones. Our younger generation is typically more expert in using these technology resources, but many communities offer classes and resources for older adults to get support and to stay technologically connected.

Two studies (Chua, Jung, Lwin, & Theng, 2013; Siyahhan, Barab, & Downton, 2010) examined intergenerational video-game play. Chua et al. (2013) investigated the role of game enjoyment on intergenerational perceptions when younger and older adults played video games, whereas Siyahhan et al. describes parent and child video-game play.

Chua et al. (2013) randomly assigned older and younger dyads to two conditions: (a) video-game condition (n=38, 19 dyads) and (b) non-video game condition (n=36, 18 dyads) to examine the effects of intergenerational perceptions on video-game play for two months. Each pair of participants consisted of one youth and one older adult. The ages of the younger participants ranged from 16-to-18-years and old participants were 60-to-86-years of age. The authors conclude that a shared activity such as video-gaming supported positive perceptions and attitudes towards interaction partners. Additionally, the results indicated game enjoyment played a role in developing positive intergenerational perceptions only for the elderly, not the younger generation.

Additional work by Siyahhan et al. (2010) confirms the potential for video-game play as a context of intergenerational play. A five-week qualitative study was conducted with 7 parent-child dyads (children ages 9–13 years). The families played *Quest Atlantis,* a 3-D video game. The parents reported the intergenerational activity allowed them to spend more quality time with their children. It also provided a way to engage with their children's thinking, character development, and learning.

The preceding studies on intergenerational play point to the benefits and rewards of shared play experiences between older and younger participants. There is little doubt that play is the unifying factor in allowing participants the opportunity to communicate and share in the joys and wonders that play provides. The literature provides a background for the present cross age study in which we asked college students to interview older adults as they reminisce about their play experiences.

To investigate this topic, we devised an interview project whereby undergraduate and graduate university students interviewed members of earlier generations about their recollections of play when they were young children. These interviews were collected in 2012 and 2013 at two different university campuses in two different states.

METHOD

Participants

Participants were 72 undergraduate and graduate students (66 females and 6 males) enrolled in a play course at the two northeastern universities and 72 older adults (55 female and 17 males). The courses took place over one term (four months) and had 3 credits assigned, distributed in 2.5 - 3 hours a week for 15 weeks. The gender of the interviewers was predominantly female (66 out of 72 or 92%) and the gender of the interviewees was predominantly female (56 out of 72 or 77%). The college students ranged in age from 19 to 28 years. The older adults ranged in age from 46 to 85 years, with an average age of 58 years. The age breakdown of the interviewees is reported in figure 4.1 with 11 respondents being between 40–49, 34 respondents between 50–59, 15 respondents between 60–69, 7 respondents between 70–79, 2 respondents between 80–89, and 3 respondents not reporting their ages.

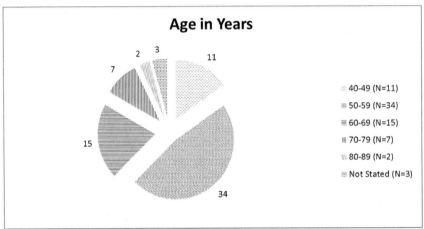

Figure 4.1.   This figure represents a percentage of ages of the interviewees. The majority of the older adults were between 50-and-59 years of age.

All but two of the interviewers reported socioeconomic status. The SES was reported for the interviewees' childhood. The predominant memories were from members of the middle class. The majority of the interviewees self-reported themselves to be middle SES (63.9%), with low SES following (25%), and high SES being the least reported (6.9%).

Procedure

The authors, who were also the students' instructors, asked students to obtain a statement from interviewees giving permission for use of the information gathered without identifying the interviewee. They were assured that their participation was voluntary and would not affect their grade if permission was not obtained. IRB approval was granted as an exempt research project.

The play interview project had three objectives corresponding to the traditional knowledge, skills, and concepts of undergraduate and graduate course work: (a) to improve the learning of developmental concepts and theories related to life span research (Erikson, 1963), (b) to enhance research-related skills, such as interviewing, (c) for college students to draw conclusions about childhood play by learning about an older adult's memories of play.

To achieve these goals, the project had the following tasks: (a) interview a person who was 25 years older by means of an open-ended interview, (b) transcribe and report the interview, (c) examine similarities and differences between their childhood play and the older adult's play, and (d) write a summary paper that combined objective reporting, connecting to theoretical concepts reflecting trends in play over at least two generations.

The conceptual and practical knowledge necessary to complete the assignment was explained in detail in sessions during the course. These sessions included the importance of play in the development of children and older adults. There was also limited practice of interviewing techniques and strategies, including how to present questions and gather play memories, how to be sensitive to interviewees' reactions and feelings, and how to avoid judgments and ethical issues related to research with human subjects. Handouts and guidelines related to the assignment were distributed and discussed.

For the data collections, the students were encouraged to meet an older person and interview him or her face to face. A few of the interviews were conducted via telephone, but all interviews were conducted during "real time" to allow for back and forth interactions between participants. Wellin (2007) suggests avoiding rules about selection of perspective interviewees. To make it easier for the students, family members were allowed as candidates for the interview, as long as they met the age requirements of a person 25 years older than the interviewer. Most of the interviewees were women (76.4%) and the age ranged from 48 to 85 years ($M = 58.3$; $SD = 9.0$). Students were to transcribe interview questions and responses verbatim whenever possible.

The students then completed a short paper that included a full description of the interview questions and responses, including where, when, with whom, and what the interviewees remembered about their childhood play experiences, comparison of their own childhood play experiences with that of the person they interviewed, and a summary of trends they discovered in intergenerational play. Students were instructed to adhere to American Psychological Association format in their papers.

Data Analysis

The authors, with the help of our graduate assistant, first read all the responses to the questions to become acquainted with the data. Then the transcribed student responses were entered into an EXCEL spreadsheet as categories emerged from the data. Specific details or units of meaning were identified in each response. The next step was to combine ideas into more specific categories, based on the repetition among threads of similarities. Using the constant-comparison method (Lincoln & Guba, 1985), first developed in their classic volume on naturalistic inquiry, a set of categories emerged and was refined by both authors. Consensus was reached between the two researchers in the coding and category system. Play categories that emerged included play memories of setting (indoors or outdoors), play memories of playmates, memories of materials used in play, and presence of technology. Importing the information into an EXCEL spreadsheet allowed for quantifying and comparing frequencies of responses, allowing patterns and trends to emerge.

RESULTS

After the 72 interview data were entered into an EXCEL spreadsheet, a number of quantitative patterns could be discerned. The following is a summary of some of the trends that emerged.

Play Memories: Setting

The types of setting where the interviewees grew up were divided into rural (including small towns), suburban, and urban. Not all of the interviewers reported on the setting, so only 43 of the 72 interviews could be analyzed. Of these, 24 (55.8%) reported memories of play in rural areas (woods, grandparents' farm, open fields, streets in a small town), 11 (26%) reported memories in urban areas, and 8 (18.6%) reported memories in suburban areas.

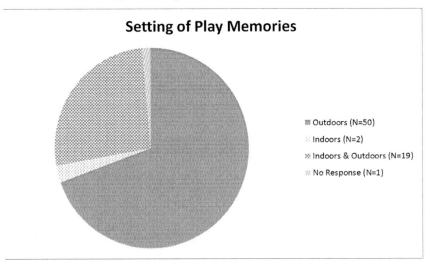

Figure 4.2.   Most interviewees reported playing outdoors during their childhood.

Related to the setting is the type of play that the interviewees reported as memorable. The majority of the play memories were of outdoor play (including school playgrounds) (70.4%), with a combination of indoor and outdoor play reported by 28.8 %, and indoor play only by 2.8%. One interviewee did not report in this category. It should be noted that the interviewees most probably played both indoors and outdoors, but when asked to recall their memories of play, 88% reported on their play out of doors.

Play Memories of Playmates

Many of the respondents reported with whom they remembered playing as children. They could have reported more than one category. The categories that emerged were neighbors (39 out of 72 or 54%), relatives (20 out of 72 or 28%), schoolmates or self (2 out of 72 or 2.7%), or non-specified (33 out of 72 or 45.8%).

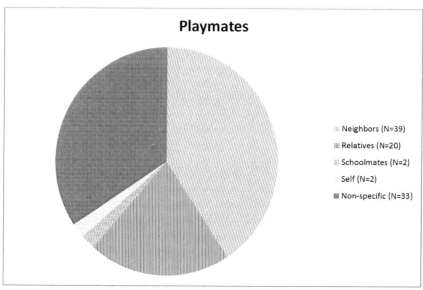

Figure 4.3. Interviewees reported memories of playmates. Most played with either neighbors or relatives.

Play Memories of Popular Toys

As part of the interview, the respondents mentioned many different types of toys or play objects in their memories of childhood play. Some of the categories that emerged from the data analysis were dolls and figurines, bikes, balls, board games, and handmade or natural materials. Respondents could list more than one of these categories in their responses. The most popular play material was natural or handmade items such as sticks, dirt, structures made out of cardboard, and so forth. This was mentioned by 43 of the 72 respondents (59.7%). Dolls and figurines were the second most mentioned item (30 out of 72 or 41.6%), with balls (24 out of 72 or 33.3%) and bikes (23 out of 72 or 31.9%) ranking third and fourth in popularity. Board games (including playing cards) were mentioned by 19 of the respondents (26%).

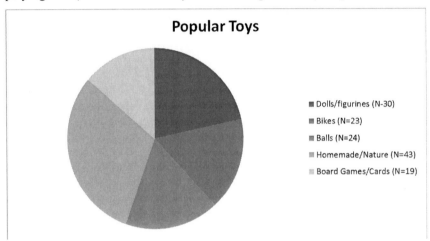

Popular Toys

- Dolls/figurines (N-30)
- Bikes (N=23)
- Balls (N=24)
- Homemade/Nature (N=43)
- Board Games/Cards (N=19)

Figure 4.4.   Percentage of play memories of popular toys. Dolls, figurines, and homemade objects were popular toys for our interviewees.

Technology and Play

Some of the interviewers asked the interviewees about memories of using technology. Forty-five older adults (62.5%) included technology or lack of technology in their play memories. Not surprisingly, 35.6 % (16 out of 45) of the respondents said they did not recall using any technology in their childhood. Television was in the homes and viewed by 48.9 % (22 out of 45) of the interviewees. The other responses included radio (4.4%), radio and television (4.4%), record player (2.2%) and Atari (4.4%).

DISCUSSION

College students were asked to interview a person at least 25 years their senior and ask them to reflect on memories from childhood play. The method described is based on Parker's (1995) continuity theory approach to reminiscence. The goal was to highlight the play experiences of older adults and examine how play appeared to them and the role of play in past generations.

The results seemed to justify the academic value based on collecting and analyzing an older person's play memories. It helped college students understand developmental concepts related to play and integrate them with theory

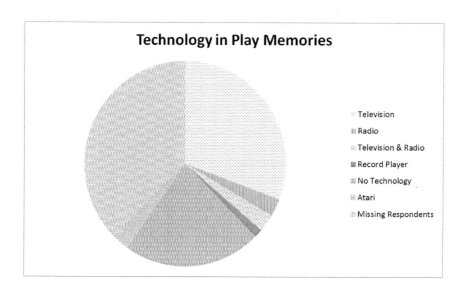

Technology in Play Memories

- Television
- Radio
- Television & Radio
- Record Player
- No Technology
- Atari
- Missing Respondents

Figure 4.5. Technology and Play. Most interviewees that responded to this question either said they did not use technology or they reported watching television.

to improve research-related skills. Similar benefits appear in college intergenerational service learning projects (Lokon et al., 2012; Penick et al., 2014) as college students learn to use art projects or conversations with older adults. Penick et al. (2014) found that when reminiscence is used in "conjunction with intergenerational service learning programs, younger and older participants share memories in an effort to gain insight into their own lives as well as into the lives of one another" (p. 28).

Therefore, using reminiscence theory to gather information on an older person's play experiences in play coursework has the potential to facilitate the attainment of our learning objectives for college students: (a) to improve the learning of developmental concepts and theories related to life span research (Erikson, 1963), (b) to enhance research-related skills, such as interviewing, and (c) for college students to draw conclusions about childhood play by learning about an older adult's memories of play. Penick et al. (2014) further notes that getting generations together can be promising but one must fully consider the activity that contributes to one's goals. In our case we wanted college students to bridge Erikson's (1963) psychosocial theory with concepts of reminiscence theory. We brought college students together with older adults to become more secure in their sense of identity as play experiences were re-experienced and similar and different perspectives were shared.

According to our results, the value of interviewing an older person about play memories goes beyond the academic aims of the assignment. College students may begin to examine the state of play in today's schools and become advocates for play, both indoor and outdoor. The data suggest that older adults shared memories of playing outdoors and in nature rather than indoors. Similarly, Sandburg (2001) reported that outdoor play created the strongest play memories from childhood when adults reported childhood play experiences. Pre-service college students may learn to challenge current academic standards and provide more outdoor play when they become in-service teachers. The findings with regard to playmates are contrary to previous play memory research (Sandburg, 2001).

The majority of our older adults (54%) reported playing with neighbors and Sandburg's (2001) adults reported mothers were primarily involved in their play activities. The differences may be Sandburg (2001) asked adults to recall memories at specific stages in childhood (i.e., 3–6 years, 7–12 years, 13–18 years and in adulthood). The stages (3–6 years, 7–12 years) in Sandburg's (2001) study are periods in a person's life span in which there is a strong attachment to mother and family members. This was described in the first 3 stages of Erikson's (1963) psychosocial stages: (a) basic trust vs. mistrust (0–2 years), (b) autonomy vs. shame and doubt (2–4 years), and (c) initiative vs. guilt (4–5 years) are periods in a child's development associated with significant relationship, specifically mother and family members. The present study did not specify specific time periods to recall childhood memories and older adults may have been recalling play memories from middle childhood, rather than early childhood years, which would explain the difference between the two studies.

Dolls have consistently engaged younger and older generations in play interactions so the results that 44.6% of the respondents recalled dolls and figurines as a popular toy preference was consistent with the Davis et al.'s (2001) research related to intergenerational learning through play. Whereas, playing with natural or handmade objects could have been connected to participant's memories of outdoor play and playing in open spaces.

Results reported from the technology questions are not surprising because the average age of the interviewee was 58-years-old. Television was recalled as a childhood memory by 48.9 % of the older adults and 35.6 % reported not using any form of technology at all in their play. At the end of World War II in the 1950s a few households had television, then between 1950 to 1960 television gained in popularity and was present in many American households. The college students interviewed mostly participants born between 1950 and 1960 when households were just beginning to purchase and watch television. The Internet, email, and on-line shopping, now changing our society and intergenerational video game play (Chua, et al., 2013; Siyahhan, et al., 2010), is a new form of play that could be used to develop and support learning and social interaction across generations.

In summary, our study in play reminiscing confirms most of the previous findings in studies on intergenerational play. Outdoor play predominated in the play memories of the older adults, play materials were often made from found materials or common objects such as dolls or bicycles, and most of the older adults remembered playing with neighbors or family members. Technology did not factor in as a major influence for nearly all of the interviewees. When technology was mentioned, it had limited use in terms of time and variety. One of the important outcomes of this study is the use of the one-on-one interview method as a means for younger generations to interact in a meaningful manner with older generations about the topic of play, which is a common component of all of their childhood experiences and memories. In other words, the method was just as important as the findings of this study for the participants.

Future Research

As a small study involving 72 interviews, the purpose was to explore the interview method for university students in their studies of play across the lifespan. This type of study, along with other service learning projects whereby college students interact directly with members of other generations needs further study. All teacher education programs build in experiences for preservice teachers to interact directly with younger generations, but few require experiences with older generations. Opportunities to bridge the older and younger generations as part of the teacher preparation program, such as in the models researched by Penick et al. (2014) need further study to determine if such models could impact the teaching profession as they learn to tap into the potential of the elder population in educating young children. Such models of teacher preparation have the potential to impact early childhood education on a broader scale if determined to be effective in future research.

Another future study could replicate the interview methodology and ask university students to interview someone from a younger generation, such as an elementary-age child, about his or her play experiences. Since one of the patterns implied in the current study was that the play patterns of the university students and the older adults had much in common with each other, interviewing a member of the current generation (i.e., children born in the last 10 years) could highlight more recent trends in play patterns since the influx of technology has taken place. Questions about the children's play settings (inside vs. outside), play materials, and play partners would allow comparative patterns to emerge between the generation of the future teachers and the generation which they will be teaching. Such research would help future teachers understand the day to day realities of children today.

Another related subject of future research could involve studying today's children playing with technology in intergenerational play venues. Several studies, such as those by Chua, et al. (2013) and Siyahhan et al. (2010) have shown that members of today's generation and past generations approach technology in very different ways. As children become more and more adapted to technological devices in their everyday lives, the play that they engage in with their elders is bound to change and adapt as well, bringing the older generations along. For example, using interactive video and audio communications allows children and grandparents the opportunity to communicate—and play—across distances in real time. How does this type of technologically-assisted play impact both partners of the dyad, the older and younger participants? For older children, playing games via the internet with members of older generations could open the possibilities for both generations to learn from each other. Children and elders can participate in word games, strategy games (e.g., chess), and other familiar and not so familiar games without being in the same room. Researching the possibilities provided by technology would be an important next step for studies of intergenerational play.

Limitations

There are a few limitations to our study. First, it was a convenience sample drawn from students in existing play courses. Another limitation was the interview data were collected by 72 different interviewers, creating inherent variability in the data collection process. As these were students with limited interviewing experience, the authors needed to keep in mind that there were bound to be some biases in their reports. Furthermore, some of the students were very detailed and comprehensive in their reporting of the interviews; whereas others were more parsimonious in their reporting of the details. Since this was an investigation into the reminiscing of the respondents and their interviewers, what the interviewee and interviewer chose to report signaled what was important in their memories and reporting on childhood play. Thus, this limitation was also considered as an important piece of the evidence as to what was memorable enough to report or reminisce about over the course of the interview and the writing of the paper.

A third limitation was the gender of the interviewers was predominantly female (66 out of 72 or 92%) and the gender of the interviewees was predominantly female (76%). Thus, the results are skewed toward female biases in the memories of play and the reporting on these memories. The interviewers were permitted to select their subjects and could include family members. The only criteria were that the interviewees must be at least 25 years older than the interviewers. So the selection of female subjects was the choice of the interviewees, perhaps due to convenience or due to identification of similar interests.

CONCLUSIONS

Intergenerational play covers a wide range of possibilities, from programs that unite the generations in play, to studies of how play changes over one's lifespan, to how play has changed across several generations. As the U.S. population ages and lives longer, the potential to use technology and other means to connect members of one generation to another grows exponentially. This study pointed to the possibilities of pre-service teachers becoming change agents in the process of tapping into the potentialities of using play, technology, and cross generational programs in the educational process of young children with positive outcomes for all participants, young and older.

NOTES

The authors acknowledge the invaluable assistance provided by Tara Cathers, Graduate Student, Edinboro University of Pennsylvania.

REFERENCES

Azar, B. (2002). Helping older adults get on the technology bandwagon. *Monitor on Psychology, 33*(3), 28.

Belgrave, M.J. (2009). *The effect of a music therapy intergenerational program on children and older adults' intergenerational interactions, cross-age attitudes and older adults' psychosocial well-being.* Retrieved from ProQuest UMI Dissertations (UMI 3385231).

Bengtson, V.L. (2001). Beyond the nuclear family: The increasing importance of multigeneration bonds. *Journal of Marriage and Family, 63*, 1–16.

Biggs, M.G., & Knox, K.S. (2014). Lessons learned from an intergenerational volunteer program: A case study of a shared-site model. *Journal of Intergenerational Relationships, 12*(1), 54–68. doi: 10.1080/15350770.2014.869981.

Butler, R.N. (1963). The life review: An interpretation of reminiscence in the aged. *Psychiatry, 26*, 65–76.

Chua, P.H., Jung, Y., Lwin, M.O., & Theng, Y. (2013). Let's play together: Effects of video-game play on intergenerational perceptions among youth and elderly participants. *Computers in Human Behavior, 29*, 2303–2311. doi: 10.1016/j.chb.2013.04.037.

Davis, L., Larkin, E., & Graves, S.B. (2002). Intergenerational learning through play. *International Journal of Early Childhood, 34*(2), 42–49.

Educational Council (2013). *Service learning.* Retrieved from www.edcouncil.org/service-learning.

Erikson, E.H. (1963). *Childhood and Society.* (2nd ed.). New York, NY: W.W. Norton & Company.

George, D.R., & Singer, M.E. (2011). Intergenerational volunteering and quality of life for persons with mild to moderate dementia: Results from a 5-month intervention study in the United States. *The American Journal of Geriatric Psychiatry, 19*(4), 392–396. doi: 10.1097/JGP.0b013e3181f17f20.

Generations United. (2007). *The benefits of intergenerational programs.* Retrieved May 25, 2014 from http://www.gu.org

Hayes, C. (2003). An observational study in developing an intergenerational shared site program. *Journal of Intergenerational Relationships, 1*(1), 113–132. doi: 10.1300/J194v01n01_10.

Heydon, R. (2007). Making meaning together: Multimodal literacy learning opportunities in an intergenerational art program. *Journal of Curriculum Studies, 39* (1), 35–62. doi: 10.1080/00220270500422665.

Heydon, R.M., & Daly, B.S. (2008). Facilitated interaction and learning opportunities in intergenerational programs. *YC Young Children, 63*(3), 80–85.

Holmes, C.L. (2009). An intergenerational program with benefits. *Early Childhood Education Journal, 37,* 113–119. doi: 10.1007/s10643–009–0329–9.

Lokon, E., Kinney, J.M., & Kunkel, S. (2012). Building bridges across age and cognitive barriers through art: College students' reflections on an intergenerational program with elders who have dementia. *Journal of Intergenerational Relationships, 10*(4), 337–354. doi: 10.1080/15350770.2012.724318.

Lo Gerfo, M. (1980). Three ways of reminiscence in theory and practice. *International Journal of Aging and Human Development, 12*(1), 39–47.

Lincoln, Y.S., & Guba, E. G. (1985). *Naturalistic inquiry.* Newbury Park, CA: Sage Publications.

Merriam, S.B. (1995). Reminiscence and the oldest child. In B. Haight, & J.D. Webster (Eds.), *The art and science of reminiscing* (pp. 79–88). Washington, D.C.: Taylor and Francis.

Parker, R.G. (1995). Reminiscence: A continuity theory framework. *The Gerontologist, 35*(4), 515–525.

Penick, J.M., Fallshore, M., & Spencer, A.M. (2014). Using intergenerational service learning to promote positive perceptions about older adults and community service in college students. *Journal of Intergenerational Relationships, 12*(1), 25–39. doi: 10.1080/15350770.2014.870456.

Rosebrook, V. (2002). Intergenerational connections enhance the personal/social development of young children. *International Journal of Early Childhood, 34*(2), 30–41.

Siyahhan, S., Barab, S.A., & Downton, M.P. (2010). Using activity theory to understand intergenerational play: The case of *Family Quest, Computer-Supported Collaborative Learning, 5,* 415–432. Doi:10.1007/s11412–010–9097–1.

Sandburg, A. (2001). Play memories from childhood to adulthood. *Early Child Development and Care, 167*(1), 13–25. doi: 10.1080/0300443011670102.

United States Department of Health and Human Services. (2010). *Healthy people 2020 framework: The vision, mission, and goals of healthy people 2020:* Washington, D.C.: U.S. Department of Health. Retrieved from http://www.healthypeople.gov.

Wellin, C. (2007). Narrative interviewing. *Gerontology & Geriatrics, 28*(1), 79–99, doi: 10.1300/J021v28n01_06.

Wong, P.T.P. (1995). The process of adaptive reminiscence. In B. Haight, & J.D. Webster (Eds.), *The art and science of reminiscing* (pp. 23–35). Washington, D.C.: Taylor and Francis.

Chapter Five

Children's Gendered Play and Toys at Preschool

Mia Heikkilä

The overall aim of this research is to develop updated knowledge on how gender is experienced in play and how toys can be seen as having an amplifying or moderating effect on gendered relations. In this article the use of toys as related to gender is taken into the analysis. Toys are central aspects of children's play and culture, or have become central since society has become more and more material and focused on technical tools and artefacts. Toy production has grown enormously during the last decades and toys have become more and more central in children's lives. In this article the analysis focuses on what role toys play in children's gendered play. The research reported in this article is an ethnographic study of the relation between gender, children, learning, and toys/educational artefacts with a child perspective. The ethnographic work was done over six months from September 2013-March 2014. Nineteen children between 3.5 and 4.5 years of age were included in the preschool group, and there was an equal mix of boys and girls.

One finding was that the toys can be placed in two main categories – *interpreted toys* and *interpretable toys*. The interpreted toys were artefacts commonly associated with toys – an artefact that an adult has decided what kind of play it should be used in/for, and also if the toy was meant for a girl or a boy.

It is clear that gender negotiation is a very vivid part of children's play. This study shows that what kind of toys children are using has an impact on how gender relations and play situations develop, and thereby on boys' and girls' learning boundaries.

The relation between play, learning, and development has been a focus in a number of studies (Dahlberg, Moss & Pence, 1999; Sutton-Smith, 2003; Lytle, 2003; Danby, 1998; Corsaro, 1997; Berthelsen, 2009; Greve, 2009). Play has been seen as a central aspect of children's ability to learn, develop, and build a culture of their own. The play arena is also a place where children are able to keep adults separated from 'their' world, their discourse, and their interpretation of reality. In this paper power relations are analysed as a central part of children's discourse and culture (Connell, 1987; Qvortrup, 2014). Power is here seen as something every child has to relate to in society since adults are still considered more influential than children.

The relationship between adults and children can be seen as a relationship where power relations are established and where children are forced to relate to power. Equity in a real sense is not present, and adults' use of power means that children's lives are also embedded into power relations both between them and adults and between them and other children. Power and hierarchies are seen as central aspects of studying culture and play. Equity and equality are seen as the other side of the equation – a situation that the children crave, but which they are prevented from attaining due to power relations and hierarchies. Equity and equality are, however, important aspects of play, and this creates a paradox. Equity is needed in play, although children seldom experience real equity. Perhaps this is why play is elevated – as a situation where equity between people is happening, without obvious indications that power is being exerted. This is perhaps also why adults in general, and researchers in particular, do not understand and see the logic of every play situation, since this form of equity is unknown to us.

Gender relations are here considered an aspect of how power relations in society are realised (Connell, 1987). As a number of research studies have shown in different ways, gender has been, and still is, one of the most central categories of social life in school settings (Danby, 1998; McNaughton, 2000; Browne, 2004; Epstein, 1998; Paechter, 2007; de Groot Kim, 2011; Uttley & Roberts, 2011). Gender matters for individuals and groups in everyday life. In this article gender is seen as something that is *done* by individuals in relations with others, not something individuals *are* just because they were born girls or boys. There are several categories that matter in social life that would be required for a comprehensive analysis of play and children's culture. In this article the focus on gender is seen to have a great impact on children's everyday lives in educational settings.

Just as other social categories are developed in society and social life, gender is also developed. People do things differently today than in the past, and gender is therefore done differently as well. This difference over time is why new knowledge of how gender matters is needed.

In this article the use of toys as related to gender is analysed. Toys are central aspects of children's play and culture. Toy production has grown enormously in recent times and toys have become more central in children's lives. This research focuses on the role toys play in children's gendered play. Previous research has not focused on how toys are central for children's negotiation in play. This aspect of toys in children's gendered play is therefore further developed in the analysis. The overall aim of this research is to develop updated knowledge on how gender is experienced in play and how toys can be seen as having an amplifying or moderating effect on gendered relations.

Research Questions

1. How is children's gendered play visible?
2. In what ways are toys a part of children's play, and how can the negotiation between toys, gender, and children's play be described?

INTERNATIONAL RESEARCH ON GENDER IN EARLY CHILDHOOD SETTINGS

The body of research around gender and play has grown, become more nuanced through different theoretical perspectives and given valuable knowledge of gender issues. Davies' studies (1998, 2003a, 2003b) of post-structural understanding about how children's gender was constructed in preschool settings have provided new ways of understanding gender relations amongst children. Her work has shown how gender is experienced by children through the use of language and social setting, and how gender relations are negotiated in play situations. Gender is not, according to Davies', a static category where norms and hierarchies are always predictable, but rather a set of patterns which indicate how individuals act. These patterns can change in different social situations, and therefore researchers need to unravel more of these patterns in order to further understand the role that gender plays in children's play and everyday life.

Thorne's work (1987) includes results in line with Davies' although Thorne offers a more specific ethnographic analysis. She shows through ethnographic analysis how gender is a category that can be understood in different ways and in different contexts since gender as a category does different types of work in different settings. Thorne also discusses how gender is subject to negotiation in play discourses. Francis (2011, 2001) and Paechter (2001) build further on these theoretical and empirical analyses within post-structuralism, and support the idea of gender being a category. How gender is understood and matters in everyday life remain an issue for further research to unravel.

Swedish Research on Gender in Early Childhood Settings

Recent Swedish research studies (Lenz Taguchi, 2000; Månsson, 2000) have focused on how gender is experienced in children's play through a post-structural perspective, and contributed valuable knowledge on the issue of gender in early childhood settings. Gender studics in Sweden have become a popular research area due to a number of government policies of gender equality in recent decades.

Hellman (2010) investigates boyishness and restrictions of gender that are visible in preschools. Her analysis highlights the floating gender borders for children in some play contexts and the very strict gender borders in other play contexts. The adults are often the ones monitoring the strict gender borders (Hellman, 2010), where crossing gender borders means risking your social position as a child. Hellman also notes that boys' atypical behaviour such as being caring, crying, and being non-competitive is seldom encouraged or even noticed by the teachers. The teachers have a tendency only to take notice of typical boy behaviour and value the boys' abilities according to that behaviour. Odenbring's (2010) analyses are in line with Hellman's study, and she also elaborates further on how negotiation is done and acted upon in relation to gender. Eidevald (2011) shows the impact gender has on children's play and lives in educational settings in general terms. One of the most recent Swedish research gender studies concerning preschool issues that has gained a lot of publicity is Dolk's (2013) study on so called norm-critical or subversive analysis, where not only gender is analysed, but also how power relations are established and enhanced through the normalisation of certain norms in a context. According to Dolk (2013) some norms are more active than others depending on the context, but the use of power is the common element of these norms. In Dolk's (2013) study the social categories gender and age were examined to determine how these categories matter throughout the preschool setting. The children in her study resisted adults' prompts to do certain things that would develop gender categories that are not exclusive to children.

BUT TOYS THEN?

Toy research is a very broad area consisting of different perspectives. In this study I have combined education, ethnography, and gender studies with a child perspective in order to further understand what role toys play when children learn and develop culture and identity. The toys are not seen or analysed as semiotic objects but rather as artefacts that are used by children in order to enhance, find meaning, and interpret their context (Kress, 2003; 2010). In this study, toys are invested with meaning through the way they are used in children's play. Trawick-Smith, Russell, and Swaminathan (2011) conducted a quantitative study in order to see the impact a number of toys had on children's spontaneous play. They identified clusters of items and three distinct factors were identified: thinking/learning, creativity/imagination, and social interaction.

There are some studies focusing on girls' and boys' preferences concerning toys, or the tendency to classify toys as girl toys or boy toys (Cherney & Dempsey, 2010; Sandberg & Vuorinen, 2008; Cherney & London, 2006; Cherney, Kelly-Vance, Gill Glover, Ruane & Ryalls, 2003; Serbin, Poulin-Dubois, Colburne, Sen, & Eichenstedt, 2001; Campenni, 1999). These studies show that gender is a significant factor concerning toys, but do not elaborate further on why or how gender signifies when toys are used by children in games.

Toys can be considered cultural tools for children to understand society and the relationships they are in, and in that sense toys are also tools that support and establish identities (Francis, 2010). The analysis here focuses on understanding how children use toys in play and how toys can establish or diminish gender norms.

METHOD

The research reported in this article is an ethnographic study of the relation between gender, children, learning, and toys/educational artefacts with a child's perspective. The obvious challenge when conducting research on children within a child's perspective (James, 2001/2008) is the risk to over interpret or put one's own understandings of the world upon the children studied. The purpose of using an ethnographic method here is to show children's own agency and how they are capable individuals in shaping their own life. As stated above, children are objects to power exerted by adults, but preschool and especially play situations in preschool, can in some respects be arenas where the power relation between adults and children is diminished. Another challenge when conducting ethnographic work is to not superimpose my own childhood on the children in the study. Being conscious about this challenge and continuously reflecting on it during fieldwork are crucial for ensuring the credible results of the study. Hammersley (2001/2008) points out the importance of understanding parallel processes when studying some ready-made categories like gender. Here the experienced ethnographer is constantly reflecting and knows how and when to use personal experiences to understand the subjects studied (Gordon, Holland & Lahelma, 2001/2008). In this research study I have reflected in text and thought with the teachers at the early childhood educational setting where the material was constructed.

A feminist approach to the research process has been helpful (Skeggs, 2001/2008) since feminist research methods are used to see power relations in the researcher's own work (Jones & Barron, 2007). Gordon, Holland and Lahelma (2001/2008) write that feminist ethnographers seek to observe processes in the construction of gender hierarchy and gender power relations at the micro level of an educational institution. This research process has also included reflections on the power relations to which research itself contributes. This reflective work has contributed to the validity and reliability of the analysis presented here.

The early childhood educational setting where the material for this study was constructed was a preschool in a Swedish multi-ethnic suburban area. The ethnographic work was done over six months from September 2013-March 2014. Nineteen children were included in the preschool group, and there was a nearly equal mix of boys and girls. The children were 3.5 to 4.5 years old when I started the ethnographic process, and the group had three teachers.

I took part in the everyday work of this preschool group, and followed each child to capture the experiences s/he had in preschool. I have, as James (2001/2008) states, tried to regard children as research participants in order for their voices to be heard and acknowledged. When conducting an ethnography within a child's perspective, this is crucial.

The analysis of this ethnographic material has transpired continuously throughout the study with additional detailed analysis being added later. In this chapter I present a number of examples that illustrate how toys are a part of children's negotiation in gendered play, and how toys become a central part of the play process at the micro level. Gendered play is defined as a play situation where gender explicitly or implicitly matters through the use of language and through the way in which the play situation is carried out by the children taking part in a game. Sutton-Smith (2003) points out the folly of endless attempts to define play and argues for viewing play an open social situation where communication in the specific context can establish play as a social event for children.

I deliberately use 'gender' as a collective word for categories that relate to people's (biological) sex. I could use femininity and masculinity to nuance gender, but that would also mean excluding people who do not identify themselves with these categories. I think feminist researchers should challenge also the way we express gender analysis in order to include all individuals in our analysis.

RESULTS

The results are presented in two main sections. The first section presents examples of how gender is done in and is visible in preschool. The second section will deepen the discussion on gendered play in preschool by relating it to how gender is done by and together with the toys used in the examples shown. The collective negotiation of meanings and relations between gender, toys, and play is discussed in relation to two main categories of toys that the analysis shows. The current research on how gender matters presented earlier in this article is a foundation for this analysis.

In educational settings one clear aspect of how gender matters is how boys and girls create gender-segregated games and play situations. It can also be said that the institutions where children play are organised in a way that restores a gender order where girls and boys are encouraged to play in a gender-segregated manner. In a world where gender would not matter, I believe that individuals would find another person to play with, hang out with, someone who they would feel comfortable with regardless of this person's gender. In a world where power shapes the relations between women and men, it applies in children's play as well. A situation where girls and boys play games together is for the purposes of the present study seen as a situation where gender is negotiated.

In everyday work in the preschool studied, roughly 15 children were present and most often divided into smaller groups where children work together with one teacher. A song or a book is put in focus when these working sessions are planned, and they can last for 20 to 90 minutes. The sessions were child-centred with the children having a great impact on both the content and the educational direction. It is interesting to note that toys are never part of these educational sessions as the sessions focus on creative processes, language development, and group processes.

Gender is experienced in all these sessions in different ways.

Example 1

Amelie, Nathalie, Ebonee, and Mirabelle sit in the studio at the preschool. They paint with watercolours and much of what they paint is coloured pink. Some of the paintings include really dark pink.

This is a very stereotypical situation in a preschool and it is still a reality that four girls sit together and paint pink paintings. Here these girls talk at the same time as they paint and their conversation concerns both paintings and other things. They have by language use and by relating to each other during this session negotiated around the use of colour. The result is that they all paint with pink, and here this is interpreted as a way of showing unity and showing friendship. Moreover, it is a way of doing gender since pink is one of the most common symbols for femininity (Ambjörnsson, 2011).

Another situation of doing gender happens after an educational session in the same room, here called the studio. Before this happens, the group has worked together and used a special kind of thin paper that makes a sound when using it.

Figure 5.1.   Stereotypical Preschool Situation.

Example 2

> Johannes comes into the studio and takes a pair of scissors and a bit of rustling
> paper. No one is here in the room. He tries to cut the thin paper but soon puts it
> down on the table. He walks up to a box of beads and puts his hand in it so that
> the beads move around inside the jar. Some fall out on the table. He does this
> with his hand a few times, and then starts to pick up the beads that have fallen
> out on the table. He picks out all the beads calmly and systematically. Then he
> screws on the cap and shakes the can as a rhythm instrument. He looks out of
> the room and sees Anne and Lukas come closer to the door. He puts everything
> back and leaves the room while Anne and Lukas come into the room. Lukas
> sits down by the same table where Johannes sat a while ago. He brings out the
> glue and starts gluing on the paper, and opens the lid of the box of beads.
> Lukas starts to glue beads onto the paper and does this very carefully, one bead
> at a time. Lukas continues to glue beads in a row with the glue stick and box of
> beads in front of him.

This example shows how gender is negotiated in another way, and that
both girls and boys can take gender positions in preschool that are perhaps
not expected. In this example, Johannes and Lukas are doing what at this
preschool mostly is considered as something girls do. But it is still an ac-

cepted thing for boys to do. They are doing crafts with small beads and glue, a very demanding thing to do for a 4-year-old in terms of fine motor skills. But this is not commented on by any adult or teacher, not highlighted or reflected on as almost any other educational session is in this preschool. It happens silently, but it is still happening. It takes at least five minutes for each of the boys to do what they do. This relates to what Davies (2003) shows in her research, where gender positions or gender orders are negotiated. Hellman (2010) also discusses what boys are allowed to do, and her analysis suggests that aspects of boyishness are seldom reflected on or viewed as part of being a real boy to the extent that stereotypical boy behaviour would.

When the children have 'time between' these planned and organised sessions or daily routines such as lunch, outdoor activities, washing hands, standing in lines, or tidying up, or when so-called free sessions take place, there are very quickly a number of toys visible. The artefacts that were defined as toys in this study were cars, building materials (lego, plus plus, domino etc.), plastic animals, kitchen devices, board games, books, etc. The definition of toys is based on the fact that the children *used* these artefacts in their play. The toys were placed by the children in a play context, and the artefacts created play contexts through the children's play in different ways.

Example 3

> A crafts book is on a table and one of the unpainted pictures inside shows the sea maiden Ariel sitting and the text below the picture says that she is 'waiting for his first kiss, paint the picture while she waits'. One of the teachers read this out loud, and says nothing, looking puzzled. This crafts book is one of the girls' own.

This example is another way of showing how tacit expectations on a girl are communicated. In this crafts book, a girl is told to sit and wait to be chosen, and heterosexual love is taken for granted as the norm. In this situation the book belonged to one of the girls, and it is possible to interpret the teacher's lack of comment as being surprised or as being shocked by the text. The book was (only) lying on one of the tables for a couple of hours, but it was still visible and communicating its pictures to both boys and girls.

Example 4

> Anish plays with her hair clips and compares how they sound when they are used. Mirabelle stands by watching.

Here Anish has got hair clips in her hair and she takes them off to listen to the sound they make when being opened and closed. This is a way of doing gender which perhaps can be seen as typical of girls since boys very seldom wear hair clips and have the possibility to listen to the sound of them. To take them off, play with them as a kind of a toy, and try out how they sound can be seen as a series of small ways of doing gender.

Example 5

> Cornelia: Do you think I 'm good looking?

The last small example of how gender is done is this simple question. Cornelia turns to me when I sit on the floor in the construction room and asks me if I think she is good looking. Just the question and the need for affirmation are here interpreted as girl things. What is not shown here is that she is wearing a dress and has some hair stuff in her hair, all coloured pink. She has, before turning to me, been standing in front of the mirror in the kitchen room. During the time of this ethnographic work I never saw a boy do this or I did not pay attention to it. Whether it is a girl or a boy asking such a question I would say it is a way of doing gender, and to say that gender matters.

TWO MAIN CATEGORIES OF TOYS

Children negotiated the meaning of the toys in their play through language use, through the use of gestures, and through trying out different possible characteristics for toys to take in a certain play situation. One finding is that the toys can be placed in two main categories – interpreted toys and interpretable toys. The interpreted toys were such artefacts that we most commonly mean when we talk about toys. Examples of interpreted toys can be cars, dolls, pitchers, plates, carts, rocking horses, trains, and puzzles. When children played with interpreted toys at the preschool the play was already designed for the children, the context for the play was set, and the toy was very dominant. The toy with its semiotic meanings had power in the play situation. Negotiation and social interaction between the children were not vivid, and use of language was almost not present at all. Thereby the level of interactive play and learning was low. Interpreted toys give children a manuscript and a dialogue that is very much like adult dialogue. Here children practice in their games the process of becoming adults. The interpreted toys are mostly used in a gender-segregated manner which divides boys and girls into different play contexts.

The interpretable toys are possible to consider as the opposite kind of toy. Although the categories are called interpreted and interpretable toys, there are still possibilities of being interpretable in very different ways. The interpretable toys, these results show, allow for more open play where children can go in and out of play, and were both girls and boys can create common play. The interpretable toys are all kinds of building blocks (including Lego, Plus Plus, domino, magnets) and paint. Construction and building are stereotypically related to boys' play and when looking at the play happening in this preschool, this is also what happens here. One of the rooms at the preschool is a construction room, and it is predominantly used by boys.

Example 6

Emil has built something with blocks and he makes a sound like shooting. Amira comes and says to him, no guns!

There is a group of toys that can be put in both categories. Lego is one of these since Lego can both encourage creative play and building as well as be connected to a manual where the result is a very interpreted toy with a certain purpose and context. This double function of Lego is perhaps the key to its popularity. In the preschool context, Lego is only used as an interpretable toy, without manuals. The Legos are organised in different boxes related to colour.

Figure 5.2. Block Building.

Another artefact that is put 'in between' interpreted and interpretable is the iPad. In some situations, it is clearly a toy when children are using it for entertainment purposes. In other situations, it is a vivid part of an educational session where an application is used to illustrate a process or to inspire a feeling.

When taking a closer look at how gender works in relation to the categories of interpreted and interpretable toys, it is interesting to see that gender is done in children's play more clearly when the interpreted toys are used in the play. The interpretable toys give children the possibility to use their own preferences more and the power aspect of the toy is not present. Since the interpreted toy communicates a meaning to children, using the toy also communicates an expectation of how gender is understood. This will be further discussed in the following analysis.

Situation 1. iPad, music and gender

> When I arrive at the preschool one morning Alina (preschool teacher) is sitting together with four children and they are dancing in the assembly room, the room with one large blue rug. Alina has the iPad in one hand searching for something on it, and after a while the music starts.
> Johannes: Nooo, it's girls. I do not like that.
> And then he walks away and hides from the others. Alina follows him and asks why he says that. He replies and says again that he does not like girls. Alina answers and says that she sings beautifully.
> Liana: Your mama is a girl. You like her of course. You wanted 'babe'?
> Johannes says that he does not want it and that it's boring. Alina and another girl are then debating on what music to choose.
> Liana: Should we take Justin Bieber instead?
> Zahra: No Alvin and the gang!
> Zahra is happy and dances around the room when the music starts. Johannes is bit by bit re-entering the group and after a while he is back dancing with the others.

In this situation Alina, the preschool teacher, is together with the children, and this is a situation which could be called an in-between time. This happens after breakfast and before the educational sessions start. Not all of the children have arrived at the preschool yet, so it is also a time of waiting for the others.

Here the iPad has the position of a toy that regulates the situation. It is interpretable, since the content of the music they listen to is negotiable and in this situation negotiated. Johannes genders the situation by saying that he does not want to dance to the 'girls' music'. He goes away and by doing so he also indicates that gender is a significant factor in this dancing game. The other children are not saying anything nor commenting on the fact that Johannes focuses on the singer's gender. While Johannes is away, Zahra goes on negotiating what music to listen and dance to, without an explicit focus on gender. Alina is trying to negotiate the meaning of gender with Johannes in this situation, and she is trying to diminish the importance of gender by relating to Johannes's love of his mother. The iPad is here in this situation used as a toy for negotiation of what focus gender can have, and it also makes gender meanings explicit for the children present.

Situation 2. Domino and doing gender

Now the children sit and build with domino blocks. They build formations along the floor. They are building and moving around the domino blocks while talking.

> Johannes: The way out! Way out!
> Teemu: She has ruined it
> Johannes: Look out Emil. You can build somewhere else!
> Teemu: You are taking too much
> Lukas and Cornelia are all of a sudden doing a high five.
> C: Not so hard!
> L: But it should sound loudly
> C: Good Lukas (when he beats gently)
> They continue building. Julian sits and builds by himself.
> Johannes: Can you help me then?
> Lukas: But then mine will break

Figure 5.3. Domino Blocks.

Cornelia: We can do a little in between
Cornelia has moved to build together with Julian and moved away from Amelie and Sofia.
Amelie and Sofia: Where is Cornelia?
Without getting an answer Sofia and Amelie walk out of the room.

Here children have the interpretable toy domino blocks in front of them. They are using them to create play and the process of using the blocks in this situation can at the same time be considered play in itself. Johannes and Teemu are building intensely and wanting the others to go somewhere else. Lukas and Cornelia are by doing a high five marking that they are doing something together and something that is not what Johannes and Teemu are doing. The play situation can be considered in terms of negotiation. Lukas and Cornelia seem not to be paying attention to gender here, since they are playing together and also by negotiating the appropriate force of a high five together. According to the results of this study this is what happens when children are using interpretable toys. Girls and boys are more likely to play together, find solutions of play dilemmas together and find common, rather than separate, arenas of communication.

The interesting twist at the end of the situation is that Amelie and Sofia seem to pay attention to gender by only asking where Cornelia is, and not wondering about the other children. Amelia and Sofia are walking hand in hand when asking this and thereby marking their unity. Cornelia does not respond to them and reverse orders her own focus.

Situation 4. Plastic animals and hula hoop

Cornelia sings a song that she made up and Teemu is trying to sing together with her. They call the song 'Song of the little cat' and they are playing with a plastic leopard, a tiger, and a small tiger while singing. They hang out and play at the shelf by the window where the domino blocks are placed in the drawers below. Teemu has a plastic leopard in his hand.
Cornelia: Stop biting me in the tail (saying it to the leopard)
The children happened to find three building ledges on the top of the shelf and Cornelia builds a kind of parking lot of them.
Zahra: Nathalie! Nathalie, the hula hoop is now inside!
Cornelia does not pay any attention to what Zahra is trying to say to her, but continues playing with Teemu.
C: Teemu, you can be in this place. We can do like this and you can come in if it's scary in there.
T: Well
C: Where do you want to go if it's scary?
Cornelia says this to Teemu showing a small opening that she made.
C: A door here instead
Johannes and Samuel come and look at their game. Johannes climbs on top of the so called parking lot.

C: Hey buddy, what are you doing here
S: Look out! We are building a car track (for me)
Cornelia makes the sound of a kiss to the big tiger Teemu now has in his hand. Then he throws it away and walks away.

In this play situation the children are mixing toys. They are using both interpreted toys – the plastic animals – and interpretable toys – the ledges and the domino blocks. The result is a play situation where some things are fixed and some are more negotiable. The leopard and the tigers frame the play by being the ones who sing, and by biting one another. Cornelia and Teemu are playing together in the situation, and Zahra, Johannes, and Samuel join them. Zahra tries to re-negotiate the content of the play by informing Cornelia of the hula hoop, but Cornelia ignores that. Her information to Cornelia could also be seen as an attempt 'to gender the play' by including Cornelia into her play with the rock ring which is a toy that reverse order used by girls. Cornelia and Teemu are building the parking lot for the animals, which makes the play situation more negotiable than without the parking lot. It is interesting to think that children might deliberately choose an interpretable toy to accompany the interpreted toy to make the possibilities of the play larger. Cornelia and Teemu discuss where the escape routes are if Teemu gets scared, which makes it possible to see how gender is negotiated. Boys seldom enter a discussion on being scared since one aspect of masculinity is to learn not to show fear (Connell, 1997). Cornelia and Teemu are here then also making the boundaries for gender larger for boys by discussing the possibility of fear. Then Cornelia performs a gendered action by kissing Teemu's animal and making the sound of a kiss. Is that what interpreted toys encourage – gender roles implemented in the toys that are 'ready'?

Situation 5. Building blocks and gender

Now Samuel, Oscar, and Martin mix Legos, figures, and magnetic building blocks and start building. Samuel, Oscar, and Martin are talking constantly while they are building. They build the play context while talking and moving around the building they have built. They follow each other both in talk and in gesture.
S: The helicopter is standing there
M: It spins around, Samuel and Oscar
S: Helicopter! vioviovio (making the sound of a flying helicopter)
O: This is a Star Wars. He finds the lamp!
M: This one is not ready to play with
O: Well this one is ready
S: It is dropping bombs there!

Building blocks are central in this play and the way they are used to shape the play. Three boys are here negotiating the process of their helicopter-play.

This situation begins with the three children sitting with the building blocks and talking constantly. They are in a play process, shaping the context, and by building and talking they negotiate the play. How each one of them is building and putting the building blocks has an impact on the others' way of building. The building play and the negotiation within it has become a play with interpreted toys where the creation of a helicopter shapes the way in which the play develops. It is not possible for the children to negotiate the content as much at the end of this play as it was at the beginning of the building process. This means that the play has created interpreted toys and also gendered the play in the sense that it is more common in this preschool that boys play with flying objects such as helicopters.

DISCUSSION

The aim of this chapter has been to develop updated knowledge on how gender is experienced in play and how toys can be seen as having an amplifying or moderating effect on gendered relations. By showing several examples of how gender is experienced and how gender and toys are creating gendered play together, I have shown how gender is experienced in play together with the use of toys. Earlier research presented also shows both that gender is present and how it is present in preschool contexts as well as in play situations.

It is clear that gender negotiation is a very vivid part of children's play. Gender can be negotiated in very different ways, and taking different directions, as previous research also shows. Toys in play have not been analysed as much as play itself has, although artefacts have been used by humans for thousands of years in all kinds of social situations. The research presented earlier in this chapter shows that the analysis of toys and gender has been focused on psychological aspects of toy preference relating to gender.

This study shows that what kind of toys children are using has an impact on how gender relations and play situations develop, and thereby on boys' and girls' learning boundaries. The meaning of gender is negotiated in different contexts and if the play situation could be an arena for individuals to grow and develop that would be a very good starting point for the social life of a child. If gender is emphasised too much in irrelevant situations, individuals and personalities can be hidden behind the gender curtains. For these reasons, it is important to have nuanced knowledge on how processes of gender, toys, and play are related to one another.

REFERENCES

Ambjörnsson, F. (2011). *Rosa: den farliga färgen.* (Pink: the dangerous color). Stockholm: Ordfront.

Berthelsen, D. (2009). Participatory learning: Issues for research and practice. In Berthelsen, Donna, Brownlee, Jo and Johansson Eva (eds.). *Participatory Learning in the Early Years. Research and Pedagogy,* (pp. 1–11). London/New York: Routledge.

Browne, N. (2004). *Gender equity in the early years.* Berkshire: Open University Press.

Campenni, E.C. (1999). Gender stereotyping of children's toys. A comparison of parents and nonparents. *Sex Roles, 40*(1–2), 121–138.

Cherney, I.D., & Dempsey, J. (2010). Young children's classification, stereotyping and play behaviour for gender neutral and ambiguous toys. *Educational Psychology, 30*(6), 651–669.

Cherney, I.D., Kelly-Vance, L., Gill Glover, K., Ruane, A., & Ryalls, B.O. (2003). The effects of stereotyped toys and gender on play assessment in children aged 18–47 months. *Educational Psychology, 23*(1), 95–106.

Cherney, I.D., & London, K. (2006). Gender-linked differences in the toys, television shows, computer games, and outdoor activities of 5 to 13-year-old children. *Sex Roles, 54*(9–10) 717–726.

Connell, R.W. (1987). *Gender and Power.* Sydney: Allen and Unwin.

Danby, S. (1998). The serious and playful work of gender: Talk and social order in a preschool classroom. In Yelland, N. (ed.) *Gender in Early Childhood* (pp. 175–205). London & New York: Routledge.

Davies, B. (1989/2003). *Frogs and snails and feminist tales. Preschool Children and Gender.* Sydney: Allen & Unwin.

Davies, B. (1998). The politics of category membership in early childhood settings. In Yelland, N. (ed.) *Gender in Early Childhood,* (pp. 131–148). London & New York: Routledge.

Davies, B. (2003). *Shards of glass. Children reading & writing beyond gendered identities.* Cresskill: Hampton Press.

De Groot K.S. (2011). Lessons learned early: Girls wait. In Jacobson, T. (ed.) *Perspectives on Gender in Early Childhood,* (pp. 231–246). St Paul: Redleaf Press.

Dolk, K. (2013). *Bångstyriga barn: Makt, normer och delaktighet i förskolan.* Diss. Stockholm: Ordfront.

Eidevald, C. (2009). *Det finns inga tjejbestämmare: att förstå kön som position i förskolans vardagsrutiner och lek.* Diss. Högskolan i Jönköping.

Francis, B. (2001). Beyond postmodernism: Feminist agency in educational research. In Francis, B. & Skelton, C. (eds.). *Investigating Gender. Contemporary Perspectives in Education,* (pp.65–76). Buckingham/Philadelphia: Open University Press.

Francis, B. (2010). Gender, toys and learning. *Gender & Education, 36*(3), 325–344.

Greve, A. (2009). Friendships and participation among young children in a Norwegian kindergarten. In Berthelsen, D., Brownlee, J., & Johansson Eva (eds.). *Participatory Learning in the Early Years. Research and Pedagogy,* (pp. 78–92). London/New York: Routledge.

Gordon, T., Holland, J., & Lahelma, E. (2001/2008). Ethnographic research in educational settings. In Atkinson, P., Coffey, A., Delamont, S., Lofland, J. & Lofland, L. (eds.). *Handbook of Ethnography,* (pp. 188–203). Los Angeles/London/New Delhi/Singapore: SAGE.

Hammersley, M. (2001). Obvious, all too obvious? Methodological issues in using sex/gender as a variable in educational research. In Francis, Becky and Skelton, Christine (eds.). *Investigating Gender. Contemporary Perspectives in Education,* (pp. 27–38). Buckingham/Philadelphia: Open University Press.

Hellman, A. (2010). *Kan Batman vara rosa?: Förhandlingar om pojkighet och normalitet på en förskola.* Diss. Göteborg: Göteborgs universitet

James, A. (2001/2008). Ethnography in the study of children and childhood. In Atkinson, P., Coffey, A., Delamont, S., Lofland, J. & Lofland, L. (eds.). *Handbook of Ethnography,* (pp.246–257). Los Angeles/London/New Delhi/Singapore: SAGE.

Jones, L., & Barron, I. (2007). *Research and gender.* London: Continuum.

Lenz Taguchi, H. (2000). *Emancipation och motstånd: dokumentation och kooperativa läroprocesser i förskolan.* Diss. Stockholm: Univ.

Lytle, D.E. (ed.) (2003). *Play and Educational Theory and Practice, Play & Culture Studies, 5*. Westport: Praeger Publishers.

McNaughton, G. (2000). *Rethinking gender in early childhood education*. London/Thousand Oaks: SAGE Publishing.

Månsson, A. (2000). *Möten som formar: interaktionsmönster på förskola mellan pedagoger och de yngsta barnen i ett genusperspektiv*. Diss. Lund: Univ.

Odenbring, Y. (2010). *Kramar, kategoriseringar och hjälpfröknar: Könskonstruktioner i interaktion i förskola, förskoleklass och skolår ett*. Diss. Göteborg: Göteborgs universitet

Paechter, Carrie (2001). Using poststructuralist ideas in gender theory and research. In Francis, Becky and Skelton, Christine (eds.). *Investigating Gender. Contemporary perspectives in education*. (Pp. 41–51). Buckingham/Philadelphia: Open University Press.

Qvortrup, J. (2014). Sociology: Societal structure, development of childhood, and the wellbeing of children. In Asher, B.A., Ferran, C., Ivar, F., & Korbin, J.E.(eds.) *Handbook of Child Well-Being. Theories, Methods and Policies in Global Perspective*, (pp. 663–707) Springer: Netherlands.

Sandberg, A., & Vuorinen, T. (2008). Dimensions of childhood play and toys. *Asia-Pacific Journal of Teacher Education, 36*(2), 135–146.

Serbin, L.A., Poulin-Dubois, D., Colburne, K.A., Sen, M.G., & Eichstedt, J.A. (2001). Gender stereotyping in infancy: Visual preferences for and knowledge of gender-stereotyped toys in the second year. *International Journal of Behavioral Development, 25*, 7–15.

Skeggs, B. (2001/2008). Feminist ethnography. In Atkinson, P., Coffey, A., Delamont, S., Lofland, J. & Lofland, L. (eds.). *Handbook of Ethnography* (pp. 426–442). Los Angeles/London/New Delhi/Singapore: SAGE.

Sutton-Smith, B. (2003). Play as a parody of emotional vulnerability. In Lytle, D.E. (ed.). *Play and Educational Theory and Practice, Play & Culture Studies* (pp. 3–18), Westport: Praeger Publishers.

Trawick-Smith, J., Russell, H., & Swaminathan, S. (2010). Measuring the effects of toys on the problem-solving, creative and social behaviours of preschool children. *Early Child Development and Care, 181*(7), 909–927.

Uttley, C.M., & Roberts, C.A. (2011). Gender portrayal in early childhood children's books. In Jacobson, T. (ed.) *Perspectives on Gender in Early Childhood*, (pp. 127–154), St Paul: Redleaf Press.

Chapter Six

The Conservation of Meaning and the Logic of Meanings

Exploring Piaget's Implicit Social Theory in the Context of Newspaper Puzzles

Keith Alward

It is not well known that sociological considerations were central to Jean Piaget's general epistemology. He is generally regarded as an "individualist" and is often contrasted with Lev Vygotsky, who was explicitly concerned with the intersection between sociological and psychological-cognitive processes. With regard to Piaget's general theory and its relationship to social life, I would say there is a relationship, but its exact character remains elusive and implicit rather than explicit.

Undoubtedly, the only writer to show an understanding of cognition that anywhere approaches the depth of Piaget's is the Russian Lev Vygotsky, who was born the same year as Piaget, 1896, yet died as a relatively young man in 1934. Nevertheless, for so short a life, he produced an incredibly large corpus of writing, much of which is still to be translated. The thrust of his work is that cognition, first and foremost, is tied to social experience and is inseparable from historical-cultural forces, which constitute the matrix of all social life (Vygotsky, 1978).

In contrast, the seminal body of Piaget's work traces the development of children's intelligence, but says relatively little about how this development is tied to social experience. In reading Piaget, it seems that understanding fundamental concepts of space and time, conservation of quantities, concepts of number and causality, and the development of logical thought are virtually independent of social experience. The theory is one of internal regulations in the dynamics of assimilation and accommodation within and between internal schemes that coordinate sensorimotor and conceptual actions on the world.

The theory purports that the intelligence of an organism is what the organism can do and that this is a function of the coordination of schemes within the organism. Piaget's theory says little about how social experience participates in this dynamic of schemes accommodating to reality and thereby furthering the grasp of intelligence and consciousness (Piaget, 1976). In addition, Piaget did empirical work to show that social experience, such as training, has little effect on the acquisition of concepts (Piaget & Inhelder, 1969). On the face of it, it would seem that Piaget is in direct conflict with Vygotsky. I, along with others, claim that this is not the case and that, in fact, both Piaget and Vygotsky are constructivists who complement one another (Beck, 2013; Nicolopoulou, 1993; Van Hoorn, Nourot, Scales, & Alward, 2016). Nevertheless, one might ask, what is Piaget's social theory? Where do we turn to find its substance, and, more important, where do we find the empirical work that fleshes out this theory?

PIAGET'S IMPLICIT SOCIAL THEORY AND THE CONSERVATION OF MEANING

There are titillating hints found throughout his writings, from the earliest to the last. For example, in "The Construction of Reality in the Child" (1954), Piaget stated in conclusion that, ". . . conceptual thought is collective (social) thought obeying common laws. . . . It is by cooperation with another person that the mind arrives at verifying judgments" (Piaget, 1954, p. 360).

His important work on moral development charted a course of social cognition tied to social coordinations and linked the onset of operational (logical) thought to social coordinations structured around normative rules of agreement and disagreement, i.e., games with rules (Piaget, 1965). His work on the elaboration of symbolic thought, *Play, Dreams and Imitation* (Piaget, 1962) linked the emergence of operational thought with social consensus regarding the meaning of signs. "Whether it is the construction of the operations which determines social coordinations or the converse, it is clear that the two processes are interdependent" (Piaget 1946, p. 239). A 1950 essay published in *Sociological Studies* (Piaget, 1995) stated that rational or operational thought depends on both mental and social coordination organized as mathematical groupings.

> It is through participation in collective (i.e., social) activity organized as groupings that the child eventually becomes capable of reason, itself organized as a grouping . . . (which is) a system of possible substitutions . . . constituting a general logic . . . which characterizes the form of equilibrium common to both social and individual actions. (Piaget, 1995, p. 94)

Elsewhere in *Sociological Studies* he stated, "Human knowledge is essentially collective, and social life constitutes an essential factor in the creation and growth of knowledge. . ." (Piaget, 1995, p. 30).

In short, throughout Piaget's long history there is a continual reference to the crucial importance of social experience on the development of cognitive functions. One can find in various English translations and in non-translated work a variety of propositions on the relationship of social experience to cognition. One that I find interesting, promising, but also paradoxical, is an assertion that both social coordinations and mental coordinations tend towards an operational grouping, making rational life possible and, without their mutual coordination, impossible.

The link between the general theory and his implicit social theory is to be found, I believe, in the domain of semiotics and, more precisely, in what I am calling "*the conservation of meaning.*" I am using the term "conservation" here in the same sense that Piaget used throughout his general theory, as referencing an invariant in the context of change.

In some broad way, Piaget's entire effort has been to account for conservation in cognition. How does the child fashion a world of permanent objects when the sensation of objects is in constant flux? How does the child fashion an "objective" time when experience is a succession of events unfolding in a temporal cascade? How does the child eventually differentiate cause and effect and conserve their respective roles? Similarly, for the construction of a uniform space that envelops all placements and displacements, and a quantitative conservation in which amounts, like quantitative number, length, substance, weight, volume, etc., are conserved even though encountered in a shifting field of deformations? For example, the child eventually grasps that the number of objects in an array is independent of their spatial arrangements, that the weight of a substance is independent of its shape, or that the amount of a substance is independent of its shape (Piaget & Inhelder, 1969).

In the same sense, the *conservation of meaning* refers to the conservation of the meaning of an action that occurs in contexts that vary from instant to instant and from one purpose to another. I link meaning to "action" because in a theory in which intelligence resides in action, so also does meaning. The meaning of an action is what can be accomplished with the action, its purpose, its function, its value. Every action has a meaning, and every meaning is manifest as an action. To attribute meaning to words, which reflects our common understanding, is also to say no more than the fact that words are implicit actions, whether in the form of conjunctions and disjunctions, verbs modified by adverbs, or nouns modified by adjectives, which, along with pronouns, must be located within hierarchies of classes and series. The actions are either explicit, as in verbs, or implicit mental acts of locating points within hierarchies of classes and series, or acts of combining and separating, as in conjunctions and disjunctions. For example, in the expression, "I went across the big, blue bay in a small, but fast, boat to attend my son's wedding to a lovely young lady," every word is either explicitly referring to an action or requires locating a point within a hierarchy of classes or series.

It is a biological given that humans are social animals from conception on, by virtue of their interdependent connection to the nurturing mechanisms of the mother; in the womb, neonately, and beyond. The link between human action and social action is strong. Although one could argue there are purely instrumental acts that have no social meaning or context, there are no social actions that do not entail a corresponding meaning. The core of social life is shared meaning, and any social theory must be able to account for the *conservation of meaning*.

PIAGET'S LOGIC OF MEANINGS

In an earlier paper I proposed that the *conservation of meaning* results from intra- and inter-individual constraints (possibilities and necessities) that function like groupings, where "groupings" are a logical clustering of substitutions (Alward, 2012). Here I extend this theme by connecting the idea of constraints to Piaget's last work, which addressed intensional logic and the concept of "relevant proximal sets" (Piaget & Garcia, 1991).

In brief, Piaget's operatory logical (lattices, the INCR group, groupings, the 16 binary operations) entail a null set, or the negation of an affirmation. To say something is an 'A' is also to state that there are other things that are 'not A', the negation of 'A'. But what is in the domain of 'not A'? Logically, it is everything that is not an 'A'. Piaget's operatory logic breaks down around this point, and to remedy it Piaget and Garcia (1991) drew from modern intensional logic and introduced the "proximal set," i.e., a reduced set of 'not A' that consists of exemplars that are "relevant to 'A'." For example, the question "What is not an apple?" might elicit an answer, "an orange," rather than something like "an aardvark." That is, in considering appleness, an orange might be more proximate and relevant than an aardvark.

However, as illustrated in Figure 6.1, an aardvark may be more relevant to an apple if the proximal set has been defined as consisting only of an apple and aardvark.

PUZZLES AND "MEANING IMPLICATION ACTIONS" (MIAS)

In the former paper on the *conservation of meaning*, I used puzzles from the daily newspaper to illustrate how constraints within the puzzle space coalesced to determine how each cell in the puzzle space must be filled, irrespective of the particular route to a solution. That is, the meaning of each cell of the puzzle is established by a set of constraints that operate on the

'A' stands for apple & aardvark.
Point to the aardvark.

Figure 6.1.   The Proximal Set Consists of Apple and Aardvark.

overall puzzle space, such that only one meaning can be applied to each cell. I further argued that these constraints operated as Piaget's groupings, with a number of different constraint paths resulting in the same outcome, or as a group of constraints that can substitute for one another. The same analysis applies whether the puzzles are word puzzles, arithmetic puzzles, or classification puzzles. The purpose of the present paper is to show that these constraints can be viewed as a *logic of meanings*, as intended in Piaget's last work, "Towards a Logic of Meanings" (Piaget & Garcia, 1991), and that these constraints function as a grouping. I am calling the act of filling in a cell a *Meaning Implication Action* (MIA).

Relevance defines the proximal set and is
inseparable from social considerations

Figure 6.2.   Relevance Is Inseparable from Social Considerations.

As a simple beginning, imagine there are four cells to be filled in a puzzle, each with a different object (see Figure 6.3).

Rule 1: If two cells are filled with an identical pair of objects, with a total of four objects to choose from, and an assumption that each cell will have a different object, what can go in the remaining two empty cells? In Figure 6.3, could cells X or Y contain either an apple or an aardvark? The answer is no because if, for example, X contained an apple, then V & W would each contain an aardvark, violating the conditions of the puzzle. The logic of Rule 1 follows from the definition of the proximal set of four different objects, each ultimately assigned to four cells. The general statement of Rule 1 is that

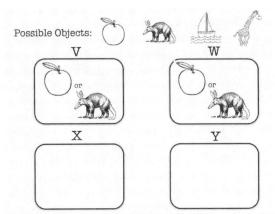

Possible Objects:

Each box must contain one object that is different from all the others.
What can be in boxes X or Y?

Figure 6.3.   An Illustration of Rule 1.

if there is a limited set of possible exemplars that must occupy a domain of cells of the same set size, such that each cell contains a different exemplar, and there are two cells in that domain with identical pairs of exemplars, then those exemplars cannot reside elsewhere in the domain.

In this particular problem, either a giraffe or a sailboat can go in cells X & Y. However, there is no logic that will tell you which object goes in cells X and Y. You simply know it cannot be an apple or an aardvark, i.e., the contents of cells X and Y are "not-apple" and "not aardvark."

Rule 2: Referring to Figure 6.4, you do know, however, that if a giraffe were to be in box X, that a sailboat would have to be in box Y because there is only one element still unassigned from the proximal set, i.e., the sailboat. The general statement of Rule 2 is that if there is a limited proximal set of possible exemplars that must occupy a domain of cells, and only one exemplar from that set is not yet applied to the remaining cell in the domain, then that exemplar belongs in that cell, e.g., if it is not an apple, it is an aardvark.

These two rules pertain to the reciprocities in the null proximate set and are sufficient to solve a wide range of daily newspaper puzzles. Parenthetically, it must be noted and also be of some interest to developmental psychologists that, while these rules can be successfully used by preoperational children, many of the puzzles dependent on these rules are well beyond the grasp of even early operational children.

Before moving on, consider the following "bead problem." Imagine there are 16 beads, 4 each of 4 different colors (red, blue, yellow, and green) that need to be arranged in a 4x4 table, such that each row and column has all 4 color beads. Imagine a starting condition, as illustrated in Figure 6.5.

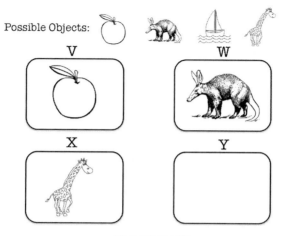

What is in box Y?

Figure 6.4. An Illustration of Rule 2.

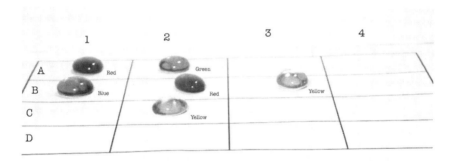

Figure 6.5. The Bead Problem.

You can see that by Rule 2, green would be assigned to cell B4 because that is the only value left in the row B; that yellow would be assigned to D1 because by Rule 1 it must be a yellow or green, and by Rule 2 it would have to be a yellow because C1 could not be a yellow and, therefore, there is no place for a yellow except D1; that by Rule 2 C1 would have to be green. The whole puzzle can be completed at a level of logical necessity expressed by the composed application of two simple rules.

Note that there is only one solution: that different *Meaning Implications Actions* (MIAs filling a cell) will lead to the same solution even if carried out in a different order; that different MIAs can be viewed as logically equivalent; and that as the problem progresses, the MIAs become cognitively easier, ultimately reduced to Rule 2, i.e., the last member of the remaining elements of the null proximate set must fill in the last remaining opportunity. In a sense, this reduces to: if it is not an A, it is a B or, as in Figure 6.1, "If it is not an apple, it's an aardvark."

Newspaper Puzzle: "Challenger"

Let me introduce our first newspaper puzzle, Challenger (see Figure 6.6), which also introduces arithmetic addition and subtraction. The puzzle consists of a 4x4 table with numbers at the end of each row, column, and diagonal. Here are the instructions: "Enter a number in each square one through nine. Rows must add to totals on right. Columns must add to totals on bottom. Diagonal squares through center should add to totals in upper and lower right." (*San Francisco Chronicle*)

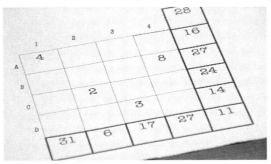

Figure 6.6.   Challenger.

The proximate set is the numerals 1–9. If you take three of the largest numbers, '9,' and add them to '4,' you get a total of '31,' which is the sum of column 1. By a logic too tedious to lay out here, it is clear that the only values that can go in column 1 are three '9's. Now there are two empty cells in row 'D,' and only the smallest number in the proximate set ('1') can go in these cells, for the same logical reasons that put '9's in column 1. There are now two numbers to be filled in column 4, and they can only be two '9's, again for the same logic. The remaining cells get filled in from Rule 2.

Notice that there is only one missing additive in the diagonal, adding up to '28' and, therefore, by an extensive quantification of Rule 2, it must be '8' (that is, 9+9+2=20; 28–20=8; therefore, '8' must belong in the only cell still to be filled). The remaining cells fill in by the application of the same rule.

Of all the puzzles to be discussed here, this is the only one where there is occasionally more than one correct solution.

Newspaper Puzzle: Sudoku

Our second newspaper puzzle is the popular Japanese puzzle, Sudoku (Figure 6.7). Sudoku typically consists of a 9x9 grid (81 cells) broken into 9 equal 3x3 squares. "Complete the grid so that every row, column, and 3-by-3 box has every digit, 1 to 9" (Knight Features, 2013). The Sudoku puzzle involves numbers, not as integers susceptible to arithmetic, but as tokens, although when the puzzle is completed, the sums of all rows and columns equal each other.

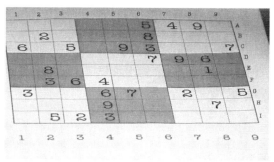

Figure 6.7. Sudoku.

A common strategy for solving Sudoku puzzles is "shading," which is a variant of Rule 2: if for a specific digit there is only one cell in a row, column, or square that can take that number, then that digit belongs in that cell. For example, in Figure 6.7, only a '5' can go into cell 5H because all other cells in that square have been "shaded" for '5'. In simple puzzles, this strategy will lead to a complete solution. More difficult puzzles might require "implicit shading," where it is known that a specific digit will have to go in a certain row, for example, even though it is not clear which cell it will occupy. Because it is, by necessity, in a certain row, however, it "shades" all the other cells in that row.

Variations on Rule 2 are: a) where a certain digit occurs only in a certain row, column, or square, it must occupy that corresponding cell. Similarly, b) where a digit may possibly occur in many cells in a row, for example, but in a particular cell it is the only possible digit, it must occupy that cell. For example, in Figure 6.8, '6' must be in cell A4 because that is the only cell in which '6' occurs. '2' must occur in cell A9 because that is the only digit possible in that cell.

By Rule 1, for any row, column, or square, if a pair of identical digits is possible in two cells, then those two digits cannot occur in any of the other corresponding rows, columns, or squares containing the two cells. If either digit was to occur in a corresponding cell, then there would be two cells with the same digits, thereby violating the rules of the puzzle that no two cells within the same row, column, or square, have the same digits in them. For example, in Figure 6.8, '1' cannot occur in cell A7 because both cells A1 and A2 contain only the pair '1' and '3'.

3	3	4	4	6 9	3	9	5	1	7	8	
1	1	2	3	2	3 5	7	5	8	4	2 4	5 2

Possible digits in one row of Sudoku puzzle

3	3	4	**4**	6 9	**3**	9	5	**1**	7	8	
1	1	2	**3**	2	3 **5**	7	**5**	8	4	2 **4**	5 2

Bold digits will be eliminated as possibilities by
the logic of meanings expressed as rules 1 & 2
and their variations

3	3	4		6 9		9	5		7	8	
1	1					7		8			2

Figure 6.8. The Reduction of Options by Rules 1 & 2.

All but the most difficult Sudoku puzzles can be solved by application of shading and inferential shading strategies, which is to say by application of Rules 1 and 2 or their variants. The purpose of this paper is not to provide a clinic on solving Sudoku puzzles, but rather to show that by a simple *logic of meanings* derived from specification of the proximate null set, *Meaning Implication Actions* (MIAs) fill each cell with the only possible meaning.

Newspaper Puzzle: Ken Ken

A third newspaper puzzle is Ken Ken, found daily in the *New York Times* (NYT), and, like the NYT crossword puzzles, gets more difficult each day of the week. This is a puzzle that involves numbers both as tokens and as integers. There are a variety of puzzles, based on the size of the matrix, typically 4x4 and 6x6.

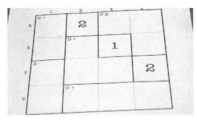

Figure 6.9. Ken Ken.

Fill the grid with digits so as not to repeat a digit in any row or column, and so that the digits within each heavily outlined box will produce the target number shown, by using addition, subtraction, multiplication, or division, as indicated in the box. A 4x4 grid will use the digits 1–4. A 6x6 grid will use 1–6. (Nextoy, 2013)

For example, in Figure 6.9, the D row of three cells with "9+" means that these cells contain three numbers that, when added, yield '9'. No other set of numbers can be in these three cells. '1' cannot be a member of this set because '1' added to the remaining two largest numbers, '3' and '4,' gives '8,' which is too small. Therefore, by Rule 2, the remaining cell must be '1'. The MIA for Cell C1 must be '3' because the only number in the set 1–4 from which '1' can be subtracted to yield '2' is '3'. But it also must be '3' because '3' cannot be an answer to, "What two numbers in the set 1–4 can be divided to give the answer '2'?"

This illustrates the key concept of this paper, which is the way that a *logic of meanings* yields an equivalent to Piaget's concept of grouping where a variety of paths of logical substitutions lead to the same meaning, or in our case, to the same *Meaning Implication Action* (MIA). This has been a feature of all the previously illustrated problems, but it is a more salient feature in the Ken Ken Puzzles, e.g., cell B1 must be '2' for a variety of arguments, all of which belong to the same grouping. For example, by Rule 1 cells A1 and B1 must either be '2' or '4' because '2' and '4' cannot be elsewhere in column 1. By a quantitative extension of Rule 2, combined with an intentional view of Rule 2, cells A1 and B1 must be '2' and '4' because the only possible two equal number combinations of digits within the set of 1–4 that yield '2' as the dividend are 2/1= 2 or 4/2=2. By Rule 2, since A2 is '2', then A1 cannot be '2' and, therefore, B1 must be '2'. But also by Rule 2, B1 would have to be '2' because this is the only open cell and unaccounted digit. The specifics may be taxing to follow, but the point is, there are a multitude of logically equivalent arguments yielding the same *Meaning Implication Action*. The following two puzzles to be discussed are seemingly a departure from the foregoing because they involve "meaning" in the more conventional sense of "words." The first is Cryptoquip (Figure 6.10).

Newspaper Puzzle: Cryptoquip

The Cryptoquip is a cipher problem, requiring the substitution of actual letters for ciphers where the resulting sentences form a quip or a play on words.

The Cryptoquip is a substitution cipher in which one letter stands for another. If you think X equals O it will equal O throughout the puzzle. Single letters,

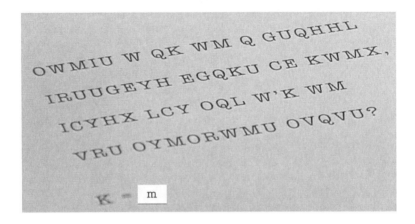

Figure 6.10. Cryptoquip.

short words and words using an apostrophe give you clues to locating vowels. Solution is by trial and error. Today's clue: K=m. (King Features, 2013)

In this particular example (Figure 6.10) the cipher K is given the value letter 'm'. From the proximate set of the English language alphabet, 'm' is therefore established, and no other cipher will stand for 'm'. I will use a convention of upper case letters for the cipher and lower case for the MIA. One of the words is composed of cipher W'K. 'W' almost certainly stands for 'I' in which case, the MIA is to replace W'K" with "I'm." There is a single letter word cipher 'Q,' which could only be an 'a' because the proximal set of single letter words consists of 'a' and 'I,' and 'I' has already been chosen. Therefore, by Rule 2, 'Q' = 'a,' which makes the second and third words "I am." This is followed by a two-letter word that starts with an 'i' that is followed by the word 'a'. The proximal set consists of 'if, in, is, it.' The only four word phrase that works is "I am in a...," therefore, M=n. That is, there is a four-member proximal set of possible four words expressions: "I am if a," "I am in a," "I am is a," and "I am it a," of which only one is prevalent in the English language. "I am in a . . .," therefore, "M"= "n". Two vowels ('I', 'a') and two consonants of the proximal set 'm' and 'n' have been determined, and of the proximal set of words that constitute the quip, six words have been determined.

The last word in the first phrase of the cipher is "minX." Of the proximal set of words (i.e., every possible word where remaining alphabet letters are substituted for "X" likely consists of only two words, "mind" and "mint"), 'd' seems the likely substitute for 'X,' yielding the word "mind." The word "mind" is preceded by a two letter cipher, 'CE'. If 'C' is a consonant, the proximal set of available letters is (do, go, so, to, we). If 'C' is a vowel, the proximate set of remaining vowels is ('of, or, up, us'). All the available likely choices that can immediately proceed the word "mind" are "to mind," "of mind." "To mind" seems unlikely and, therefore, 'C' = 'o' and 'E' = 'f'.

In any corpus of English text, there is a limited number of letters that occur frequently: the vowels 'a, e,' and the consonants 'n,' 's' and 't' are strong candidates. The only remaining cipher in our quip that occurs with any frequency is 'U'. 'U' cannot be 'a' or 'o' or 'n' because these have already been determined; and unlikely 's' or 't', and, therefore, most likely 'e'. We guess that: 'U' = 'e', but we guess with some assurance. If 'C' = 'o', it is likely that the word 'CE' = 'of'. Deciding that 'E' = 'f' gives "Game" for the phrase "of mind." The only likely substitute for 'G' is 'r,' giving "frame of mind."

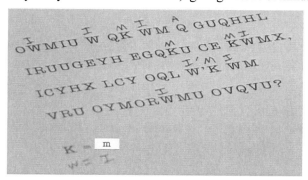

Figure 6.11. Cryptoquip 2.

By the same process of establishing proximal sets of possible letter substitutes, words, phrases, and expressions, it is inevitable that one arrives at, "Since I am in a really cheerful frame of mind, could you say I'm in the sunshine state?" While the instructions say the process is "trial and error," in fact, those who do this puzzle seldom make an error. It is not solved by trial and error. It is solved by a *logic of meanings*.

It is clear that there are many different paths that lead to the solution and, as such, different MIAs that can logically substitute for one another. It is also clear that as the solution progresses, there is a coalescing of solutions, such that the probability of achieving a solution becomes higher. There are also increasingly defined proximal sets of common English expressions and a possible quip: "Since I am in," "a really cheerful frame of mind," "could you say?" "sunshine state." Lastly, it is clear there is only one solution and that the solution is logically necessary, from which it follows that there is certainty as to the correctness of the solution.

Newspaper Puzzle: Crossword Puzzles

The last newspaper puzzle, which closely aligns with our conventional sense of meaning, is the crossword puzzle (CWP). There are many variations

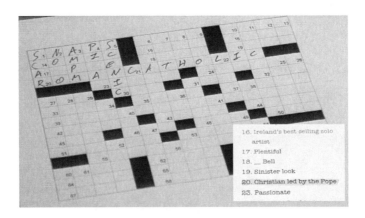

Figure 6.12.   Cryptoquip 2.

of CWPs. They typically consist of a grid of rows and columns blocked into groups of open cells, which are to be filled by words. The words are suggested by clues for rows (across) and columns (down). Every cell is an intersection between a row and column, and the letter in that cell must fit with the corresponding "across" and "down" words. As in all the other puzzles, the MIA that fills a cell draws from two proximate sets that contain a common element.

In a former paper I analyzed the conditions that governed the solution of CWPs as a variety of constraints. These constraints varied from simple associations, like "oil and water," to common names, like "Orson Welles" or "Taco Bell," to popular or recognized cultural icons ("Abe Lincoln," "Marilyn Monroe"), known geographical names ("Ural mountains," "Texas Panhandle"), names of popular sports or entertainment figures, and so forth. In part, I drew upon a concept of "cultural redundancy," a concept I conjured up years ago as a way of thinking about co-incident events. The further point of this paper is simply to recognize these constraints as resulting from proximal relevant sets and, hence, corresponding with Piaget's analysis of a *logic of meanings*. For example, if the across clue is "ginger cookies" for a five letter word, and the down clue for the first letter is "Capone facial marks" for a four letter word, the two relevant proximal sets are: any five letter plural word that associates with "Ginger cookies" that shares the same first letter with a four letter word that relates to Capone's facial mark. The latter becomes: "What is a facial mark on a gangster?" The word "scar" comes to mind and "snaps" for "ginger snaps," with their shared initial letter 'S'.

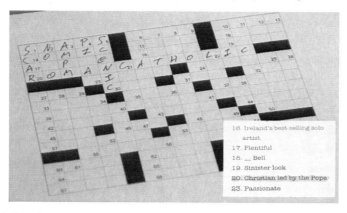

Figure 6.13.   Crossword Puzzle 2.

CONCLUSION

For some years I have been exploring the social aspects of Piaget's theory, which I have called his implicit social theory. The concept of the *conservation of meaning* is a critical junction in this quest. Piaget's last major works, the two-volume series on *Possibility and Necessity* (Piaget, 1987) and *Towards a Logic of Meanings* (Piaget & Garcia, 1991), deepen our understanding of how meaning is established and conserved. Daily newspaper puzzles serve as both examples and metaphor.

The puzzle space consists of a matrix of cells of unknown meaning that must be filled and, when filled properly, are conserved by the fact that they are the only possible answers compatible with the overall matrix. The *Meaning Implication Actions* (MIAs) that fill each cell are mental acts that establish and derive from relevant proximal sets of possibility and entail selecting necessary choices through the operations of a *logic of meanings*. The *logic of meanings* is the familiar elements of Piaget's operatory system of groupings, lattices, 16 binary operations, INCR, etc. In some instances, the required inferences are complex and belong to the mechanisms of formal operational intelligence, whereas in other instances they are simple and accessible to pre-operational intelligence, e.g., "if it is not an apple, it is an aardvark."

The *logic of meanings* derives from the coordination of affirmation and negations, along with conjunctions and disjunctions, both being embedded in the establishment of the relevant proximal sets. Turkey sandwiches are relevant to the clue "gobble gobble," whereas cheese sandwiches are not. The common words "and," "or," "not," "neither," "can't," "might," "could," "never," "only," "either," "nor," capture the psychological reality of this logic.

In going beyond the confines of the puzzle, we can claim that, in general, each *Meaning Implication Action* (MIA) is embedded in a series of possible substitution arguments that take on logical properties. A *conservation of meaning* that takes the form of true concepts will draw upon concrete operations, whereas those requiring hypothetical deductions will draw upon the mechanisms of formal operations. Simpler substitutions are possible with pre-operational manipulations. In all instances, however, we find the establishment of the proximal set of relevant possibilities that is inseparable from social considerations. The relative relevance of a turkey sandwich versus a cheese sandwich lies in the social domain rather than in the logical domain. The establishment of the proximal set and its participation in negation and affirmation, along with conjunction and disjunction, corresponds with my earlier description of a coherence of constraints, is isomorphic with Piaget's operational logical, and forms the core to understanding Piaget's implicit social theory.

REFERENCES

Alward, K. R. (2012). The conservation of meaning as a function of constraints in the social context of puzzles: Piaget's social theory revisited. In L.E. Cohen & S. Waite-Stupiansky, (Eds.), *Play and Culture Studies, Vol. 12*, pp. 121–132.

Beck, S. (2013, June). *A critical-constructive discussion of Piaget and Vygotsky's theories of teaching and learning.* Paper presented at the Jean Piaget Society, Chicago, IL.

King Features Syndicate, Inc. (2013). *Cryptoquip Puzzle.*

Knight Features. (2013). *Sudoku Puzzle.*

Nextoy, LLC. (2013). *Ken Ken Puzzle.*

Nicolopoulou, A. (1993). Play, cognitive development, and the social world: Piaget, Vygotsky, and beyond. *Human Development, 36,*1–23.

Piaget, J. (1954). *The construction of reality in the child.* New York: Basic Books, Inc. (Original work published 1937).

Piaget, J. (1962). *Play, dreams and imitation in childhood.* (C. Gattegno & F. M. Hodgson, trans.) New York: W.W. Norton and Co., Inc. (Original work published 1946).

Piaget, J. (1965). *The moral judgment of the child.* (Marjorie Gabain, trans.). New York: The Free Press. (Original work published 1932).

Piaget, J. (1976). *The grasp of consciousness: Action and concept in the young child.* (S. Wedgwood, trans.) Cambridge, MA: Harvard University Press. (Original work published 1974).

Piaget, J. (1987). *Possibility and necessity* (Vols. I & II). (Helga Feider, trans.). Minneapolis, MN: University of Minnesota Press. (Original work published 1981).

Piaget, J. (1995). *Sociological studies.* (Terrance Brown, trans.) New York: Routledge. (Original work published 1965).

Piaget, J., & Garcia, R. (1991). *Towards a logic of meanings.* (Helga Feider, trans.). New Jersey: Lawrence Erlhaum Associates. (Original work published 1987).

Piaget, J., & Inhelder, B. (1969). *The psychology of the child.* (Helen Weaver, trans.). New York: Basic Books, Inc. (Original work published 1966).

Van Hoorn, J., Nourot, P., Scales, B., & Alward, K.R. (2016). *Play at the center of the curriculum, Sixth Edition.* New Jersey: Pearson Education, Inc.

Vygotsky, L. S. (1978). *Mind in society: The development of higher psychological processes.* Cambridge, MA: Harvard University Press.

Chapter Seven

Geriatrics, Aging, and Play

Marcia Nell and Walter Drew

As the world proportion of people age 60 and over grows, there is an increasing concern for their health and well being in later life and finding effective interventions that enable them to lead a life of high quality and well-being. This paper investigates the issues surrounding quality of life for older adults, play, and the implications of a play intervention using the self active play process with older adults. The authors investigate quality of life factors that influence the cognitive, physical, emotional, and social aspects of older adults. The paper addresses barriers to positive aging, resiliency in aging, and different theoretical aspects of play and creativity in aging. The authors then describe a specific type of play, self active play, as an intervention with older adults. The implications from these research findings suggest the positive potential for use of the self active play process with older adults and families that may be suffering from Alzheimer's Disease.

> And so you set your course with your face to the rising sun, your eyes alert for the slippery loose stones, your breath reluctant to maintain the pace. You are forced to slow down and reconfirm your decision to proceed. Always the syntonic and dystonic impulses, to proceed or to give in, wrestle for control and the will to make good. You are challenged and tested. This tension, when it is focused and controlled, is the very root of success. Every step is a test of syntonic sovereignty and will power. (Erikson & Erikson, 1997, p.128–129)

According to the Association for Gerontology in Higher Education (AGHE), "*Gerontology* is the study of the aging processes and individuals as they grow from middle age through later life. It includes the study of physical, mental, and social changes in older people as they age, the investigation of the changes in society resulting from our aging population, the application of this knowledge to policies and programs. As a result of the multidisciplinary focus of gerontology, professionals from diverse fields call themselves "gerontologists" (AGHE, 2012). As an addition to this field of study *"Geriatrics* is the study of health and disease in later life and the comprehensive health care of older persons and the well-being of their informal caregiver" (AGHE, 2012). Since the field of gerontology includes many varied perspectives, it is considered to be a widely multidimensional field of study. These authors are concerned with the study of health in later life and the interventions that enable older adults to lead a life of high quality and well-being. This paper will investigate the issues surrounding quality of life for older adults, play, and the implications of a play intervention using the self active play process with older adults.

THE FOCUS ON AGING

There is a focus on the aging population today, not just within the United States but also worldwide. According to World Health Organization (WHO, 2002), "Worldwide, the proportion of people age 60 and over is growing faster than any other age group. Between 1970 and 2025, a growth in older persons of some 694 million or 223 percent is expected" (p. 6). This increase in the proportion of older to younger ages is due to the increase in life expectancy and the decline of birth rates among industrialized and developing countries. Life expectancy rates for the United States one hundred years ago was 47.3 years of age while today the life expectancy rate is 77 years of age (Tahmaseb-McConatha, Volkwein-Caplan, & DiGregorio, 2011).

The American Geriatrics Society, (2011) report *Profile on Aging,* states that in the United States there were 35 million persons in the 65+ population age range in 2000, another 5 million were added to this age range by 2010, and there is a projected figure of 55 million of 65+ people by the year 2020. The number of people in +85 year range will increase from 4.2 million in 2000 to 5.7 million in 2010 to a projected 6.6 million in 2020. With this expected increase in the aging population there will be significant impacts on society and therefore planning for this future increase in the older age range needs to take place now.

In *Active Ageing: A Policy Framework* (WHO, 2002) a "dependency ratio" is calculated by dividing the population age 60 and over by the population age 15 to 60. This dependency ratio could then be used in helping policy makers, economists, actuaries, and those dealing with the management and planning for elder care services to make informed decisions. But there is an assumption that is hidden within this line of thinking, which assumes that "older" means needy or dependent. What if the older population was not in need of social services but continued to be productive and independent members of society?

Answering this question, then, entails examining those traits that enable an older population to live more productive, independent lives; while at the same time prevents or delays disabilities and chronic diseases that have economic and social impacts on the individual, families, communities, and the health care system (WHO, 2002, p. 9). Multiple researchers in various fields of study have examined traits, which provide a multidimensional insight into the process of aging and at the same time an optimistic outlook in the ability of individuals and societies to live meaningful lives considerably farther than previously experienced (Tahmaseb-McConatha, Volkwein-Caplan, & DiGregorio, 2011).

Quality of Life Issues for Older Adults

One issue that emerges from the research literature is the term *quality of life*. Defining Quality of Life (QoL) is a more difficult task than one would expect due to its wide spread usage in diverse fields of study and therefore various perspectives associated with those fields of study. According to the World Health Organization (WHO), as cited in Malderen, Mets, and Gorus (2012, p. 1), QoL is broadly defined as "An individual's perception of his or her position in life in the context of the culture and value system where they live, and in relation to their goals, expectations, standards and concerns" (1993). Based on this definition then, QoL includes an individualistic view as well as the social value systems in relation to the individual.

In work conducted by Walker (2002) the term "active aging" (AA) began being used when discussing QoL issues. WHO built upon Walker's work by encouraging older adults to take an "active" part in different aspects of their life such as health and security concerns. Increasing an older adult's activity level has a direct outcome upon their QoL since the individual remains a "resource to their families, communities, and economies" (WHO, 2002, p. 5). Based on the belief that older adults can and should remain a resource, not only from the individual's perspective to promote QoL beliefs, but also from a social and economic perspective, the WHO (2002) created a Policy Framework to promote awareness of issues surrounding the ageing process that promotes AA and therefore QoL. The Policy Framework highlights key determinants that impact the health of an older adult and then makes recommendations for policy makers that address these influences.

Two of the seven determinants, culture and gender, are considered to be "cross-cutting determinants", which means that they influence the other five. Culture plays a huge role in how an individual experiences the aging process, based on the values and expectations set by the other members of that particular culture. According to the World Health Organization (2002, p. 20) "When societies are more likely to attribute symptoms of disease to the aging process, they are less likely to provide prevention, early detection and appropriate treatment services." In other words, it is the cultural norm to just expect for disease to be part of the ageing process and therefore it would be a waste of time, energy, and profit to try to make a change to something that is inevitable.

Gender also has a major influence on how actively one is able to participate in the aging process and thus resulting in an increase in QoL. For
example, women and girls in many cultures are considered as having less
status within the culture, are confined to care giving roles within the house-
hold, are less likely to have access to healthy foods, and health services.
Table 7.1 below shows the seven major areas for consideration when making
policy or decisions regarding active aging to promote QoL for older adults
(WHO, 2002, p. 19–20).

Health: Cognitive, Physical, Emotional and Social Aspects in Aging

When looking at dynamic variables in the pursuit of quality of life in the
older years, one cannot ignore the importance of addressing the health issues
associated with aging. Promoting cognitive, physical, emotional, and social
health in the elder years is of prime importance to the individuals, families,

Table 7.1. Quality of Life Factors

Factors	
Cross-cutting	Culture
	Gender
Health & Social Services	Health promotion
	Disease prevention
	Curative services
	Long-term care
	Mental health services
Behavioral	Tobacco use
	Physical activity
	Healthy eating
	Oral health
	Alcohol
	Medications
	Adherence
Personal	Biology and Genetics
	Psychological
Physical Environment	Safe housing
	Falls
	Clean water, air and safe foods
Social Environment	Social Support
	Violence and abuse
	Education and literacy
Economic Environment	Social protection
	Income
	Work

and communities. For example, research has documented the importance of exercise on the preservation of physical fitness, but research has also shed light on the importance of exercise on the cognitive and emotional wellbeing of an aging adult (Tahmaseb-McConatha, Volkwein-Caplan, & DiGregorio, 2011; American Geriatrics Society, 2011; Decker & Reed, 2005; Kahana, Kelley-Moore, & Kahana, 2012; & Malderen, Mets, & Gorus, 2012).

In a study conducted by Kahana, Kelley-Moore, and Kahana (2012) three proactive adaptations: exercise; planning ahead; and gathering support, were examined to determine the impact on quality of life outcomes. Exercise was found to promote not only physical wellbeing by staving off physical demise associated with old age but also to the maintenance of psychological and social functioning. In this study planning ahead and dealing with the future, were ways to provide participants the opportunity to develop more effective action plans. The third proactive adaptation, gathering support, enabled the participants to reach out to family, friends, and other social agencies, as they become resources for the older adults. An interesting finding of this study was the importance of "anticipation". The active participation in the decision-making process of the individual impacts the results. This finding supports the WHO (2002) recommendation for older adults to take part in "actively ageing".

Psychological Well-Being in Aging

Psychological research has previously focused heavily on negative mental processes. There has been an assumption, though, that if an older adult does not exhibit any of the negative processes, such as stress or depression, then that older adult is adapting to their life in positive and adaptive ways. But that is not necessarily a correct assumption, and therefore some researchers are focusing their work on defining and understanding what does it mean to have well-being. According to Urry, Nitschke, Dolski, Jackson, Dalton, Mueller, Rosenkranz, Ryff, Singer and Davidson (2004) there are two main research focuses in psychology on the understanding of well being for individuals. One research focus is entitled "eudaimonic well-being" and is supported by the research by Ryff and Keyes, 1995, which highlights how the person expresses their well-being in terms of "levels of autonomy, personal growth, positive relations with others, purpose in life, and self-acceptance" (as cited in Urry et al., 2004, p. 367). The other focus for the research is called "hedonic well-being" and is exemplified in the research by Diener (2000), which focuses on the "affective and cognitive evaluations of their lives" (as cited in Urry, et al., 2004, p. 367). There are four basic components to the hedonic well-being research which include "life satisfaction, satisfaction with important domains (e.g., work), frequent pleasant emotions, and infrequent unpleasant emotions" (as cited in Urry et al., 2004, p. 367).

Psychosocial Development in Aging

Erik Erikson, renowned developmental psychologist, provides valuable insight into the aging process, not only through his research but also through his own personal journey into aging. The focus of Erikson's work was on developing an increase in quality of life factors through the enjoyment, engagement, and understanding of this transitional period of the human life cycle. Erikson & Erikson (1997) describe this time of the life cycle as gero-transcen*dance* with a highlight on the end syllable *dance*. A time of doing, a time to make meaning in life even to the very end...new knowledge in every moment of life, ready for the taking, ready for the understanding, ready to provide truth, peace, and contentment that all humans seek. Why am I here? Especially now, with a body that does not work as it did, with a mind that is not as sharp as it was, but with a spirit that is still searching for understanding, meaning, and connection. Erikson said it so well.

As cited in Erikson, Lars Tornstam and fellow workers at Uppsala Universitet, Sweden: "we suggest that human aging, the very process of living into old age, encompasses a general potential towards gerotranscendence. Simply, put gerotranscendence is a shift in meta perspective, from a materialistic and rational vision to a more cosmic and transcendent one, normally followed by an increase in life satisfaction...According to the theory, the gerotrancendent individual experiences a new feeling of cosmic communion with the spirit of the universe, a redefinition of time, space, life and death, and redefinition of the self" (Erikson & Erikson, 1997, pp. 123–124).

In relation to developing a new sense of self, & Erikson describe how society encourages older adults "to let go" of the life they knew, but does not encourage older adults to "seek a new life and role—a new self...we must discover the freedom to go beyond limits imposed on us by our world and seek fulfillment" (Erikson & Erikson, 1997, p. 126).

One of the meanings for the word transcendence is to move "beyond or before an experience; a priori" and when combined with the prefix "gero",

---

Table 7.2. Psychological Aspects of Well-Being

Eudaimonic	Hedonic
High level of autonomy	Life satisfaction
Environmental Mastery	Satisfaction with important domains (e.g., work)
Personal Growth	Frequent Pleasant Emotions
Positive relations with others	Infrequent Unpleasant Emotions
Purpose in life	
Self-acceptance	

which means "old age" one would then have a word meaning "before old age". This then would imply also that there is some preparation needed in order to meet this stage of life. The implication is to allow a change of attitudes and preparation for the possibilities of "old age" before reaching that stage of the life cycle. The sense of loss that many older adults feel as they face the 9th stage of the life cycle could be averted or eliminated with some "preparation" prior to reaching that stage. All people will reach it, unless of course we leave earlier! One aspect to consider then is how are we preparing ourselves to meet the demands of "old age"? Erikson & Erikson (1997) shed some fascinating light using his own experience with the reality of "being" old and his reflections on the term "transcen*dance*".

They continue by saying "Transcendance may be a regaining of lost skills, including play, activity, joy and song, and above all, a major leap above and beyond the fear of death. It provides an opening forward into the unknown with a trusting leap" (p. 127). So, to move "beyond the fear of death" and to leap into the unknown with trust, there needs to be ways to develop skills in thinking, imagining, and being that are not what is culturally prevalent. These new ways of thinking, imagining, and being are awakened when engulfed in artistic expression, the act of creating not only the product of the creative process but the process itself reveals the skills needed to develop new and unique ways of thinking, imagining, and being. Erikson states, "Transcen*dance*—that's it of course! And it moves. It's one of the arts, it's alive, sings, and makes music, and I hug myself because of the truth it whispers to my soul…Transcen*dance* calls forth the languages of the arts; nothing else speaks so deeply and meaningfully to our hearts and souls. The great dance of life can transport us into all realms of making and doing with every item of body, mind, and spirit involved" (p. 127).

Erikson concludes his discussion of the ninth stage of life with these words of wisdom for life's journey, "And so you set your course with your face to the rising sun, your eyes alert for the slippery loose stones, your breath reluctant to maintain the pace. You are forced to slow down and reconfirm your decision to proceed. Always the syntonic and dystonic impulses, to proceed or to give in, wrestle for control and the will to make good. You are challenged and tested. This tension, when it is focused and controlled, is the very root of success. Every step is a test of syntonic sovereignty and will power" (p. 128–129).

Understanding, accepting, and moving beyond the commonly accepted role of the older adult is a struggle that requires new ways of perceiving one's self—creating a new image. Creating a new image entails imaging new possibilities and the expressing of one's self through the creative process provides the experiences necessary in developing the skills needed for reimagining the possibilities. As Erikson states, "I am persuaded that only by doing and making do we become" (Erikson & Erikson, 1997, p. 127).

Erikson's theory of psychosocial development is based on finding the balance between syntonic and dystonic influences. During the last stage of development, integrity and despair are the syntonic and dystonic influences that play out toward the balance or strength known as "wisdom". Erikson (1986, p. 37–38) defines wisdom as "detached concern with life itself, in the face of death itself. It maintains and learns to convey the integrity of experience, in spite of the decline of bodily and mental functions." But Erikson also reminds us that every stage of development has its focal, epigenetic balancing.

If the true meaning of the word "gerotrancendence" includes the preparation for becoming older, then one of those ways to prepare for becoming older is to have role models of older adults making positive transitions towards high quality of life and well being in old age. One is able to prepare for old age, therefore, by watching living models and anticipating or imagining how to "be old" in a more positive and productive manner. One way children make meaning of the world for themselves is through their active participation in play. Play is the context by which individuals, both young and old and all the others in-between, learn to make meaning of the world around them. They interact.

BARRIERS TO POSITIVE AGING

As mentioned above, cultural influences that impact the QoL experiences of older adults can many times be based on shortsighted stereotypes and cultural biases. Especially prevalent in western culture, the view of older adults is one of negativity the expectancy for disease, which leads to fewer opportunities for "prevention, early detection, and appropriate treatments" (WHO, 2002, p. 20). Even clichés used in everyday language depict stereotypes that perpetuate this bias against older adults. Such terms as: "over the hill", "old as dirt", "all washed up" or "old geezer" exemplify a negative connotation associated with aging also known as ageism. Stereotypes are also perpetuated through the media by depicting older adults as lacking memory, set in their ways, dependent, helpless, unproductive, and demanding. As older adults seek ways to fight against ageism, their need for play becomes even greater. As Brown and Vaughn (2009) explained, when "In an unpredictable, changing world, what we learn from playing can be transferred into other novel contexts" (p. 43–44). Using play's foundational components of variability, flexibility, and autonomy provides the safe context for older adults to reinvent their self thus connecting the biological drive to play with the emotional pleasure derived from playing thus enacting optimism and creative problem solving. In many cases for the older adult this process of engaging in play could be considered as becoming resilient.

RESILIENCY IN AGING

Richardson (2002) developed a resiliency model to facilitate an understanding of the process of change. This model helps to explain how individuals, groups, families, organizations, or systems manage or react to change. According to this model there are four possible reactions to change: resilient reintegration, reintegration back to status quo or equilibrium, reintegration with loss, or dysfunctional reintegration. Resilient reintegration as a reaction to change enables the gaining of some insight or personal growth due to the disruption or change. The second reaction is reintegration back to status quo or equilibrium, which means the individual bypasses opportunities for personal growth by remaining within the comfort zone. In the third reaction to change, reintegration with loss, the person gives up because the life disruptions are too overwhelming—lack of hope, drive, or motivation. The fourth option, dysfunctional reintegration, is described as responding to life disruptions by abusing drugs or other destructive coping mechanisms.

Richardson (2002) explained the necessity for disruption in order for resiliency to be activated within an individual or an organization. Reacting to change in a resilient manner means there will be growth and those resilient qualities developed today provide added support when the next disruption appears. Understanding the "process" associated with developing resiliency has clear implications for the need to develop interventions or programs that enable resilient skills to be experimented with and practiced by older adults.

PLAY IN AGING

When defining the word play as with "quality of life" or "well-being", there is difficulty in reaching a functional definition. Play cuts across numerous fields of study and theoretical foundations making it nebulous. Play has multiple types, facets, and obscurities. Robert Fagen states, "The most irritating feature of play is not the perceptual incoherence, as such, but rather that play taunts us with its inaccessibility. We feel something is behind it all, but we do not know, or have forgotten how to see it" (as cited in Sutton-Smith, 1997, p. 2). Sutton-Smith continues by stating that "theoretically speaking, play is difficult to understand because it is ambiguous…these ambiguities are instigated by the seven systems of value here called the ideological rhetorics of progress, fate, power, identity, the imaginary, the self and frivolity…Because forms of play, like all other cultural forms, cannot be neutrally interpreted, it is impossible to keep ambiguity from creeping into the relationship between how they are perceived and how they are experienced" (1997, p. 214–215). This ambiguity presents a paradoxical issue in that words seem to fail us when creating a definition but most of us are able to recognize play when we see it or participate in it. To some, this then is the "wordless wonder" of play. The seven rhetorics of play as described by Sutton-Smith provide a way of understanding the various lines of research and the functions, forms, and fields of study for each. Sutton-Smith concludes by stating, "that variability is the key to play, and that structurally play is characterized by quirkiness, redundancy, and flexibility" (1997, p. 229).

Stephen Jay Gould, suggests in his work on biological evolution that "Precise adaptation, with each part finely honed to perform a definite function in an optimal way, can only lead to blind alleys, dead ends, and extinction…an evolutionary potential for creative responses requires that organisms possess an opposite set of characteristics usually devalued in our culture: sloppiness, broad potential, quirkiness, unpredictability, and, above all, massive redundancy. The key is flexibility, not admirable precision" (as cited in Sutton-Smith, 1997, p. 221). Play allows flexibility to be experienced, which according to Gould provides the player with the ability to creatively adapt to new situations in optimal ways. This development of flexibility through play then provides a context in which to practice the possibilities or as Sutton-Smith describes the "potentialities" that then lead to actualities. It is the safety and freedom to explore the "potentialities" that enable adaptation to be possible and thus survival. Elizabeth Jones states, "Play is choosing what to do, doing it, and enjoying it. You may not enjoy the process, but choosing is the doorway to genuine play. So you have to make choices! Just as children do in preschool. Playing is a skill to be practiced. People who can play with possibilities—"What shall I do now, and what will happen if I do?" - will go further in life than will people who wait to be told what to do" (Jones, 2007, p. 27). This idea of play creates a possibility for the generativity of play throughout the whole human life cycle.

Table 7.3.   The Seven Rhetorics of Play (Sutton-Smith, 1997, p. 215)

Rhetoric	Function	Form	Discipline
Progress	Adaptation, growth, socialization	Play, games	Biology, psychology, education
Fate	Magic, luck	Chance	Math
Power	Status, victory	Skill, strategy, deep play	Sociology, history
Identity	Communitas, cooperation	Festivals, parades, parties, new games	Anthropology, folklore
Imaginary	Creativity, flexibility	Fantasy, tropes	Art and literature
Self	Peak experience	Leisure, solitary, extreme games	Psychiatry
Frivolity	Inversion, playfulness	Nonsense	Pop culture

According to Huizinga one definition of play is that, "it is fully absorbing, includes elements of uncertainty, involves a sense of illusion or exaggeration, but most importantly, true play has to exist outside of ordinary life and only for its own sake" (as cited in Gordon, 2009, p. 1). The second major aspect of play that needs to be considered then is the idea that play lifts itself outside ordinary life, into what is considered an altered state of being, the play space. Play then provides the context or opportunity in which to experiment with possibilities, similar to what Gould and Sutton-Smith were suggesting but with an added flavor that the player "knows" when they are playing. The player believes what and how they are playing are part of the play space and not of their "realities". This idea that the play exists outside one's reality is foundational to the player's ability to develop a sense of safety while in the play space. It is this sense of safety within the play space that enables the player to experiment, take risks, and meet their basic need for freedom or autonomy.

According to choice theory (as cited in Sullo, 2007), developed by William Glasser, humans are driven by five basic needs: survival, love and belonging, power, freedom, and fun. When looking at meeting these five basic human needs, it is clear that play provides a context in which to meet all of these needs, especially in the older years. As mentioned above, understanding that play provides safety is paramount to satisfying the basic need for freedom or autonomy. To survive includes not only the meeting of physical needs, such as food, water, shelter, but also the emotional needs thus play provides the context in which older adult are able to pay attention to those emotions that lay right below one's conscious awareness. Needing to belong or connect with others motivates the player to develop relationships and cooperate with others and is satisfied when players are in cooperative play experiences. The innate need to belong promotes the self-regulation skill development in order for the play to continue and flourish. This phenomenon is present in the play of young children but also with older adults.

The basic human need for power, as described by Glasser, is satisfied through object play with open-ended materials as the player creates order out of the chaos. When the player physically manipulates open-ended materials into something of their own choosing, thereby creating order from the chaos, then the player's need to feel competent is satisfied. This need is not only felt within the player, but the open-ended materials provide visual evidence of the change that was created by the player, from chaos to order. This sense of accomplishment or competence is then translated in to other aspects of the player's life.

Play also is foundational in promoting satisfaction in meeting the basic human need for fun. It is simply fun to play! The self discovery, the development of a sense of competence, the relational potentialities, the sense of freedom are all present and enlighten the player but there is a specific basic need to have fun. Research by Jaak Panksepp, has isolated the impulse to play as originating in the brain stem of rats, which is where "survival mechanisms such as respiration, consciousness, sleep, and dreams originate" (as cited in Brown & Vaughn, 2009, p. 61). Playing for the sheer sake of the fun meets what Glasser calls the innate or hard-wired need to have fun. The fact that the fun is derived on so many different levels and in so many different ways during the human experience of play that is exactly what Brian Sutton-Smith means when he speaks of play's ambiguity. It is this ambiguity that has fascinated both researcher and players for centuries.

Thomas Henricks (2009) suggests looking at play through a rhetoric of time. Using Henricks' line of thought then, play may be considered in the context of time such as play being a "preparation for the future, a revisiting of the past, and an effort to remain precariously in the present" (2009, p. 15). There is a strong parallel between Henricks' idea of play as "preparation for the future" and Sutton-Smith's rhetoric of progress. Through play then, one seeks novelty, choice and self-determination, "In other words, play-as-progress rhetoric is preoccupied with the future—or rather with the thousand unknown futures lying just beyond the present" (p. 19). Play-as-regression rhetoric is then the opening of past experiences through play. It is "an act of re-discovery or remembrance, an attempt to reclaim what is nearly gone" (p. 20). In play-as-regression the player is not only able to re-experience positive memories but through the play is able to re-address less positive experiences from the past and find resolve. Henricks states "the past expresses itself or even erupts (in sometimes embarrassing ways) into the present. Unresolved issues, desires, and strategies come tumbling out" (p. 23). Play-as-regression then, like psychoanalysis theory, is a way in which to recapture the past and control it. Play in the present then provides the player a way of capturing the moment. It becomes a context in which to "disregard or defy" commitments of the present or to sustain or relish them.

Gordon (2009, p. 8) defines play as: "Play is the voluntary movement across boundaries, opening with total absorption into a highly flexible field, releasing tension in ways that are pleasurable, exposing players to the unexpected, and making transformation possible. Transformations occur as frames bisociate and the parts and the whole interpenetrate, increasing the differentiation of the parts, the integration of the whole, and the range, coordination, and spontaneity of movement between and among them." This definition of play encompasses many aspects that have been discussed above but Gordon continues by stating what play is not. When an activity does not allow freedom, becomes "rigid, unconscious, habitual, or compulsive" it is not play. But more importantly, for these authors, Gordon states that play does not have to stop with childhood. Play can and should continue throughout the human life cycle.

Sutton-Smith (1997, p. 226), "The very fact that play contains so much nonsense, so much replication, and is so flexible certainly suggests that it is a prime domain for the actualization of whatever the brain contains....play is typically a primary place for the expression of anything that is humanly imaginable."

PLAY, ART AND CREATIVITY

Using a biological and evolutionary aspect associated with play, Brown and Vaughan (2009) state, "Play seems to be so important to our development and survival that the impulse to play has become a biological drive. Like our desires for food, sleep, or sex, the impulse to play is internally generated" (p. 42). This biological drive, when activated and then connected to strong pleasurable emotions, is the defining factor between play and other activities. When our brains experience "enough play, the brain works better. We feel more optimistic and more creative. We revel in novelties—a new fashion, a new car, a new joke. And through our embrace of the new we are attracted to situations that test skills we do not need now" (p. 43). It is this very element of the biological and the resultant emotional state derived from play that supplies the magnitude for the importance of play throughout the human life span. The brain does not stop growing and developing once one enters adulthood, therefore, the need to explore and understand continues throughout the human life cycle. The resultant emotional state associated with play for an older adult has significant impact on developing positive skills and dispositions for aging (Brown & Vaughn, 2009).

Brown and Vaughn further elaborate on the biological connection between play and creativity in adults by stating, "Art and culture have long been seen as a sort of by-product of human biology, something that just happens as we use our big, complex brains. But the newer thinking is that art and culture are something that the brain actively creates because it benefits us, something that arises out of the primitive and childlike drive to play" (Brown & Vaughn, 2009, p. 61). Through play and creative endeavors, adults are able to connect their inner thoughts and express them to others, thus providing the cultural connection to which Brown describes as a benefit to adults. Since play, according to Brown's definition, is a state of being, then it is not difficult to understand his theoretical connection between play and creativity, which is also a state of being. The process of play and creativity may have an end product, but more importantly it is the brain's process for discovering, understanding, and expressing novelty from one's inner world. According to Brown and Vaughn (2009), "Art is part of a deep, preverbal communication that binds people together. It is literally a communion. This 'belonging' is an outgrowth of early social play among kids" (p. 62).

Why is it important for older adults to see themselves as being creative? Being creative is defined as being original and adaptable. As stated earlier, studies have shown that being creative is a strong predictor as to whether or not a person can reintegrate in resilient ways (Dunn, 1994; Espinoza, 2010; Garmezy, 1991; Richardson, 2002). Using resilient reintegration to react to change means positive growth associated with that change, aging. Related to positive aging, being creative means finding original ways of solving problems associated with aging and making the necessary adaptations. Therefore, providing ways for the development and transference of strategies, skills, and dispositions toward creativity will impact the resilient ways in which older adults react to aging disruptions within their lives. Finding creative, resilient ways to meet the needs of older adults happens when empowerment to be creative and resilient are strategically implemented using targeted interventions.

The creative process as defined by many creativity researchers (Plucker, Beghetto, & Dow, 2004; Csikszentmihalyi, 1996; Goleman, Kaufman, & Ray, 1992) incorporates four basic steps. The steps for the creative process used for creative problem solving outlined by Goleman, Kaufman and Ray (1992) include:1) *preparation* 2) *incubation* 3) *illumination* and 4) *implementations*. During the first step, *preparation*, the person jumps totally into the problem and immerses himself or herself into the problem and according to Goleman, Kaufman, & Ray (1992) pushes "your rational mind to the limits" (p. 18). During the second step of the creative process, *incubation,* one lets the problem simmer. This is the time when unconscious understandings seem to wiggle their way into conscious awareness. According to Csikzentmihalyi (1996), "Because of its mysterious quality, incubation has often been thought the most creative part of the entire process...it is important to let problems simmer below the threshold of consciousness for a time" (p. 98).

During the third step, *illumination,* is then when "all of a sudden the answer comes to you as if from nowhere" (Csikzentmihalyi, 1996, p. 22). The time spent during incubation where the subconscious mind makes connections between seemingly trivial ideas, the "aha" moment arrives, without circumstance or reason. Csikzentmihalyi continues by stating "The insight presumably occurs when a subconscious connection between ideas fits so well that it is forced to pop out into awareness, like a cork held underwater breaking out into the air after it is released" (p. 104).

The fourth step, *implementations,* is when the illuminations are put into action. According to Goleman, Kaufman, and Ray (1992, p. 23) "the act of creation is a long series of acts, with multiple and cascading preparations, frustrations, incubations, illuminations, and translations into action." It is important to understand that the creative process is not a lock-step process. It involves varied amounts of iterations back and forth between the steps in order to reach a truly creative solution to a problem.

"Creativity involves generating that which is new, original, unique. We live all too often in molds, tight grooves, and to find the freedom necessary to break out of these restrictions we need a sense of playfulness which allows experimentation and change. . . . Change, admittedly, is hazardous. It serves both construction and destruction. But the un-cracked mold stultifies growth and breeds stagnation" (Erikson, 1988, p. 46–47).

Self Active Play

Self active play, is one of the targeted interventions being researched in the pursuit of QoL and well-being in the aging process. Self active play is defined as a process that is based upon seven guiding principles, which have grown out of the extensive professional development work done through the Institute for Self Active Education over the last thirty years. These principles lay the foundational beliefs and the theoretical framework that inspire and continue the work for creative play, leadership, and advocacy known as self active play. These principles acknowledge a creative energy within everyone, regardless of age, that is experienced during play, and the establishment of a safe context for constructing meaningful self-knowledge. This creative energy is released as the players discover new roles or new possibilities. The altered state of being that occurs during play is recognized as the "play space," and ignites or rekindles strong feelings between players and within players and those feelings are pervasive beyond the play space, thus making them transferrable to other situations and contexts.

Playing within a safe context enables the player to experiment with possibilities thus promoting planning, problem solving, adaptability, caring, tolerance, and communication all recognized as characteristics present within resilient individuals but also characteristics that promote positive aging. As discussed earlier, positive aging that promotes QoL encourages exercise, planning ahead, and gathering support. Through the self active play process using open-ended materials, players experiment with new ideas and possibilities within the play space and these ideas and possibilities are transferrable to the player's "reality" world. Self active play provides a time for subconscious understandings to surface, much like the illumination step of the creative process. It is the self active play process with open-ended materials that unlocks and facilitates connection making between ideas and feelings which encourages self awareness.

The physical nature of self active play with the open-ended materials begins a transformation process that according to Wilson (1998, pp. 5–6) explains the unique connection between fiddling with materials and profound personal understanding in the mind. "When personal desire prompts anyone to learn to do something well with the hands, an extremely complicated process is initiated that endows the work with a powerful emotional charge.

Principles of Self Active Play

Principle 1: Play is a source of creative energy, a positive force and safe context for constructing meaningful self-knowledge and revitalizing the human spirit across the continuum of the human life cycle.

Principle 2: Hands-on play and art making with open-ended materials reconnect the individual with earlier stages of human development, spontaneously balancing and strengthening hope, will, purpose, competence, fidelity, love, care, and wisdom.

Principle 3: The play space is a state of being which is self-constructed or co-constructed based on the players' previous experiences and their perceptions of the levels of safety and trust leading into the play space.

Principle 4: Experiences within the play space elicits strong affect toward the play space such as feelings of protectiveness, a yearning to return, and desire for further exploration of higher levels of understanding and self-awareness.

Principle 5: The creative energy released within the play space is accelerated as players assume new pretend roles and as players thrill in discovering "Who will I be next?" and "What will I do next?"

Principle 6: Play is a source of energy for rekindling love, passion, and intimate relationships with other people and between players. These feelings are pervasive not just isolated to the play space but rather move forward as the player moves beyond the play space in their realities.

Principle 7: Play's intrinsic qualities include spontaneity of the spirit, thinking deeply, feeling intensely, and building a trust in one's intuitive self.

Figure 7.1.   Principles of Self Active Play.

People are changed, significantly and irreversibly it seems, when movement, thought, and feeling fuse during the active, long-term pursuit of personal goals." At the onset of the play experience, when the hands begin to play with the open-ended materials, there is powerful emotional, physical, and cognitive interaction between the domains, thus making the play experience more of a whole, integrated experience. As is noted in the research on children and their development, it is imperative to provide integrated experiences in order for them to understand (Copple & Bredekamp, 2009, p. 11). Utilizing a wholistic approach during the self active play process is the feature that makes self active play so impactful to the player as evidenced through anectdotal reflective journals, personal interviews, observations, photographs, video taping, and focus groups.

Play and Aging

As mentioned above, the aging process requires active participation on the part of the individual. Many studies have shown the importance and significance for older adults to exercise, plan ahead, and gather support as part of being proactive in their aging process. The research on well-being suggests the importance of having a high level of autonomy, personal growth, purpose, and self-acceptance, which is connected to QoL factors such as psychological and social factors. Through self active play, these factors and psychological aspects of well-being are nurtured and provide the older adult with a mechanism in which to develop coping and new possibilities. The transference quality of self active play enables the older adult to bring forth with them the ideas, feelings, and creative potentialities that are enlightened as a direct result of the play.

Capacity Building Responses to Self Active Play

Self active play is a stimulus that elicits predictable capacity-building responses (CBR) from multiple-aged participants. Thousands of reflective journals, photographs, videos, and focus group interviews collected over the past thirty years have been analyzed to derive these five types of CBRs. As a specific intervention for enhancing the quality of life in aging, this practice of self active play engages and strengthens these five human capacities. These CBRs enable the players to generate and maintain optimism as well as a sense of balance when faced with difficult change and ambiguity in life.

Self active play nourishes cognition and feelings by engaging one's hands, heart, and mind; much like what healthy food does for one's physical body. Self active play enables awareness of one's inner being as an expressive force, which is always present to inform and guide when one is engaged in focused practices. Self active play is a key to developing awareness of one's power to enjoy the world and to find ways of positively influencing that world through joyful interaction. The following are the five capacity-building responses experienced during self active play.

1. Capacity to focus and concentrate.

Self active play generates interest, initiative, and extended attention. The relaxed, focused mind enters the play space and opens the flow of creative contemplation. The mind with full assistance of the senses begins to explore and arrange the novel objects. Whatever the age or ability level, whatever the background or personal preference, gradually the mind becomes one-pointed and purposeful in the kinetic expression of creative energy. The mind in a sense is placed within the relaxing focused state of play with purposeful attention and concentration on the curious three-dimensional objects in hand.

2. Capacity to imagine, reason, and elaborate.

The abundance and uniqueness of open-ended materials stimulate the brain to wonder, imagine and construct elaborate physical relationships. Ideas, associations, and connections arise during the purposeful act of creating. This process of imagining, reasoning, and elaborating enables one to uncover purpose, meaning, and values, which then leads to feelings of power, self-determination, and authority. Play with open-ended materials encourages the player to initiate, take charge and make choices. In very simple, safe, appropriate ways this experience strengthens competence.

3. Capacity to clarify intuitive insights.

The play process helps to clarify the connections and relationships between the outer experience with the open-ended materials to the inner experience of meaning making and understanding. These connections and relationships serve as reciprocal personal metaphors corresponding to happenings and relationships experienced in life. These multi-sensory metaphors between the outer and inner experience then provide the foundation for intuitive insight that inform personal understandings, feelings, thoughts, and values.

4. Capacity to choose and regulate.

Self active play is the practice of choosing and regulating the mind to accomplish an enjoyable physical open-ended task, which strengthens the power of the mind to regulate thought. There is a kinetic "transference" of the mind regulation practices experienced in the play to the applied awareness and practice in "real life". The associated enjoyment and regulation of materials, the rendering of harmony and order, and the meaningful flow of knowledge presents the realization that a more positive state of mind is achievable through self active play.

5. Capacity to appreciate wholeness.

The wholeness of self active play revitalizes the inner connection with higher order thinking and deeper feelings of peacefulness and wellbeing. The mind remains focused, fully present and alert yet tranquil and inspired during play. The wholeness of hands, heart and mind unified in joyful play fills the player with enthusiasm and a sense of completeness.

When comparing self active play capacity-building responses to other research components discussed earlier in this paper, such as psychological well-being and the seven rhetorics associated with play research, there are many parallels that arise between each of these. In Table 7.4, all five CBRs relate to at least one of the psychological aspects highlighted in the two types of well-being research. There is a strong connection between the CBRs of self active play to the seven types of play rhetorics developed by Brian Sutton-Smith. So, not only does self active play stand on its own in the integrity of its research findings, but it also is associated with others in their research pursuits of play and psychological well-being.

Table 7.4. Capacity Building Response Comparison Chart

Commonalities of Research Perspectives

Self Active Play	Psychological Aspects of Well-Being		Brian Sutton-Smith
CBRs	**Eudaimonic**	**Hedonic**	**Rhetorics**
1. Focus and concentrate	Personal Growth		Progress
2. Imagine, reason, & elaborate	Autonomy		Imaginary
3. Clarify intuitive insights	Self Acceptance	Frequent + Emotion	Fate
4. Choose and regulate	Environmental Mastery	Satisfaction with important domains	Identity, Power
5. Appreciate wholeness	Purpose of Life	Life Satisfaction	Self, Frivolity

Cross Keys Village

A pilot study using the self active play process was conducted at Cross Keys Village in Pennsylvania. The study was conducted with six older adults in an assisted living facility. The study participants engaged in the self active play process using open-ended materials and painting as creative expression. Each intervention took place for approximately 20 minutes during which time there was soft piano music playing in the background. Participants chose their own open-ended materials and began to play quietly by themselves with one material. After the play, reflective journals were given to each player and they wrote down what they experienced during the play. Each participant then painted while soft music was playing in the background. The participants shared their perceptions of the experience with the whole group, as a focus group. Many of the participants discussed the reminiscing of meaningful experiences from their past and re-discovery of their creative ability. As noted in some of the comments, "The buttons reminded me of my mother working in the coat factory" and "When I was growing up, I was interested in model airplanes. This one is Japanese, from WWII". Another participant stated, "Do you like my Van Gogh? He painted a starry night. This is my sunny day."

Each participant was given an individual interview regarding his or her creative experiences. One participant, who had recently suffered from a stroke, spoke of her painting and reminisced about her childhood. She recalled that her family would go to the beach and as a mother she spent time at the beach with her own children. She recalled the smell of the beach air and her eyes were closed as if she were there at the beach that very moment. Her vivid recall of such times, showed visibly, as her eyes lit up when she spoke of her loving family. She then spoke of going there again with her children and a smile broke across her face. She had tapped into a time when she was fully present and the recall brought back to her those cherished memories. This self active play experience with creative arts materials highlights the impact and provides evidence for Principle 2, which states that individuals spontaneously reconnect with earlier stages of human development as they balance and strengthen hope, will, purpose, competence, fidelity, love, care, and wisdom. Another participant spoke of her feelings of peace and hope as she reminisced about her sister who had just passed away. The self active play provided the context in which this participant could reconcile her emotions of loss into a sense of peace and hope. And as mentioned earlier, providing older adults with ways of gathering support is an important element in well-being.

One response after the pilot study from the facilitator of Cross Keys Village suggested her perspective on the value of this experience. "Sometimes we forget what talents we still have, if we are never given a chance to use them." This reminds us of the importance of staying active during the aging process. Through the active use of one's talents and skills, one can be reminded of the vitality and possibilities that are still present. The results of this pilot study are encouraging and have prompted the authors to seek a more in-depth study in order to fully understand the connections between self active play, QoL perceptions, and well-being in older adults. An extension of this research is to compare the results of using self active play as an intervention with healthy older adults but also extending the research with use with older adults suffering from Alzheimer's Disease.

Play and Alzheimer's Disease (AD)

Wollen, (2010) reviewed studies that examined interventions, such as pharmaceutical, nutritional, botanical, and stimulatory, for Alzheimer's disease (AD) patients and practitioners. Wollen stated that the studies found that "Physical exercise increases the blood supply to the brain and regulates chemicals such as insulin that are necessary for a healthy brain. Recent reviews of studies on exercise indicate that exercise may facilitate learning and memory, improve vascular function, reduce inflammation, improve metabolism, elevate mood, delay age-related memory loss, speed information processing, increase brain volume, aid hippocampal neurogenesis, increase synaptic plasticity, increase brain-derived neurotrophicfactor, increase dendritic spines, enhance the glutamatergic system, and reduce cell death" (p. 235). Wollen continues the review by looking at stimulatory therapies using music as a way to relieve stress, anxiety, and depression in mild to moderate cases of AD. Finding interventions that clearly link these types of factors associated with AD to self efficacy, palliative care, and QoL in well-being are at the forefront of research in geriatrics. Self active play is one of these interventions that could clearly impact QoL and well being for AD patients as well as providing support for the AD patient caregiver.

Brown and Vaughn (2009 p. 71) "For instance, various studies have shown that only a small part of the risk of getting Alzheimer's disease is determined by genes. The majority of the risk of Alzheimer's is attributed to lifestyle and environmental influences. One prospective study done at Albert Einstein and Syracuse Universities showed that for people who had the most cognitive activity (doing puzzles, reading, engaging in mentally challenging work), the chances of getting Alzheimer's disease were 63% lower than that of the general population. If we stop playing, we share the fate of all animals that grow out of play. Our behavior becomes fixed. We are not interested in new and different things. We find fewer opportunities to take pleasure in the world around us."

CONCLUSION

The use of self active play with older adults is an intervention used to promote well-being and positive aging. Capacity-building responses are awakened during self active play. Self active play, then, is an expressive system that acknowledges and encourages the innate human need for creativity throughout the life span. Internal awareness of this need for creative expression enables us to perceive it in others and thus to realize its universal connectedness. Self active play is a context to build one's capacity to deal with the inevitable ambiguity of life.

REFERENCES

American Geriactrics Society. (2011, July). *Quality Measures and Complexity.* Retrieved June 24, 2012 from American Geriactrics Society: www.americangeriactric.org
American Geriatics Society. (2011). *Profile of older adults.* New York.
Association for Gerontology in Higher Education. (2012). *What is Gerontology? Geriactics?* Retrieved July 30, 2012 from Association for Gerontology in Higher Education: http://www.aghe.org/500217
Brown, S., & Vaughn, C. (2009). *Play: How it shapes the brain, opens the imagination, and invigorates the soul.* New York: Avery Publishing.

Copple, C., & Bredekamp, S. (2009). *Developmentally Appropriate Practice in Early Child-hood Programs: Serving Children from birth to age 8.* Washington, D. C. : National Association for the Education of Young Children.

Csikszentmihalyi, M. (1996). *Creativity: Flow and the psychology of discovery and invention.* New York: Harper.

Decker, I., & Reed, P. (2005). Developmental and contextual correlates of elders' end-of-life treatment decisions. *Death Studies, 29,* 827–846.

Dunn, D. (1994). Resilient reintegration of married women with dependent children: Employed and unemployed. *Unpublished doctoral dissertation.*

Erikson, J. M. (1988). *Wisdom and the senses: The way of creativity.* NY: Norton & Company.

Erikson, E. H., & Erikson, J. M. (1997). *The life cycle completed.* New York: W. W. Norton.

Erikson, E., Erikson, J. M., & Kivnick, H. Q. (1986). *Vital involvement in old age.* New York, NY: W. W. Norton & Company.

Espinosa, L. (2010). *Getting it right for young children from diverse backgrounds: Applying research to improve practice.* Washington, DC: National Association for the Education of Young Children .

Glasser, W. (n.d.). *The William Glasser Institute.* Retrieved September 16, 2012 from The William Glasser Institute: http://www.wglasser.com/the-glasser-approach/choice-theory

Goleman, D. (1995/2006). *Emotional intelligence: Why it can matter more than IQ.* New York: Bantam Dell.

Goleman, D., Kaufman, P., & Ray, M. (1992). *The creative spirit.* NY: PLUME.

Gordon, G. (2009). What is Play? In Search of a Definition. In D. Kuschner (Ed.), *From Children to Red Hatters: Diverse Imags and Issues of Play* (Play and Culture Studies ed., Vol. 8, pp. 1–13). Lanham, MD: University Press of America.

Gould, S. J. (1996). *Full house: The Spread of excellence from Plato to Darwin.* New York: Harmony Books.

Henricks, T. S. (2009). Play and the rhetoric fo time: Progress, regression, and the meaning of the present. In D. Kushner (Ed.), *From Children to Red Hatters (R): Diverse Images and Issues of Play* (Vol. 8). New York: University Press.

Jones, E. (2007). *Teaching Adults Revisited: Active Learning for Early Childhood Educators.* Washington, D. C.: National Association for the Education of Young Children.

Kahana, E., Kelley-Moore, J., & Kahana, B. (2012). Proactive aging: A longitudinal study of stress, resources, agency, and well-being in late life. *Aging and Mental Health, 16*(4), 438–451.

Malderen, L. V., Mets, T., & Gorus, E. (2012). Interventions to enhance the quality of life of older people in residential long-term care: A systematic review. *Ageing Research Review.*

National Advisory Council on Aging. (2008). *BSR Review Committee Report.* Washington, DC: National Institute on Aging.

National Institute on Aging. (2011). *Biology of Aging: Research Today for a Healthier Tomorrow.* Washington, DC: National Institutes of Health, US Department of Health and Human Services.

Plucker, J. A., Beghetto, R. A., & Dow, G. T. (2004). Why isn't creativity more important to educational psychologists? Potentials, pitfalls, and future directions in creativity research. *Educational Psychologist, 39*(2), 83–96.

Richardson, G. E. (2002). The Metatheory of resilience and resiliency. *Journal of Clinical Psychology, 58*(3), 307–321.

Sullo, B. (2007). *Activating the desire to learn.* Alexandria, VA: Association of Supervision and Curriculum Development.

Sutton-Smith, B. (1997). *The ambiguity of play.* Cambridge, MA: Harvard University Press.

Tahmaseb-McConatha, J., Volkwein-Caplan, K., & DiGregorio, N. (2011). Culture, aging, and well-being: The importance of place and space. *The International Journal of Sport and Society, 2*(2), 41–48.

Thompson, W., Zack, M., Krahn, G., Andresen, E., & Barile, J. (2012). Health related quality of life among older adults with and without functional limitations. *American Journal of Public Health, 102*(3), 496–502.

Urry, H. L., Nitschke, J. B., Dolski, I., Jackson, D. C., Dalton, K. M., Mueller, C. J., et al. (2004). Making a life worth living: Neural correlates of well-being. *Psychological Science, 15*(6), 367–372.

Walker, A. (2002). A strategy for active ageing. *International Social Security Review, 55,* 121–139.

Wollen, A. K. (2010). Alzheimer's disease: The pros and cons of pharmaceutical, nturitional, botantical, and stimulatory therapies, with a discussion of traetment strategies from the perspective of patients and practitioners. *Alternative Medical Review, 15*(3), 223–244.

World Health Organization. (2002). *Active Ageing: A Policy Framework.* Policy Framework, The Second United Nations Assemby on Ageing, Madrid.

Section III: Playing into the Future

Chapter Eight

Memories and Remembrances of TAASP/TASP (1973–1989)

Ann Marie Guilmette

What follows can be attributed to the Past-President's panel that Phil Stevens organized for the 2014 TASP Conference, (40th Anniversary meeting), held at The Strong National Museum of Play in Rochester, New York, April 23–26, as well as an invitation I had received earlier from Michael Patte for a submission to the *International Journal of Play*.

I am Ann Marie Guilmette, and in 2012, Patte wrote "I am thrilled to hear you are willing to offer a reflective piece describing the playful past of TASP (TAASP) with both words and pictures. I am very pleased that you will consider contributing your beautiful memories." Michael had sent this message in reply to an earlier invitation, in which he asked that I write a reflective piece on the importance of TASP (TAASP) to me personally and professionally since its inception, and through which some of the "old" traditions ("Great Debates," roasting of TASP Presidents, provocative Keynotes, and bawdy Presidential addresses) could be resurrected and reinstated.

As well, this article has been inspired by Brown & Patte's (2012) interview with Brian Sutton-Smith, in which Brian describes his latest book *Play as Emotional Survival* (Sutton-Smith, in Progress) and in which Brian identifies his interest in combining play with humor and stories. On the basis of Sutton-Smith's recommendation, I offer the following memories and reflections of TAASP/TASP and the Past-President's from 1973 to 1989.

In 1975 at the University of Windsor in Canada, I entered the doctoral program in psychology with Dr. Lawrence La Fave serving as my dissertation advisor. La Fave was a social psychologist and well-known researcher in the study of humor (La Fave, 1980; La Fave & Mannell, 1976). He encouraged me to consider how play and humor might be related as concepts.

Additionally, La Fave believed that all research should be grounded in the context of culture. Indeed, at his urging, a cross-cultural approach was included by most of his students in exploring these inter-relationships (Tsang & Guilmette, 1980).

Earlier in 1973, as a Master's student (also at Windsor but in physical education), Dr. James Duthie became my mentor. He conducted research on play, games, sport, and leisure, and like many thesis advisors was more of a 'tor-mentor'! Although, as you can imagine, none of his students made advising easy for him! Nevertheless, Duthie was another social psychologist who similarly encouraged his students to pursue an inter-cultural understanding of play (Duthie, 1976).

To this end, in Chinese culture, we are in the year 4048 (rather than 2014) and the celebration of the Chinese New Year occurs in January or February of each year, rather than on the fixed date of January 1st. As well, in Chinese astrology the year in which you are born is considered as important as the month of your birth.

In this story of the TAASP/TASP Presidents who served before me, we must first be transported to the temple where The Lord Buddha has called the animals to him, and promised to name a Year in honour of each upon their arrival. In the Chinese zodiac then, there are 12 animals used to represent "The Year of" the Rat, Ox, Tiger, Rabbit, Dragon, Snake, Horse, Goat, Monkey, Rooster, Dog, and Pig.

In 1973 and 1974, Allan Tindall participated in a series of meetings through which The Association for the Anthropological Study of Play (TAASP) was founded. Unfortunately, Allan did not survive long enough to become a Past-President, so in this journey of remembrances Allan Tindall will be our TASPian Lord Buddha, who will call the TASP animal Presidents to him, and honour them by proclaiming their special contributions to the study of play.

So, this story also is based on my memories of the 12 Presidents who served TAASP/TASP, before me in 1989, and from whom at that time I had requested a picture, and a copy of their Presidential addresses.

The first TAASPian president is represented in the Year of the Snake, which means he was limber and maneuverable as he slithered his way into our consciousness. In human form, he also was mystical and meditative, with a passion for music and books. Like a snake, Michael Salter was a charmer who could draw you in to the study of play. Colleagues and students alike were crushed by the overwhelming number of publications through which Mike would channel information on the "Great Ball Games of the Mayans." Duthie (my Master's thesis advisor) and Salter (a graduate course instructor) were colleagues at The University of Windsor, so they invited me to participate in the first TAASP conference held in 1975 in Detroit, Michigan (located directly across from the Canadian border). I submitted my Master's thesis research to the program, and after my presentation, prepared an article for publication in the proceedings (Guilmette, 1976).

Another of the TAASP Presidents represents the Year of the Horse. So, while 2014 is not only TASP's 40th Anniversary conference, but this year also just happens to be the Year of the Horse.

As we currently celebrate all things equine, I distinctly remember the conference with the most horsing around to be the 1979 meeting in Henniker, New Hampshire. I drove with Duthie and Salter for 19 hours to get there, and most everyone was lost. Edward Norbeck, a distinguished TAASPian, who had delivered the first Johan Huizinga address as a Keynote in 1975 (Norbeck, 1976), claimed that he could not even find an airport in New Hampshire. So he flew from Rice University in Texas to New York City, and from there hired a limousine to take him to Henniker. Regrettably, the driver took him to Henniker, Massachusetts, causing him to miss the Wednesday evening reception, and the first day of papers on Thursday, on which he had been scheduled to present. Even more uproariously, at this 1979 conference, I met the TAASP President who epitomizes the Year of the Horse. Phil Stevens was then such a serious scholar of play that he became an easy target to be the "butt" of much of my humour. Thank goodness Phil's research (Stevens, 1991) focuses on similar examples of this type of "sanctioned, permitted, disrespect," characteristic of funeral ceremonies among the Bachama. In seeing this characterization, I am certain that Phil is now wishing for my funeral. Yet, if he accepts my role as a *gboune* who is engaging in sanctioned "public horseplay," and during which he is expected not to take offense, then he will understand that in our "joking relationship," he actually enjoys elevated status and is held in the highest esteem by me and our Association.

The next year to be celebrated is the Year of the Dragon, and perhaps from having just seen my Stevens' tribute, you can understand why Helen Schwartzman was reluctant to send me her picture. In actuality, Helen sent her Presidential address, but did refuse to send a picture, by telling me "I don't give head." Nevertheless, like the fire-breathing dragon, Helen's focus on the transformative nature of play (Schwartzman, 1978) scorched the academic community and razed/raised the awareness of many scholars who then joined the quest in pursuit of play.

The next animal is the Year of the Ox. This character is a gentle giant, who is methodical and broad shouldered. He is considered to be the hardest worker among all of the twelve animals. Jack (John) Roberts was just such a character. He left a rich legacy for TAASP in identifying the enculturation processes (cultural values of achievement motive, sacred governance, and obedience to authority) through which games of skill, chance, and strategy (respectively) came to prevail in the lifestyles of specific cultures in a society.

Another animal is featured in the Year of the Tiger, and what a special lady our TAASPian tigress was. Alyce Cheska, a sleek, stylish, striking, and fiercely protective academic, had a keen mind and was an active listener. She was my role model for what a TAASP President should be. You couldn't miss her elegant and professionally coiffed shock of white hair. Alyce was especially comforting, supportive, encouraging, and inclusive with members who were new to the Association. She was formidable, or as the French say *formidable*, which means bold. Her research on the games of Aboriginal and Inuit cultures in North America were exhilarating and illuminating.

The next animal is represented in the Year of the Pig, and here we find the most intelligent in the Zodiac. This President's research was anything but 'boaring' (boring). His chapter on the cultural politics of the "Caribana" festival in Toronto, Canada became required reading in the course I taught on play and culture.

At Frank Manning's 1987 conference in Montreal, Canada, I nearly stayed away from his Presidential address. I was shocked to see that he was presenting on sport, which was clearly outside Frank's comfort zone in his paper titled "Jocks and Boxers." I should have known that Manning would not disappoint, and his presentation went well beyond the comfort zone of many in the audience. I am sure that most of you will have read Manning's (1988) article that appeared in the first edition of the TASP Journal. If you have not, I highly recommend you to it, as the jocks to which Frank refers are those TASPians who wear jockey shorts or briefs, and thus he suggested produce mostly quantitative research, as opposed to those who prefer boxers, which then he suggested would more likely be inclined to qualitative studies in play. Manning's Presidential address could have been titled "Panty Play" and would have been in keeping with another series of Presidential addresses that had equally provocative titles.

In the Year of the Rat, we find an overachieving, enterprising character who likes to experience most everything firsthand. Gary Alan Fine epitomizes the Year of the Rat. He too was reluctant to send me his picture, but did so, and wrote, "Please note that in this picture, I am fully clothed as I engage in play." His address titled "Dirty Play" was derived from his first-hand observations and field notes on the bullying and cheating he witnessed during his fieldwork with boys' little league baseball teams. Later, Gary regaled us with his first-hand accounts of the exotic mushroom hunters in the muddy woods, who broke all of the rules in search of a psychedelic and hallucinogenic nirvana.

The career diplomat can be found in the Year of the Goat, as one who seeks harmony above all else in his personal and professional life. He is the peace-maker in the zodiac. John Loy epitomizes the Year of the Goat, in referring to most of us as kids, although to me he usually just bleats, Nah! In his address, titled "Coercive Play," John talked about the need for formal, institutionalized, inflexible, and unchanging rules and roles in the governance and regulation of sport. His detailed and extensive descriptions of these codified rules and roles are exhausting and exhaustive.

Then there is the Year of the Rooster, who represents the senior statesman. He is the energetic, cocky, passionate, and well-spoken messenger in the zodiac. He also reluctantly sent his picture, and with much trepidation begged me to try to preserve his administrative dignity as the President of a University. Kendall Blanchard is our TASPian President who can be aligned with the Year of the Rooster. He is a President who was a President. He is our most effective communicator, a bit cocky, but the best at crowing about our achievements and accomplishments in TASP. I will never forget his creative and articulate non-Presidential address titled "Obscene Play," during which he recited an eleven-page ditty of hand-crafted, albeit fairly explicit dirty verse.

TASPians are ideally situated for the Year of the Monkey given that our logo, depicts a skeleton at play with a gorilla. Only a skeleton will remain because any TASP President will likely be long gone before we can fully understand and explain play. The gorilla or monkey is a unique problem solver who is persistent, detailed, and deliberate. Barney Mergen is our TASP President for the Year of the Monkey. His address was titled "Forbidden Play," and Barney's research typically provided an extensive and historically rich chronicle of the role of toys and play in defining a society (Mergen, 1991). During his term in office, Mergen was well known for organizing a series of special, additional seminars and workshops for TASP members.

I was fortunate to attend a session in the 1980s at the opening of the first interactive children's museum, which ironically has since come to be known as "The Strong."

The next is the Year of the Dog. This animal is quite companionable and loyal, but he is the worrier in the zodiac. He is a perfectionist who sets extremely high standards and becomes intolerant of anyone who does not also give 100%. Jay Mechling is our TASPian President for the Year of the Dog. After Manning's "Panty Play," Fine's "Dirty Play," Loy's "Coercive Play," Blanchard's "Obscene Play," and Mergen's "Forbidden Play," Jay's address titled "Morality Play" (Mechling, 1989) seemed a welcome relief. Nevertheless, Jay asserted that play was like religion in exerting a moral order, but is transcendently both subversive and joyful. From this perspective, what remains is both nasty and messy, and we are left in a circumstance wherein neither science nor philosophy is viewed as particularly helpful to our understanding of play.

Finally, in the Year of the Rabbit, we find the most playful and prolific member of the zodiac. Interestingly, Albert Einstein was born in the Year of the Rabbit. Nevertheless, Brian Sutton-Smith is our TASPian President who most assuredly resembles this year. Brian continues to be our most influential and recognizable TASPian. I thought that he wrote *Play as Emotional Survival* (Sutton-Smith, in progress) just for me, but I recognize that there are many who could relate to the awesome power of play in transforming our lives from the ordinary to the extraordinary. I am grateful to know Brian. On more than one occasion during our exchanges (skirmishes some may have called them), I have shared and enjoyed our mutual interests in play, humor, and stories. Sutton-Smith is a prolific scholar, and the "Ambiguity of Play" (Sutton-Smith, 1997) still resonates as central and germane in recognizing, understanding, and interpreting the elusive nature of this entity we have all committed to studying, which is play.

Thank you for allowing me to share these memories and reflections of the early years of TAASP/TASP, and congratulations to The Association for the Study of Play on our 40th anniversary.

NOTES

I am very appreciative and owe a debt of gratitude to Sanghee Chun, Diane Doneff, Bonnie Gallagher, Sandy Notar, Arlene Purpura, Shalini Singh, and Lynn Wolbert. They are colleagues from Brock University, as well as family and friends, who provided me with the time, patience, assistance, support, and encouragement needed to complete this manuscript. If there are errors or omissions, I am entirely and solely responsible for them.

REFERENCES

Brown, F., & Patte, M. (2012). An interview with Brian Sutton-Smith. From the streets of Wellington to the Ivy League: Reflecting on a lifetime of play. *International Journal of Play*, *1*(1), 6–15.

Duthie, J. (1976). Play/non-play determinants. In D. Lancy and A. Tindall (Eds.), *The anthropological study of play: Problems and prospects* (pp. 217–220). New York: Leisure Press.

Guilmette, AM. (1976). Binocular resolution as a function of the play identification class. In D. Lancy and A. Tindall (Eds.), *The anthropological study of play: Problems and prospects* (pp. 211–217). New York: Leisure Press.

La Fave, L. (1980). De-ethnocentrizing humor theory. In H. Schwartzman's (Ed.), *Play and culture* (pp. 293–299). New York: Leisure Press.

La Fave, L., & Mannell, R. (1976). Ethnic humor as a function of reference groups and identification classes. In D. Lancy and A. Tindall (Eds.), *The anthropological study of play: Problems and prospects* (pp. 227–239). New York: Leisure Press.

Manning, F. (1988). Academic underwear: Getting down to play. *Play and Culture*, *1*(1), 70–76.

Mechling, J. (1989). Morality play. *Play and Culture*, *2*(4), 304–316.

Mergen, B. (1991). Ninety-five years of historical change in the game preferences of American children. *Play and Culture*, *4*(3), 272–283.

Norbeck, E. (1976). The study of play—Johan Huizinga & modern anthropology. In D. Lancy and A. Tindall (Eds.), *The anthropological study of play: Problems and prospects* (pp. 13–22). New York: Leisure Press.

Schwartzman, H. (1978). *Transformations: The anthropology of children's play.* New York: Plenum.

Stevens, P. (1991). Play and liminality in rites of passage: From elder to ancestor in West Africa. *Play and Culture, 4*(3), 237–257.

Sutton-Smith, B. (1997). *The ambiguity of play.* MA.: Harvard University Press.

Sutton-Smith, B. (In Progress). *Play as emotional survival.*

Tsang, S.Y.W., & Guilmette, AM. (1980). Interactive incongruity humor theorydepicted in social-normative humor experiments. In H. Schwartzman's (Ed.), *Play and culture,* (pp. 305–310). New York: Leisure Press.

Chapter Nine

Transcultural Study of Play

Turkish and Saudi Mothers' Beliefs about Play

Monirah Al-Mansour, Serap Sevimli-Celik, and
James E. Johnson

Play is complex with multifold manifestations as is its study. Within this expanding diversified context the rising importance of play and play studies as cultural phenomena is easy to detect in the literature. Play and culture are receiving increasing scholarly attention over the past few decades with investigators employing many different methods. Earlier studies of play and cultural variation relied primarily on observational, questionnaire, and interview methods Schwartzman (1978), Smilansky (1968), and Whiting and Pope-Edwards (1988). More recently, researchers are using a range of innovative, sophisticated techniques to generate data including drawing tasks, participatory photography, participatory observation and videoing, and videoconferencing (see Johnson, Al-Mansour, & Sevimli-Celik, 2015).

Equipped with new methods those interested in childhood play around the world are able to pursue divergent goals and aims of study. A dominant strand has been parental beliefs about play (Roopnarine & Davidson, 2015). Summing up, Roopnarine and Krishnakumar (2006) assert that "play participation in different cultural communities depends, in part, on the adjustments children make to accommodate the childrearing goals and expectations of their parents" (p. 276).

Conceptual underpinnings for the research come from the historic-cultural perspective in which the study of play is situated in a person's contexts and reflects historical, economic, social, and cultural factors. Within this research tradition many studies show cultural differences in children's play behaviors (Cote & Bornstein, 2009; Goncu, Mistry & Mosier, 2000; Suizzo

& Bornstein, 2006). For example, Holmes (2011) indicated that adults in Lana'i culture valued play that fosters social skills such as cooperation and sharing which is an integral part of collectivist ideology. In another study, Suizzo and Bornstein (2006) compared French and European-American children and their mothers on exploratory, symbolic, and social play and interaction. French children engaged in more exploratory play, whereas US children engaged in more symbolic play. French mothers less frequently solicited symbolic play and offered less verbal praise than did US mothers.

Reviews of the literature (Roopnarine & Davidson, 2015) note the complexity of the connection between play and culture. Parents' views on the meaning of play for child learning and development vary considerably. Discussions of them typically include reference to variables within cultural settings including the relative importance ascribed to different family values and goals for children, which themselves are linked to history as well as current circumstances. Roopnarine has examined maternal thoughts and concerns about play. For instance, in an important multi-national study, Singer, Singer, D'Agostino, and DeLong (2009) interviewed 2,400 mothers in 16 countries and asked 49 questions relating to how children from the earliest years of life through age 12 years spend their time each day. In general, the results supported the assertion that mothers are similar to teachers in their worry about the quality of children's play experiences and the compression or loss of childhood. For example, nearly half (47%) reported dismay over how little children play outdoors and over half (64%) about the connection between loss of playtime and childhood obesity. Overall, 72% of the mothers reported that their children watched TV (most common activity reported), compared to 58% and only 27% for playing outside and engaging in imaginative play, respectively.

Similarly, IKEA (2010) carried a research-driven project across 25 countries to investigate the children's development and play. A total of 7,933 interviews with parents (parents of 0–12 years) and 3,116 interviews with children (aged 7–12 years) were conducted via the Internet. The state of parenthood, the state of childhood, and play were the main topics for interview questions. Study results showed the very high agreement (93%) on the developmental benefits of play. However, 45% of the parents interviewed felt that they struggle to find time to play with their children. Parents especially in the *time-poor* countries like China, Portugal, Hungary, Russia, Italy, Ireland, and France stated that they do not have time to play with their children. In addition to time constrain, parents also stated their concerns about stranger danger (49%), traffic (43%), and bullying (38%).

This chapter highlights findings from our transcultural study of play project (TSPP) that commenced in August 2010 and involved faculty and graduate students from the USA, Iran, Belize, India, Taiwan, South Korea, China, Turkey, Kuwait, and Saudi-Arabia. Two cases are presented, one from Turkey and the other from Saudi-Arabia. All studies used similar methods and shared a common purpose.

TSPP's overall aim is to promote international dialogue and research on play and culture while contributing to faculty and graduate students' social networking and increased mutual understanding of play with culture, especially with respect to development, education, and early childhood education. TSPP continues in the Early Childhood Education Emphasis Area in the Department of Curriculum and Instruction in the College of Education at The Pennsylvania State University at University Park.

METHODS

TSPP uses three methods to generate data: interviews, drawing tasks, and focus groups. The interviews took place either in person or by Skype. Interviews lasted about an hour and were always carried out with the interviewer and the interviewee being of the same gender and from the same culture. Interviews allow researchers to verify, clarify, or alter what they thought happened, to achieve a full understanding of an incident, and to take into account the 'lived' experience of participants (Seidman, 2006). In addition, semi-structured interviews allow for elaborated in-depth responses as participants reconstruct and report their experiences.

Results reported here used such interviews which attempted to put the participants' experiences in context by asking them to describe themselves and their child in the past, present, and also to predict the future of play. In this study we also asked the participants to elaborate on their play beliefs and concerns.

The two drawing tasks embedded in the interview facilitated thinking about what play is now and how it has changed over time. The tasks were specially devised and adapted from similar ones found in published studies from Mälardalen University, Sweden, by Sandberg and her colleagues (Sandberg, 2001; Sandburg, 2003; Vickerius & Sandburg, 2006; Sandburg & Tammemä-Orr, 2008). These investigators posit that to fully understand play in the present, a memory exercise on the development of play over time should be conducted. The technique served to motivate respondents giving them opportunities to elaborate and think deeply about their play memories. Also by drawing from memory participants were afforded chances to reveal their points of view on play in what soon always became a relaxed situation; this served well the over-all purpose of the interview. The play memories as drawn and spoken provided a base to continue the interview to extract a deeper understanding about play now and then. Drawings provide the participant with a visual comparison to examine similarities and differences in the kind and quality of play between self and own child, between play past, present, and future.

The procedure entails a number of steps. First, respondents complete a drawing task that focused on parental memories of their own play as a young child, middle age child, teenager, and adult. Follow up questions asked parents to elaborate and evaluate their play. The next step was a second drawing task in which parents are asked to draw a picture of their child (age 5 to 10 years old) playing now (top half of paper) and in five years (Bottom half of paper). Follow up questions were asked about the drawings.

The final step is asking additional questions to conclude the interview. What play reflects your own culture? What play contributes to the well-being and growth of your culture? An additional aim was to obtain reports of mothers' memories of their own play histories to compare with data about their children's current and projected play activity preferences.

The researchers asked questions and engaged in conversation with the participants prior to the first drawing in order to help the mothers reflect on their own play and their children's play as separate from their own and to view the child as an individual. Fonagy and colleagues call this concept "reflective functioning", which is defined as the ability to imagine mental states in self and others. Through this capacity for reflection, one develops the ability to understand one's own behavioral responses and the responses of others as a meaningful attempt to communicate between inner mental states. Fonagy describes reflective function as a uniquely human capacity to make sense of each other (Fonagy, Gergely, Jurist, & Target, 2002). Project data collection used audio-recorded interviews with recordings transcribed shortly after each interview. The researchers' field notes also were considered to help explain the interviews and to broaden the researcher's mental picture.

TSPP also used focus group sessions. Groups or subgroups of interviewers came together to share their views and reflect upon the views of the mothers interviewed. For example, one time a focus group was conducted with the interviewers from Taiwan, South Korea, China, and another with the interviews from Turkey, Iran, and Saudi-Arabia. A third focus group brought all six together to generate data for transcultural analyses. The questions were open-ended (*e.g., What elevator speech about play would you give to the top government leader in your country?*) Using open-ended and carefully crafted questions and follow-up probes, a similar emergent, spontaneous manner of stimulating dialogue was followed in each focus group. An important objective was to have all participants engaged in the discussion and interacting with one another. Data from the focus groups are not presented in this chapter, but some comments at the end of this chapter are based on what we learned from the focus groups.

What follows comes from extended work by two former TSPP members who are co-authors of this chapter. They share some findings from their interviews with mothers from Turkey and Saudi Arabia.

FINDINGS

Turkish Case

Seeking a broader empirical base on parental beliefs about play, using the aforementioned research methods, data were generated from 13 Turkish mothers either living in the United States ($n=6$) or in Turkey ($n=7$). The interviewer's intent was to obtain information which would exemplify the changing face of mothers and children's play over time across different settings, revealing different types of play and playthings, and suggesting values given to play and maternal concerns about it. The semi-structured interviews were conducted face-to-face (mothers living in US) or via Skype (those living in Turkey).

All mothers noted the limited amount of time today's children spend outdoors, and remarked that they played outside more often than to their children now reminiscing about staying outside for long periods until their moms called them in for dinner. The following statements reflect a difference with the current situation of their children:

> We used to play outside a lot. We used to climb trees, play dodge ball, marbles, hide and seek. However, my kids are much more supervised because the world is a different place. And my son rather spent the day in front of the computer instead of going outside. He has a bicycle and he rarely rides. Sad but true (Mom O)
>
> We were playing outside not inside. Now, my son barely goes outside and plays. He has not many friends to play. We were playing as a whole neighborhood. It was all going outside and play most of the time. We knew each other very well. Our moms knew each other very well. Now it is different (Mom N)

Although worried about their children's limited outdoor playtime, most mothers were reluctant to let them play outside due to the safety issues. Particularly, seven mothers who were living in the metropolitan cities in Turkey emphasized the lack of access to safe outdoor play areas in their neighborhoods as a barrier.

> We are living in a big city and our neighborhood is not very safe to play due to the traffic. I cannot allow her to go outside by her self so I need to supervise her all the time. She does not have balls since I don't want her to run after the ball in such a dangerous street. She does not have a bicycle either for the same reason (Mom A)

In addition to the safety concerns, these mothers also indicated poor playground designs as a barrier. For instance, some mothers criticized the lack of proper fencing around the playgrounds and shaded areas for hot weather. They noted concerns about surfacing such as asphalt, concrete, or other hard surfaces lacking shock-absorbing properties, and the scarcity of open grassy areas for running, kicking, or rolling. When on rare occasion coming across such grassy areas they often encountered a "Keep off the Grass" sign. This raised tension between the mothers and persons responsible for caring for the grassy areas. In contrast Turkish mothers living in small rural areas in the United States were not concerned about this issue, being in communities that can afford safe and open play areas for the children.

In addition to environmental issues adversely affecting play the mothers living in Turkey frequently mentioned academic pressure and increasing competition for college acceptance as play barriers. Some opined that it is never too early to start thinking and preparing their children for the national university placement exam.

> I can't let her play all the time. To be honest, she does not have time to play. Her schedule is busy. She goes to the school from noon to 5:30 pm. In the morning she is doing tests and at night she is doing her home-works. At the weekends she has to go to additional courses. She is busy with studying for exams most of the time. If she wants to be admitted to a good university she will work even harder (Mom S)

Another mother commented:

> She'll study more and more for the exams. I want her to be admitted in one of the prestigious universities. She'll continue to study harder and play less (Mom F)

Most mothers also reported technology as important. The Turkish mothers living in Turkey and in the United States articulated that technology has changed play preferences in one generation. For instance, dominant play patterns when the 13 mothers were children included: (1) active/physical play ($n=13$), (2) make-believe play ($n=13$), (3) creative play ($n=13$), (4) constructive play ($n=10$), (5) rough and tumble play ($n=8$), (6) games with rules ($n=8$), (7) language play ($n=6$) and (8) risk-taking play ($n=5$). In contrast, the reported play habits of their children were: (1) virtual/computer play ($n=13$), (2) organized sports ($n=13$), (3) arts and music classes ($n=12$), (4) educational play ($n=10$), (5) constructive play ($n=9$), and (6) traditional Turkish games ($n=5$).

Generally, the types of play children engaged in were reported to be similar in Turkey and the US; but interestingly the mothers living in the US often discussed one type that was not mentioned by the mothers living in

Turkey: traditional Turkish games. Turkish mothers living in the US acknowledged their responsibility to preserve and promote cultural heritage through teaching such traditional games as Hacivat and Karagoz shadow play, Nasreddin Hoca tales and role-plays, and folk dances. Providing opportunities for intergenerational play via Skype or face-to-face interactions, the mothers also stated that they aimed to carry on the family traditions. For some mothers, it is through play that children adopt family values and ideals specific to their culture and keep their traditions alive:

> While I'm talking with his grandmother over Skype, I also want him to bring his toys and join our conversation. My mom has toys at her house as well. She brings them and he asks her to play such and such. Most of the time they are pretending to get on a plane and going to Turkey or coming to the states. It's taking almost 2 hours to finish the game. He always wants to play with his grandmother over Skype. I think this is wonderful for both of them to know each other. It's also a great way to keep family bonds (Mom H)
>
> They need to know their Turkish culture well. We read books about Turkey and watch cartoons or documentaries to learn more about foods, dances, clothes, or music specific to some regions. They take folk dance and Turkish courses. I'm teaching them some games from my childhood. They know how to play five stones, whose hand on my back, catching the kerchief, and blind man's bluff. In our cultural festivals, they have a chance to watch Hacivat and Karagoz shadow play or Nasreddin Hoca role play through which they learn to respect each other while having fun at the same time (Mom Z)

Turkish mothers' play memory drawings for themselves and their children also illustrated differences between the types of play in which they engaged. The mother's responses to the interview questions suggested that the materials used in children's play have changed in one generation. All 13 mothers stated that they had played with natural, inexpensive, open-ended, and hand-made materials. But their children seldom do. Instead they are drawn to highly commercial, structured, and technological toys. One of the moms commented on her concern for her child's not being as creative as herself due to the ready-to-use-toys.

> The main difference between our play is the toys. I did not have toys and we were trying to create our own toys. For example, when it was raining, this was a chance for us to go outside and play with mud since we did not have play dough. I did not have any kitchen utensils but I could find something to use for my play. I could find and play with my mom's old and broken utensils. She has a lot of toys but she still does not have any idea what to play or how to play. Unfortunately, she'll never be as creative as I am (Mom P)

Regarding play materials, the mother's central focus was the heavy influence of technology and media in the lives of their children. All the mothers agreed on how technology has changed the way their children play and communicate.

> He spends most of his time in front of the computer. I was spending all my time outside playing with friends, real friends. My son has many virtual friends they met online but they never saw each other in a real environment. They are just virtual friends and he likes to spend time with them. Unfortunately, he is not a very social child (Mom R)
>
> He wakes up very early in the morning and sits and plays silently so we don't hear him playing. He is playing spider man games and he can sit in front of it up to 2 hours. However, he can easily get bored while playing with his toys. He only plays with them once and then throws them away. I always try to encourage him to go outside and meet with friends. When we go outside, he cannot initiate play or continue playing. When they have problems we as their moms need to intervene and solve their problem (Mom Y)

In addition, 10 of 13 moms specifically stated being worried about increasing aggressive behaviors and violence due to the excessive use of computer and video games. Common problems mentioned included: inability to control their negative emotions (n=10), lack of tolerance to others (n=8), lack of empathy for others (n=7), and social isolation (n=6). Mothers further believed that too much screen time is a leading cause of sedentary lifestyles and less time spent outdoors. These latter findings are consistent with the 16 nations study (Singer et al., 2009).

The mothers clearly endorsed the importance of play for their children's development, expressing the need for a wide variety of play and to encourage certain types. For instance, seven mothers living in Turkey favor educational play as an enjoyable means of providing learning opportunities. Examples included puzzles, board games, memory games, word games, and letter games. The mothers valued the intellectual skills these games encouraged such as thinking, reasoning, understanding, problem-solving – all foundational for academic success. Further, the mothers indicated organized sports, arts, and music activities to improve their children's self esteem and self-discipline.

> I like him to be successful at least in one of the sports. He's going to a tennis course and he's really good at it. It's a very competitive sport and I think he's facing winning and losing all the time. When he learns to cope with these feelings, his self esteem and confidence grows. He is also gaining work ethic, discipline, and responsibility (Mom K)

For the two mothers, proficiency in one of those organized activities is also an important element of their social status and approval of society:

She is taking swimming, violin, and dance classes. It is important for her to learn a variety of skills at the same time so that her personality grows stronger. The more she knows about everything, the more she'll be respected by the society (Mom R)

She takes piano lessons for 2 years. To be honest, I forced her to take the lesson and then she liked it very much. She's even giving mini-concerts to our relatives and friends. I'm so proud to see her while she's playing and I'm pretty sure that she'll be very successful and represent our country in the future (Mom H)

The six mothers living in the United States specified pretend, cooperative, and traditional play as one of the ways to teach traditional values, social rules, and cultural expectations. For them, pretend play provides a means of teaching what is right or wrong and what is acceptable or unacceptable in virtue of the traditions, customs, and practices of their culture. For example, one mother deemed her daughter's tea ceremony pretend play as a way for practicing one of the everyday Turkish traditions. Another mom saw his son's cooperative play as a way for understanding and respecting others, being patient, and helping others in need. Due to the concerns about maintaining group interdependence and sensitivity to others, three mothers commented on the benefits of this type of play to push back against the competitive and individualistic way of life. To become familiar with traditions, five mothers in the US also talked about their efforts to include traditional play (e.g., folk dances, Hacivat Karagoz shadow play, Nasreddin Hoca pretend play) into their children's lives through participating in Turkish festivals or cultural events.

Besides the benefits, all thirteen mothers expressed their concerns about the types of play that might be harmful for their children. All mothers agreed that virtual play can be detrimental when it encourages children to become socially isolated and inactive, causes them to behave violently, decreases their creativity, or corrupts their cultural values and traditions. The mothers worried about the transformation of play from a hands-on to a computer-controlled experience. Interestingly, six mothers living in the United States also expressed their disapproval of playing with imaginary friends, a play form extremely rare in Turkish culture. They stated that having an imaginary companion might be a sign of a problem requiring intervention and that children with an imaginary friend should be redirected toward different activities. Mothers living in Turkey did not bring up this topic.

To sum up, the findings suggest differences between the mothers' childhood play experiences and those of their children. Academic pressure, lack of access to safe play areas, poor playground designs, and technology were mentioned as the leading factors that have caused a decline in both indoor and outdoor play time. Mothers judged some play types as beneficial and others as harmful for their children, recognizing some forms as supportive of children's physical, social, and intellectual development, as well as reinforcing cultural values. Other play that had violent and antisocial themes, or was inactive, was labeled as harmful and unhealthy for children. Generally, play was seen as an important factor for their children's intellectual and social development, as well as a means to embracing cultural traditions.

Turkish parents and communities need to increase support for children's play compared to the previous generation. Developing programs of research and projects, as well as formulating policies concerning play would be helpful to preserve and promote the child's right to play.

Research studies examining children's play in terms of parental attitudes, mother and child relationships, value given to play, and societal changes in play over time are rare. The results support the involvement of Turkish parents in their children's play (Göncü, Mistry, & Mosier, 2000; Isikoglu & Ivrendi, 2008). Continued research is needed to better understand the meaning and importance of play in Turkish cultural communities (Göncü, 1999).

For example, it is of utmost importance to improve children's play areas. Consider the apartment style living found in urban cities of Turkey; obviously there is the need for well-maintained, developmentally appropriate, safe, and secure play areas. This is especially crucial for children who have limited play opportunities at home. There is also a need for well-developed playground safety guidelines that enforce standards for outdoor play areas. Another goal is to assist parents to understand the value of children's play and to support the creation of opportunities and affordances for a wide variety of play types, rather than focusing efforts on only specific types of play.

Saudi Arabia Case

Semi-structured interviews with the embedded drawing tasks were conducted with 10 Saudi mothers of 5–10 years old children. Five mothers were English-speaking and currently reside in the U.S. and five mothers are currently living in Saudi Arabia and speak little to no English. The interviews were conducted in both languages, Arabic and English. The participants were selected through a snowball sampling method. The main categories emerging from data analysis were: climate and ecological factors, technology and modernized life, family bond, public expectation and public manner, and tradition and globalization.

Climate and Ecological Factors

Often mothers expressed disappointment over reduced play time, academic pressures, too much technology, and television watching. Ecological, temporal, and climate factors also appeared as influencing childhood play in the Saudi culture studied. In the winter, children spend most of their day doing schoolwork, preparing for examinations, and racing to the top which provides limited opportunities to play in their lives. During summer, children have no school. However, playing during the daytime seems impossible because of the heat. The weather in the summer is not helpful for outdoor play so people prefer to play outdoors when the sun sets. Night camping is a very popular Saudi activity. People go out of the city and find a quiet spot to camp. Usually they go in groups and have lots of fun being away from the restrictions in life, noise, and everyday pressures. Most of Saudi families respect and appreciate nature because it gives one power and energy as one of the mothers emphasized.

A Saudi mother residing in the U.S. said that her son's play is like everybody else there. He goes outside, plays with neighbor kids, goes to the park, and joins organized sport teams. However, she predicts in 5 or 10 years her child's play will be different:

> . . . on one hand he will be older and on the other hand, he will be in Saudi Arabia. Accordingly, he will play with what will be provided for him. So if I am in Saudi Arabia right now he will be like everybody else there playing with whatever the community is offering. More importantly, my child will be playing according to the weather. If it is hot he will remain indoors and will most likely do more activities at evening time. Unlike here, we only go outing during the day time (Mom 10).

Technology and Modernized Life

The Saudi children prefer different types of e-games nowadays. Some mothers, especially the young mothers between 28 and 29 years of age, have different points of view on play and technology. At least one mother, 29 years old, said that she is interested in computer games such as Mario car races. However, she put emphasis on the computer games as bad for self, children, and society when they are out of control, encourage violence, or are sexualized. Another younger mother, 28 years old, had a stand on technology and play that was quite different than the rest of the mothers who were in their 30's or 40's:

> . . . perhaps the electronic games now will be considered old fashion play for this new generation's future. Every generation they have their play and games that suit that era. I cannot say that my mother's or grandmother's games were good, maybe it was good for them and entertaining for them at that time; their games might be beneficial, but does it fit this generation's needs? I doubt it! I doubt that it would benefit us. We can't even play the way they played because play is disappearing and in the future 'play' will be limited to technology! What we notice now is no PLAY only TECHNOLOGY . . . maybe this is the type of play that children now like . . . . This is the 'era of speed or age of speed'! Everything needs to be hurried and everything needs to be done in a

fast manner. In the past people used to carry toys and things with them when they go places to entertain their children; now you get an IPOD or Nintendo and it has thousands of games that you can fit it in your pocket (Mom 4).

Saudi mothers in their 30's or older viewed electronic games as negative, meaningless, and stressful. Such play does not help children to become better people. One mother described such technologically oriented play as lacking in imagination. She said:

> . . . . From my observation there is not imagination in children's play there (in Saudi Arabia) . . . they all have some kind of electronic devices such as DS and/or IPads! . . . I can tell that my son can be good at video games because he is sharp, but I don't want him to get started and I try to delay it as much as I can (Mom 3).

Another mother of a five-year-old (Mom 1) had decided on delaying electronic games for her son so he can use his imagination and play freely. Yet another mother who currently resides in the U.S. highlighted the use of technology nowadays and commercialized toys as a part of the materialistic world. She blamed the diminishment of old-fashioned play to adults who themselves yearn to catch up with the world's market! She summed it up, saying:

> . . . this new generation is always bored and cannot entertain themselves. The reason for that is that they are spoiled. They have *everything* and all those toys ban them from being creative and entertaining themselves. In the past, we used to play with recyclable items to entertain ourselves but this generation wants everything to come from this brand or that store. They are effected heavily with commercialism; they are not creative when they are playing. Anything they ask for, it is there for them 'on a golden plate'. I bought the computer games for her that I personally condemn. The problem is us 'the parents'.. They have everything because we want them to be like everybody else (Mom 9).

One of the issues that arose while discussing the importance of play, especially amongst mothers living in Saudi Arabia, was that play can be 'a waste of time'. One mother said that her daughter never had time for play because she was busy with her school work starting on it right after school. However, if her daughter has any free time before bed, she prefered to watch television or play computer games. The mother felt that this type of play wastes her daughter's valuable time that could have been used for studying.

Family Bonds

Saudi mothers are attached to their family and expressed happiness seeing their children happy. Most of the mothers said that they like to solve hard puzzles or to be involved in trivia questions with their family. At least one mother thought that amusement parks are not good for her or for others, because they are loud, hurt, cause pain, and do not mean anything. However, this mother reported a lack of resources and that sometimes she would go to amusement parks just to satisfy her children's need to play and to take advantage of opportunities for socializing with other families at the park.

Most of the mothers, while reflecting about themselves at 20 years of age, said that college life and other developmental and personal goals were more important than play. There were many responsibilities to worry about then. But now, they all said that they have gotten back to play and are enjoying it. Most of them also said that they enjoy playing with their own family and children.

Group play is another theme that was unearthed from the data. Most mothers emphasized the importance of playing as a group either for themselves as adults or for their children. One mother said:

> A lot of games vanished but we kept on playing and found a way to be together, it doesn't matter with what . . . I enjoy the most at this age to play cards and board games with my family . . . I like to be in group play and we laugh, talk, and socialize. The rides are not always there for us so we have to go to it occasionally but the board games and cards are there daily. I really enjoy playing with big groups of people . . . (Mom 5).

Another mother said "my kids like games that involve everybody. I think group play is really good for my children . . . " (Mom 1).

Not only playing as a group in general but also more particularly playing with members of one's nuclear and extended family was highlighted. This mother believed that group play helped her to become an open-minded person and flexible:

> I came from a family that supported play, I used to play a lot with children and with adults, play as a group, play with family and extended family . . . . all of that makes me feel united and supported . . . we are together always in good days and bad days . . . . Group play helped me to be open minded and flexible . . . (Mom 8).

Public Expectations and Good Manners

Public expectations, especially when visiting relatives' or friends' houses, were highlighted by most of the mothers' interviewed. Children are expected to behave displaying their best manners because they are representing their family. Their clothes have to stay clean and their hair has to be neat at all times. Even adults have to act this way.

The importance of cleanliness and neatness was discussed with several mothers. One of the mothers (who resides in the U.S.) had a strong opinion toward playing with sand, and thought that playing with sand should be by the beach and that the children should be dressed up accordingly. Getting dressed up for school is different. Children should be presentable, well dressed, and have a clean appearance in school. She said:

> . . . when I wake up in the morning and I dress my daughter up with nice and neat clothes to go to school and she comes back to me with sand on her hair, that's what I don't really like. I even told my daughter's teacher not to let my daughter play in the sand box because it is not clean. It is dirty and kids put it in their hair and mouth . . . those sandboxes are contaminated and not clean because they never change the sand and you don't know what is in it, children step on it . . . I got disgusted by it . . . .it is different than the sand at the beach . . . (Mom 6).

Another mother, however, had a different point of view in terms of playing with dirt; she viewed the beach as the best place for unstructured play that we are missing these days. She shared:

> I still believe that playing with sand and water gives your child a unique feeling using all senses. So what I decided to do is that I provided him with a sand box and water as a substitute. I am trying to provide the environment that encourages digging and playing with dirt (Mom 7).

Another mother expressed a similar concern that the cultural expectations interfere sometimes and become somehow a restriction to what she wants for her son. Another mother examined this issue from a different angle. She thought that culture and public expectation affects the way people behave and accordingly affects the way they play. She stated:

> I like to see myself still be able to jump on the trampoline. Unfortunately, in our culture, people are put in templates that restrict this hope. I wish that we become more spontaneous. They are the ones who push you to do something that is out of the ordinary (Mom 2).

Tradition and Globalization

One of the mothers who lives in Saudi Arabia indicated that there are some concerns with the disappearance of traditional games and that people are not spending any effort to keep them. She said: " . . . Maybe there are lots of play and activities starting to disappear and all we observe now are activities that are shared with everybody else around the world" (Mom 9).

Some of the mothers living in Saudi Arabia have a strong opinion that there are no games and play activities that represent the Saudi culture anymore. All games played now are universal. One mother said that the market is full of Disney products and that sort of thing. Another mother shed light on what she called 'global games,' that all games are shared with everybody around the world. These mothers have no concerns about play itself, but their major concern is that their children would lose their identity, if no effort was spent to keep it. So they believe that play can be a bridge that brings the two cultures together if families exerted some effort to encourage play rather than being ashamed of it. Most of the mothers residing in the U.S. encourage the openness for their children, yet want them to be presentable and act like ambassadors of their country. One of the mothers repeated:

> . . . no play is bad play. It is really what we (adults, community, and the environment) endorse our children to do and that play should help the child to live in this world along with everybody peacefully... When my son plays outside with the neighbor kids, I always stay around to make sure he is not misbehaving because he is not only representing himself, he represents his family and his country.. (Mom 7).

Another mother believes that it is a huge responsibility to keep their heritage and folklore games alive while living in a place where people are not necessarily informed about their culture. To keep the culture visible and understood by others, she recommended participation in heritage days, festivals, creative events that encourage the sharing of culture, food . . . etc. These are some of the activities that Saudi mothers find themselves engaged in while living in the U.S. As one of the mothers said, being involved helps her connect with cultural roots, conquer homesickness, transfers the Saudi heritage, and teaches children to be proud of themselves. This mother stated that if she were living now in Saudi Arabia this would not be of a concern.

In short, mothers living in the U.S. and in Saudi Arabia viewed play as a means of enculturation and preparing children for living in a global society in the future. With some disagreement over many toys and games in the market coming as they do from somewhere else in the world, they are still there for children to play with in Saudi Arabia. Perhaps part of the reason for parental acceptance of this is a yearning to catch up with the world, so Saudi children will not fall behind. Indeed, "the globalization is here whether we like it or not, so we have to face it", as a young Saudi mother exclaimed.

DISCUSSION

Play is a challenging notion that requires understanding in diverse cultures like Saudi and Turkish communities. Adults create an ideal image of their childhood by overestimating and misrepresenting some memories. Furthermore, adults influenced by all the religious, political, and philosophical ideas formed while growing up remember no longer the same childhood that they really had. The Turkish and Saudi mothers no doubt spoke with some exaggeration about changes concerning the way in which children play today. Kristjánsson stated that adults' uncertainties concerning change is obvious when it comes to the family, hence they are unable to recognize that family and childhood have always been influenced by the continuing development of society (as cited in Sandberg, 2003).

Turkish and Saudi mothers seem to have gained some insight and high appreciation about their children's play from participating in this study, and some may strive to improve their children's current play. We conclude that the drawing task served as an intervention that spurred participants to reflect on themselves and their own children, helping mothers see the mother/child relationship in a new way and value it. The drawing task helped mothers to be reflective instead of being reactive, and to act thoughtfully in regard to play. This capacity of understanding and making sense of each other helped mothers to view their children as separate and as individuals with their own mind set; it enlarged their scope and their ability for play and exploration. This study helped mothers to speak openly about themselves and their children without a threat or fear of any sort.

Some mothers living in Saudi Arabia and Turkey seemed more consistent with their responses when it came to talking about play itself. These mothers made explicit their concerns and ideas about how to encourage play and bring it back into their children's lives. They gave suggestions on how to advocate for play and advice about where children should play. They discussed some play issues and trends in context of their culture and sought to find some solutions that would be best fit for their nation.

The Turkish and Saudi mothers who reside in the U.S. generally indicated that play itself is not a concern, although certain types of play are. These mothers believe that their children would play with whatever the environment offered them. What concerned them the most seemed to be the apprehension of losing their identity, heritage, language and even their culture. Consequently, Turkish and Saudi mothers in the U.S. strive to keep the culture alive through their children's play and participation in their community.

The small sample of this study makes it difficult to draw coherent or generalizable conclusions about mothers' beliefs concerning play in Turkey or Saudi Arabia or Turkish-American or Saudi-American contexts. Nevertheless, play scholars and practitioners hopefully can glean from the study some value such as more awareness about the importance of looking at Turkish and Saudi children's play with different lenses. Play and culture studies looking ahead need more information about other nations, cultures, and cultural communities. As Göncü and colleagues point out, Western and non-Western middle class income families provide time, space, and materials for children's play, but how it is being conducted presents cultural variation (Göncü et al., 2007; Göncü et al., 1999). Both *etic* (outsider's) and *emic* (insider's or indigenous) research is needed.

Some mothers in the present study emphasized the importance of starting from within the person. One suggested that parents should start advocating for their children's right to play starting with personal actions and intentions. The importance was noted of setting a good example for children by being playful as adults and as parents. Children basically do 'what we do' and not 'what we say'. It is important to show our children to face the technological world and embrace it in ways that do not discourage play and in ways that will help them live a balanced life. The study of play and the uses of play should proceed from bases *within different cultures.* Play policies and practices in nations thereby can be informed in the most advantageous way.

Most mothers expressed disappointment about play within their cultural contexts. A few opined that, indeed, a very long and difficult journey is ahead to encourage play properly. The vision and hope that they shared throughout the study was that there must be more effort to promote play for all ages. This is not only the government's responsibility, but a shared responsibility across scholars, educators, and most importantly the parents themselves; all should advocate for play. The hope is that through research, scholars can make discoveries and society can use the results of research in applied settings to make changes in play practices and policies. Play studies as a community of inter-disciplinary play scholars are positioned well to contribute real world 'wicked' problems that are by nature complex and messy and require attention and problem-setting/solving from multiple academic and other vantage points.

Communities have their local goals with societal practices supporting or interfering with children's play in ways that are tied to values and beliefs (Gaskins, Haight, & Lancy, 2006; Gaskins, 1999; Johnson et al., 2005). Evaluating whether these practices are adaptive requires an understanding of the culture. Adaptation cannot be separated from the beliefs and values. What works for one culture, might not work for another.

For example, in some situations a need exists for more recreation centers, clubs, and organizations that support intergenerational play, since it is missing or exclusive to certain groups. Saudi mothers expressed that play places can be good for adults and children considering their very hot daytime weather and their hurried lives. Play places can teach their children to be organized, develop a sense of sportsmanship, how to be engaged in the community, and more importantly, play spaces encourage group play. Guided and organized play would reflect and contribute positively to the Saudi culture.

Practical Needs of Early Childhood Practitioners

Teachers would benefit knowing more about play patterns of children from different cultures. Parent-teacher communications can serve as a tool to help teachers rethink their practices and to "act and think both globally and locally" (Johnson et al., 2012). Play studies indicate that western viewpoints of play might lead to inadequate analysis of children's play globally (Göncü, 1999). Children might feel isolated and underappreciated if not understood, so it is important for early educators to plan for children's play bearing in mind multiculturalism, and to move beyond the western theories of play (Dockett & Fleer, 2002; NAEYC, 2009).

Play and cultural studies can be a good source of information for practitioners regarding specific enculturation and global socialization processes. Constructed understandings from evidence garnered by interdisciplinary and inter- or trans-cultural research teams would serve to empower teachers and other professionals for more responsive communication and sensitive uses of play in practice and policy. These studies would place a premium on the voices of cultures different from the west and north. Adding more research in the east (*e.g.* Asia) and south (*e.g.* South America) will help the community of play scholars and professional practitioners construct new frameworks and begin to see other ways to work with diversity in various fields.

CONCLUSIONS

Transcultural interests in play bringing together investigators from diverse cultures have important benefits. Opportunities for delving into each data set and comparing beliefs and concerns about play across the mothers studied was rewarding. Such work is needed to complement the large scale questionnaire or survey studies (*e.g.* Singer et al., 2009) through analysis and interpretation of qualitative data within and between cultural settings. Play studies need further work seeking descriptions that are contextualized, nuanced, and multi-layered, yielding information on topics germane to play and culture.

Future play studies moreover hold promise for producing evidence and encouragement for fulfilling plans to build more indigenous theorizing and model building on play, policies, and practices in different locations across the globe. Further TSPP and other investigations can continue to spur discussion among researchers, many whom were or are international graduate students from universities in the U.S.A. Many of these beginning researchers are preparing to return to their countries of origin where they can work to advance play studies through research projects, including creating journals and other publication outlets for the dissemination and utilization of information. Goals that were stated in TSPP focus group discussions included the intention to use insights from research to enhance play spaces in communities, children's museums, playgrounds, and other locations. In addition, ways need to be found to energize education by developing and using pedagogies of play. Focus group discussions stressed the need for translating technical information expressed in academic language into the everyday vernacular so that the concepts and uses of play can become understood by everyone.

Lastly, we have also discovered during our TSPP work what we think is an important way to contribute to our globally networked world. The context and medium of play expression itself, the research on play we embark upon, and our reflections on play and its situational enmeshments and communicative channels have the potential for building cross-cultural fluency (Portera, 1998). Transcultural play research, actions and thoughts, can enlarge and deepen visions, and point a direction into the future. Play scholars on this mission can contribute to the next steps, aiming to illuminate the value of play across professional disciplines and practices over all nations during the 21st century.

REFERENCES

Cote, L.R., & Bornstein, M.H. (2009). Child and mother play in three U.S. cultural groups: Comparisons and associations. *Journal of Family Psychology, 23,* 355–363. doi: 10.1037/a0015399.

Dockett, S., & Fleer, M. (2002). *Play and pedagogy in early childhood: Bending the rules.* Australia: Nelson.

Fonagy, P., Gergely, G., Jurist, E., & Target, M. (2002). *Affect Regulation, Mentalization and the Development of the Self.* New York: Other Press.

Gaskins, S. (1999). Children's daily lives in a Mayan village: A case study of culturally constructed roles and activities. In A. Göncü (Eds.). *Children's engagement in the world: Sociocultural perspectives* (pp. 25–37). New York: Cambridge University Press.

Gaskins, S., Haight, W., & Lancy, D. (2006). The cultural construction of play. In A. Göncü and S. Gaskins (Eds.), *Play and development: Evolutionary, sociocultural, and* functional perspectives (pp. 179–202). Mahwah, NJ: Lawrence Erlbaum.

Göncü, A. (1999). *Children's engagement in the world: Sociocultural perspectives.* Cambridge: Cambridge University Press.

Göncü, A., Mistry, J., & Mosier, C. (2000). Cultural variations in the play of toddlers. *International Journal of Behavioral Development 24,* 321–329. doi:10.1080/01650250050118303

Göncü, A., Tuermer, U., Jain, J., & Johnson, D. (1999). Children's play as cultural activity. In A. Göncü, (Eds.). *Children's engagement in the world: Sociocultural perspective* (pp. 148–170). Cambridge University Press.

Göncü, A., Jain, J., & Tuermer, U. (2007). Children's play as cultural interpretation. In A. Göncü, & S. Gaskins (Eds.). *Play and Development: Evolutionary sociocultural, and functional perspectives* (pp. 155–178). Mahwah, NJ: LEA.

Holmes, R. M. (2011). Adult attitudes and beliefs regarding play on Lana'i. *American Journal of Play, 3,* 356–384.

IKEA. (2010). *Playreport: International summary of research results.* Family, Kids & Youth. International Summary Report.

Ivrendi, A., & Isikoglu, N. (2008). Erken cocukluk doneminde cocugu olan anne ve babalarin oyuna yonelik goruslerinin incelenmesi. *Cagdas Egitim Dergisi, 355,* 4–12.

Johnson, J., Al-Mansour, M., & Sevimli-Celik, S. (2015). Researching play in early childhood. In O. Saracho (Eds.). *Handbook of research methods in ECE: Review of research methodologies* (pp. 473–506). Charlotte, NC: Information Age Publishers.

Johnson, J., Al-Mansour, M., Sevimli-Celik, S., Ko, Y, Cheng, M-F, & Rafie, F. (2012). *Trans-Cultural Study of play during early and middle childhood years.* Global Summit on Childhood, Association for Childhood Education International, Arlington, VA.

Johnson, J., Christie, J., & Wardle, F. (2005). *Play, Development, and Early Education.* Boston: Allyn & Bacon.

NAEYC. (2009). *Developmentally appropriate practice in early childhood programs serving children from birth through age 8: A position statement of the National Association for Young Children.* Washington, DC: Author. Retrieved from: www.naeyc.org/files/naeyc/file/positions/PSDAP.pdf

Portera, A. (1998). Multiculture, identity, educational need and possibilities of (intercultural) intervention. *European Journal of Intercultural Studies, 9,* 209–218. doi: 10.1080/0952391980090211

Roopnarine, J., & Davidson, K. (2015). Parent-child play across cultures: Theoretical considerations and suggestions for advancing play research. In J. Johnson, S. Eberle, T. Henricks, & D. Kuschner (Eds.). *The handbook of the study of play* (pp. 85–100). Lanham, MD: Rowman & Littlefield.

Roopnarine, J., & Krishnakumar, A. (2006). Parent-child and child-child play in diverse cultural context. In D. Fromberg & D. Bergen (Eds.). *Play from birth to twelve: Contexts, perspectives, and meanings, Second edition* (pp. 275–288). New York: Routledge.

Sandberg, A. (2001). Play memories from childhood to adulthood. *Early Child Development and Care, 167,* 13–25. doi:10.1080/0300443011670102

Sandberg, A. (2003). Play memory and place identity. *Early Child Development and Care, 173,* 107–221. doi: 10.1080/03004430303091

Sandburg, A., & Tammemä-Orr, H. (2008). Drawing and conceptions of play by children ages 7–12. In P. G. Grotewell & Y. R. Burton (Eds.). *Early childhood education: issues and development* (pp. 127–143). New York: Nova Science Publishers, Inc.

Schwartzman, H. (1978). *Transformations: The Anthropology of Children's Play.* New York: Plenum Press.

Seidman, I. (2006). *Interviewing as a Qualitative Research: A Guide for Researchers in Education and the Social Sciences.* New York: Teachers' College Press.

Singer, D. G., Singer, J. L., D'Agostino, H. & DeLong, R. (2009). Children's pastimes and play in sixteen nations: Is free play declining? *American Journal of Play, 1,* 283–312.

Smilansky, S. (1968). *The Effects of Sociodramatic Play on Disadvantaged Preschool Children.* New York: John Wiley.

Suizzo, M. A., & Bornstein, M. H. (2006). French and European American child–mother play: Culture and gender considerations. *International Journal of Behavioral Development, 30,* 498–508. doi: 10.1177/0165025406071912

Vickerius, M., & Sandberg, A. (2006). The signification of lay and the environment around play. *Early Childhood Development and Care, 176,* 207–217.

Whiting, B., & Pope, E. C. (1988). *Children of Different Worlds: The Formation of Social Behavior.* Cambridge MA: Harvard University Press.

Chapter Ten

Playing into the Future

Thomas Henricks

When we play, we create and respond to challenges. Sometimes, as Piaget (1962) maintained, those play behaviors represent attempts to consolidate life-strategies we're trying to develop. At such times, play is a form of practice or refinement, a repetition-based improving of our abilities to comprehend the world. However, play can also feature, as Sutton-Smith (1966) emphasized in his critique of Piaget's model, a much more spirited—and irregular - reinvention of self. In that second view, play is less an attempt to gain assurance about what one already knows than it is a process of discovering what one does *not* know. At such times, players court opposition, uncertainty, and surprise. Familiar pathways are abandoned for experiences of the new.

This essay argues that scholars of play should approach their topic with a curiosity that is equally wide-ranging. To be sure, there is much to be said for steady progress along carefully chosen routes. As other chapters in this volume have shown, scholars of play can take pride in their collective accomplishments. Much has been learned about play's character and implications. Worthy research agendas have been established. Play advocates remain steadfast in their commitment to defend the creative possibilities of every person and to develop play-environments that maximize those possibilities. Play studies move forward within the terms of well-considered narratives.

However, it is also the case that many opportunities for play studies are not being pursued, or at least that those studies are not being integrated into the major play organizations and their journals. To that extent, play—one of the most fundamental, and necessary, forms of human expression—continues to elude the wider scholarly attention that it merits. What follows then is a call to invoke the spirit of play in its scholarly formulations. One of play's most appealing qualities is its restless spirit, its encouragement to players to de-stabilize their own understandings and inhabit new circumstances. Intentionally players erect challenges that test, refine, and expand their abilities. When those challenges are mastered, new ones (of differing types and levels of complexity) are created; and the process is started again. Participants define themselves by the obstacles they place in their own way. In much the same fashion, scholars of this subject should play themselves into the future.

CELEBRATING PLAY'S MULTIDISCIPLINARY HERITAGE

More than a half-century has passed since C.P. Snow (1961) declared that the two "cultures" of the sciences and humanities had divided, so dramatically that representatives of one side had difficulty understanding the most rudimentary formulations of the other. Worse, they were no longer interested in bridging that divide. Snow attributed that change to the severe specialization—and hidebound attitudes—that flourished in the academic world, particularly in his country Great Britain. Careers there were made by knowing more and more about less and less - and by securing professional relationships within ever-smaller social circles. Even in the same field of study, theorists separated themselves from empiricists; those doing applied work were another category yet.

Snow (1961, p. 3) admitted that he overdrew his distinction for the purpose of provoking debate between the two camps. He noted the significance of the social sciences as an intermediary (or "third") culture and offered some examples of combined approaches. Still, his general thesis remains pertinent, even in our putatively post-modern age that recognizes the legitimacy of multiple perspectives and the possibilities of joining these in interdisciplinary ventures. For the most part, advanced scholarship continues to be carried forward by academic specialists trained (and granted positions) in recognized disciplines. Those training processes result in approved topics of study, favored theoretical and methodological approaches, selective acknowledgement of forbearers, arcane terminologies, and related forms of "focus." It is difficult enough keeping up with scholarly writing in a specialized field of study and in conducting research that communicates with that literature. To attempt to span multiple fields is to find oneself, almost immediately, outside the zone of professional competence.

As scholars who concentrate on play know well, disciplinary specialization has worked against the study of play, for other topics have been deemed more important by those disciplines. Even in academic fields where play has received considerable attention—such as psychology, education, health and recreation, and animal behavior studies—that topic is usually subsumed by what are thought to be more important concerns; namely learning, physical and emotional well-being, and "development" seen in broadest terms. Pointedly, no discipline claims play as a topic significant in its own right.

This lack of disciplinary oversight is not entirely a negative matter, for it makes play studies amenable to contributions from many disciplines. Varieties of research are welcomed at play studies meetings and in the annuals and journals affiliated with these. Still, it should be acknowledged that those gatherings tend to be dominated by scholars of early childhood and by advocates of the child's right to play. The centrality of that group is not inappropriate for these professionals insure that there is a stable base for the continued development of the field, as well as a strong commitment to maintain the public profile of play in the broader culture. But it also means that persons with other interests in play tend to exist at the margins of those events, find a limited range of colleagues with shared interests, and (by consequence) attend those conferences sporadically. In the case of the Association for the Study of Play, there has been a marked decline in the participation of anthropologists (the group that began the organization), historians, and scholars of sport and leisure (Stevens, 2014).

In this author's opinion, the continued advancement of play studies depends on the recognition of varieties of disciplinary contributions and on strategies to integrate these. Once again, the importance of a psychological perspective is not to be disputed. Play is typically understood to be a self-sponsored (and monitored) activity; the relationship of that behavior to personal thought and behavior will always be a fundamental concern. However, development—as Vygotsky (1976) and Mead (1964) emphasized—is not a solitary affair. People become themselves through interaction with other people. More than that, a clearly sociological perspective means recognizing the importance of groups and organizations in shaping play behaviors (Henricks, 2006). Indeed, play is sometimes organized on the basis of concerns quite different from those of the players themselves. That issue—the intersection between organizational and individual visions for activity—has been central in educational studies that explore the best uses for play in schools (Johnson, Christie, and Wardle, 2004).

Also fundamental to play—and play studies—are cultural resources, both symbolic and material. Human play occurs under the auspices of publicly maintained meaning systems, though the expression of these may feature patterns of escape or rebellion as well as socialization or reproduction. Those taking historical and anthropological approaches (Huizinga, 1955; Caillois, 2001; Roopnarine, Johnson, and Hooper, 1994; Lancy, 2008) have insisted that play be seen in all its societal applications. Without this overview, play studies become trapped in the mythology of childhood distinctive to advanced industrial societies.

Critical also are contributions from the physical sciences and the humanities, Snow's two poles of academic expression. To consider the first of these, play studies require the natural sciences. Behaviors of every type are physical occurrences which manifest the workings of bodies. It is important to understand the evolution of those physical abilities (as frameworks for living) as well as the physical operations of other species (Burghardt, 2005; Power, 2005). Inevitably, play involves both muscular-skeletal commitments and patterns of neurophysiology (Panksepp, 1998). Changes in bodies and brains produce changes in play. The reverse is true as well.

A full understanding of play also means embracing the commitments of the humanities. People negotiate ideas just as they negotiate natural contingencies. Play involves symbolic framing, story-telling, and make-believe (Paley, 2005; Singer and Singer, 1990). Even the simplest forms of physical play ("What would happen if I tried to hop on one leg?") feature supposition and self-imposed constraint. More complicated forms of play (sometimes developed as "games") draw out these narratives. Much play uses culturally circulated artifacts that change dramatically through the years. Much requires subtleties of language to position players symbolically as well as physically (Garvey, 1990).

Because the direction of play studies has been influenced strongly by social and behavioral scientists—who are interested in how people behave toward one another—probably too little attention has been given to the involvement of people in highly artificial cultural formats including electronic games. This is striking because computer-based games and social network sites are critical settings for contemporary expression and are the basis of an extensive literature (Wolf, 2008; Wardrip-Fruin, 2009). But this literature usually does not communicate directly with the types of play studies described above. Much the same can be said for studies of sport, tourism, shopping, hobbies, food culture, sexual expression, clubbing, gambling, and other forms of often highly organized amusement. Obviously, people of every age engage in many kinds of play. Too few studies of that spirited, creative, self-motivated activity finds their way into the camp of "traditional" play studies.

This specialization of interest has not always been the case. Many of the classic theorists of play (Groos, 1898; Huizinga, 1955; Sutton-Smith, 1997; Caillois, 2001) possessed very wide-ranging visions of their topic. Play was understood both as the simplest patterns of physical expression and as the deepest forms of symbolic engagement. Music, art, dance, and religion were recognized as fields of play. Imagination was simultaneously public and private. Aesthetics, even the pursuit of beauty itself, was fore-grounded. Some contemporary writers continue this tradition (Fagen, 2005; Henricks, 2015). But much more needs to be done.

REMEMBERING SUTTON-SMITH'S RHETORICS

In the field of play studies, perhaps the book that best articulates the importance of diverse perspectives is Sutton-Smith's *The Ambiguity of Play* (1997). In that work, he argues that play scholarship features at least seven major approaches, which he describes (in a literary fashion) as narratives or "rhetorics." Each of these is seen as a legitimate way of thinking about play. Each is based on certain guiding assumptions and tends to draws its support from certain academic disciplines.

The dominant tradition is the rhetoric of "play as progress" (Sutton-Smith, 1997, p. 9). This view is central to the disciplines that currently dominate play studies associations and journals; namely, psychology, early childhood education, physical education, and animal behavior studies. It guiding theme, applicable to both humans and animals, is that play fosters forms of development that aid survival. Those adaptations include cognitions, skills, physical capabilities, social sensitivities, and forms of emotion management. Creatures possessed of the ability to play (at least during key periods of their lives) are thought to have improved opportunities to flourish in open, complicated environments where food-seeking, shelter-making and social support are problematic. For many species, behavioral flexibility—assisted by capabilities to envision environments widely, assess one's standing within these, remember, plan (and evaluate) action strategies, pause behavior, and cooperate with others—is advantageous.

To that extent, and as Groos (1898) argued long ago, play is part of a series of evolutionary changes that freed individuals from many of the controls of "instinct" and other narrowly biological directives. In that spirit, generations of play scholars, advocates, and therapists have emphasized how play offers a pattern of self-motivated learning that (under the best circumstances) leads to creative, thoughtful, and socially-sensitive adults.

Sutton-Smith's theme is that this is not the only way to see play. His six other rhetorics, each the subject of a chapter in his book, are "fate," "power," (community) "identity," the "imaginary," the "self," and the "frivolous." Scholars focusing on modern, or modernizing, societies tend to emphasize the rhetorics of self, the imaginary, and progress. Taken together, these three perspectives stress the developing curiosities and capabilities of individuals. By contrast, scholars focusing on traditional societies emphasize the rhetorics of fate, power, community identity, and frivolity. That is, they stress how play is a public exploration of social and cultural patterns. Traditional approaches also emphasize that adults as well as children play. Under such circumstances, play is seen less as a project of personal advancement than as a discovery of how communities are embedded in forms and forces that shape their lives. This older view of play is also central for postmodern theories, which typically show how contemporary people are embedded in diverse, conflicting, and continually changing world conditions that defy systematic control (Spariosu, 1989).

Sutton-Smith's work is remembered here not only because it is a classic formulation but also because it poses a continuing challenge for play studies. The play-as-progress rhetoric may rightly deserve its leading role, for it addresses the need of children to creatively support their own development amidst the formally organized, adult-dominated organizations central to many contemporary societies. But other viewpoints - reflecting other aspects of those societies - must be honored as well.

BOTH MODERNISM AND POSTMODERNISM

Like most academic pursuits, play studies express the commitments of modernism. Since the Renaissance (itself a reclamation of selected themes from the classical world), emphasis has been placed on the enterprising individual. Modern persons are allowed to separate themselves from centuries-old beliefs and customs and from the equally well-established groups (such as families and communities) that embody and enforce these. Inborn capacities, especially the ability to reason and reflect, are stressed. So are rights, based increasingly on conceptions of personhood rather than group affiliation. In modern societies, it is anticipated that people will leave their settlements of birth and wander from one place to another in search of better circumstances. Like Dickens's (1991, p. 1) David Copperfield, one is encouraged to become the "hero" of his or her own life.

This general viewpoint - that individuals should achieve their places in the world rather than accept what is granted them by religiously ordained institutions—features some related changes. One of these is the ascendancy of an "associational" style of interaction and relationship (Kahler, 1956). In pre-modern societies, persons understand themselves to be the living representatives of ancient groups that both define them and provide the terms of their living. People cannot conceive of themselves outside this surround. Under conditions of modernity, relatively independent individuals (possessed of ideas about their own character, rights, and "interests") make judgments to create, sustain, modify, and destroy social forms. Congregational churches, businesses, parliamentary governments, public schools, and sporting clubs are examples of this process.

Modernist versions of play reproduce the above themes (Henricks, 2006, pp. 90–100). That is, emphasis is given to the developing individual, along with notions of rights, freedoms, and skills. In keeping with this vision, players are encouraged to engage in activity that is constructive, orderly, and unidirectional and to erect and support rule systems voluntarily. Rationality is emphasized; so is "fair play," understood as the equilateral extension of opportunities to participants. Inter-individual competition is often stressed, but this is ritually framed from beginning to end. When people play, they are said to build and inhabit models of society. At the same time, they build models of themselves.

Another aspect of modernism is its emphasis on increasingly wide frames of abstract conception and regulation. Nation-states, communities, businesses, and schools grow large. Bureaucracies (pyramids of administrative control featuring written policies and impersonal relationships) become the dominant organizational type. And individuals understand themselves in very broad terms, as citizens of societies or even as members of a human community (who deserve compassion and support for that reason alone).

In its darkest manifestations, that fascination for universalistic principles and centralized control, what Lyotard (1986) described as grand totalizing narratives, leads to militarism, imperialism, monopolistic business practice, narrowing of belief, de-valuing of marginal groups, and other forms of bureaucratic surveillance and discipline. In its best forms, modernism identifies the qualities and conditions shared by all people and devises (and continually revises) schemes for creating a widely established, well-regulated "civil" society.

For the most part, play studies participates in this way of seeing the world. Most research on play, and most play advocacy, focuses on the qualities shared by all children, even if this means only their shared rights and possibilities as persons. It is presumed that research performed on one group of children is applicable to another group; general conclusions about human character and possibility are drawn. Academic associations (and professional books and articles) are recognized to be the vehicles by which these understandings are established, disseminated, critiqued, and revised.

Contemporary play studies also address modernism's dark side by encouraging various forms of independence by players and by calling for more enlightened policies by organizations. Children should be "free" to express themselves outside of bureaucratic, adult-dominated regimes. Such play is not merely aimlessness or "fooling," to use Dewey's (1910, p. 218) term, but rationally guided behavior that determines if one action-strategy is better than another.

In contrast, postmodern scholarship tends to reject the prospect of a universal, centrally coordinated model for living. No one-size-fits-all model can respond adequately to the varieties of human circumstance. In part this is because, as Derrida (1976, 1981) emphasized, cultural systems of belief and rule are never logically complete or coherent. Always there are inconsistencies and oppositions; implicit assumptions rule discourse; things left out are as important as things said. Inevitably also, the interests of only some social groups are given precedence. Others (marked as different by ethnicity, age, gender, class, sexual orientation, religion, and nationality) are subordinated or pushed to the side. The Enlightenment dream of a rationally governed, highly-coordinated world has not materialized; or rather, it has floundered amidst conditions of economic depression, world war, state and non-state terrorism, environmental degradation, and continuing global injustice. Taking its place now is a resurgent pluralism, exalting old ethnic and religious divisions as well as new interest-based communities. Both of these developments are supported by advances in electronic communication.

So conceived, the contemporary world is said to exhibit cultural fragmentation, conflict, pluralism, and change. De-centralization is more descriptive of human affairs than centralization; randomness or chance trumps sturdy determinism; conceptions of underlying structures (that give form to behavior) are replaced by looser images of how relationships coalesce and dissolve. In the view of many postmodern thinkers (Jameson 1984, Rosenau, 1992), this proliferation of diverse perspectives is not a condition to be mourned. Instead, it is the basis for new, more integrative styles of thinking that respect the various ways in which people are situated and that honor the complex living conditions that mark the contemporary era.

A similar perspective can be applied to individuals themselves. Modernist images of a firmly positioned subject confronting an equally established object-world are replaced in postmodernism by a more fluid, situated, or even "saturated" self (Gergen, 2000). That self does not exhibit a stable center; instead (and like society and culture), it is de-centered or pluralistic. People find themselves transformed by their involvements in changing circumstances. It becomes pertinent to speak of the many roles they play or masks they wear (Gergen, 1995).

The more extreme versions of postmodernism follow Heidegger in insisting that there is no isolated vantage point from which subjectivity can appraise the world; each of us is conditioned, even constituted by the occurrences that swirl around us at every moment of our lives. Selfhood is only the sense of being positioned at these intersections. We feel these connections as much as we perceive them rationally. Stated in strongest terms, radical postmodernism declares the "death" of the self (Bertens, 1995, p. 166). What we imagine to be the self is only a position in language or effect of discourse (Flax, 1990).

A more "affirmative" style of postmodernism, to use Rosenau's (1992, p. 14) term, retains the modernist view that people have relatively stable, ongoing commitments but emphasizes that people are situated differently and bring different perspectives and issues to their involvements. In addition, affirmative approaches emphasize the importance of people's recognizing their connections to others and of their working together to build communities that honor pluralism, open communication, and social justice.

Postmodern conceptions of play illustrate both the radical and affirmative views presented above. Some of those play theories reflect postmodernism's foundations in post-structural philosophy and literary theory (Hans, 1981; Spariosu, 1989; Kuchler, 1994). Emphasized is the relative openness of meaning that prevails in both physical and cultural relations. Relationships are understood to be transient, superficial, largely unpredictable, and subject to arbitrary (and thus alterable) conventions. To that extent, worldly events resemble "games" (Kuchler, 1994) and players of these find that they are in play (that is, subject to largely uncontrollable conditions) as much as they manage their own constantly changing positions within them.

Such theories embrace selected themes of pre-modern societies, especially the idea that people willfully enter and ride the energy of tumultuous public events that they have no prospect of directing on their own terms. But it should also be pointed out that this contemporary style does *not* include the pre-modern emphasis on a powerful sacred realm that gives meaning to every type of worldly activity. Instead, postmodern people assemble meaning in the fashion of players, that is, provisionally, strategically, and with the sense that the conventions of one event are different from those of another.

Affirmative postmodernism is more common to behavioral and social studies of play. Looking to Vygotsky and contemporary performance theory among other sources (Schechner, 2002; Edmiston, 2008; Newman & Holzman, 2006; Lobman & O'Neill, 2011), this approach stresses the utility of sponsoring social situations that allow participants to play unusual roles and, in the process, to come to new understandings about themselves. Open dialogue is important; so is respect, commitment to the group, and egalitarianism. Play of this sort is less a pattern of expression (in which the players vocalize or act out pre-existing thoughts and feelings) than it is a discovery of often unrecognized or latent abilities. Pointedly, it is the act of performing (as behavior) that moves the person from one pattern of awareness to the next. Because of its focus on social inclusion and non-authoritarian relationships, this approach is especially useful for developing a sense of community among underprivileged or marginalized populations. It is also valuable as a substitute for more authoritarian, talk-based styles of therapy.

Not surprisingly perhaps, modernist and postmodernist scholars advocate distinctive methodologies for studying play. For its part, modernist scholarship emphasizes the extent to which the world is orderly, structured, and continuous. Human behavior is patterned; so are the conditions (both physical and symbolic) in which humans operate. Much of what happens seems to be influenced by a limited range of identifiable, "external" causes. Past events are thought to lead to current occurrences. For such reasons, research approaches drawn from the natural sciences (positivism) seem especially useful in confirming these chains-of-causation. Simpler explanatory frameworks (as narratives) are preferred to more complicated ones, if large portions of the occurrence's variance can be accounted for. What scholars, policy makers, and practitioners desire is feelings of assurance for how the world—and especially behaving humans - operates. Fundamental questions that people ask—who, what, when and where, how, and why—are transcribed categorically. That is, they shift to concerns about what kind of subjects do what kinds of things in what kinds of ways under what kinds of conditions—and for what kinds of reasons.

Guided by the above commitments, modernist approaches seek to discover key factors or structures supporting play, and especially the play of young humans and animals. These factors may be environmental, physiological, psychological, social, and cultural in character. Stable patterns *within* individuals—that is, psychological and physiological—are typically given emphasis. Once formed, these patterns are thought to guide the various life forays of those individuals and even to provide the foundations for later stages of life.

As important as this tradition is, it is critical to sustain the opposite vision, as postmodernism does. Human behavior may be patterned, but people are extremely malleable in their orientations. In particular, they recognize and accommodate themselves to the demands of situations, which may also be volatile, confusing, and conflict-ridden. Some patterns of meaning may be relatively narrow or stipulated but many more arise from the evaluations and commitments of the persons involved. Because of that, it is difficult to categorize—and thus predict - what any event will be like or what any person will do in that event. With the matter so conceived, positivist explanatory models seem less useful than interpretive approaches that focus on the sense-making commitments of differentially situated persons. People do not operate *typologically* in a predictable world with clearly marked boundaries. They "make something" out of their involvement, in the spirit of players.

In such ways, postmodernist accounts of play remind us that individuals do not confront an objectified external world from the vantage point of fully formed creators and combatants. They willfully embed themselves in events; they acknowledge the satisfactions of that immersion; they focus more on the present than on the past or future. Such a view fully embraces the possibilities of adult play. People do not go to dance clubs, play tennis, surf the internet, and engage in video games with the principal motivation of turning themselves into something other than what they are now. They do so with the intention of experiencing the color and dynamism of life. To that degree, human involvement resembles a game. But no two instances of game-playing—be these moves on a dance floor or serves in a tennis match - are ever the same.

Once again, it is not the spirit of this essay to proclaim the supremacy of either the modernist or postmodernist approach. Both are useful for understanding contemporary play; each calls attention to selected issues and forwards valuable lines of thought. The challenge for the play studies community as a whole is to recognize and integrate those contributions.

EXPANDING THE CONCEPT OF DEVELOPMENT

Arguably, play studies has been dominated by the concept of development. According to that idea, young children and animals are somehow strengthened and led forward by playful behavior. Such movement occurs on many fronts and results in new platforms of understanding and competency. In the view of Peter Smith (2010, pp. 27–28), that commitment to play's transformative impact, and especially to its long-term effects on improved functioning, is perhaps as much an "ethos" as a factually substantiated claim.

On the one hand, Smith's concern means that those working in the development tradition must continue to demonstrate linkages between play activities and changes in players. Part of that project involves continuing attempts to define how play is different from other behaviors. For too long play has been studied apart from other similar activities such as ritual, work, and communitas (or patterns of communal bonding). Sometimes play is conflated with physically or mentally vigorous activity. It is difficult to know play's causes and effects without guiding distinctions.

It is not to be expected that a uniformly supported definition will emerge; but there is already, at least in this author's view, loose agreement among scholars about the general qualities of play. Play's qualities—transformative, consummatory, unpredictable, contestive, self-regulated, and episodic to reproduce one summary of scholarly definitions (Henricks, 2015, p. 63) - distinguish play from similar behaviors, promote its special pattern of meaning construction, and support a distinctive sequence of emotions. Play is not different *in every way* from other behaviors but rather in the way in which its qualities *combine.*

A more important outcome of any listing of qualities is the possibility this creates for analyzing different types or patterns of play behavior (expressing kinds and levels of predictability, self-regulation, consummation, contestfocus, episodic organization, and so forth). A more differentiated approach of this sort would counter the tendency in play studies to treat play as a unitary phenomenon, a practice that results in researchers exploring the causes and consequences of "play in general." As the preceding pages have indicated, play appears in many guises and is described from many perspectives. By acknowledging that variety one acquires a clearer vision of the whole.

Several other issues—each with implications for a revised view of development—are to be emphasized. The first of these is the importance of seeing development as a life-long process. This, it may be recalled, is Erikson's (1963) famous contribution. Human playfulness extends through the life course; the last stages of life deserve as much attention as the first. To be sure, the early years feature challenges of their own sorts and produce rapid changes in players; but every stage offers its own kinds of obstacles. When people play, they replicate and manage these. To continue the theme of the paragraph above, what seems appropriate is to understand better why different kinds of play are developed and sustained in response to those evolving life-challenges.

A second issue concerns the directions of development. Only sometimes does play align itself with a path of incremental improvement, whether this is self-sponsored (Piaget, 1962) or socially supported (Vygotsky, 1976). To repeat Sutton-Smith's theme, "progress" is not the only way to think about play (Henricks, 2009b). Oppositely, some play can be considered "regression" (that is, a return to earlier circumstances and patterns of awareness). Particularly for older adults, play can be a revisiting of long-ago life stations. Sometimes, it is intentionally simple-minded or puerile, to use Huizinga's (1955, pp. 205–206) term.

Play can also take the form of "introgression." That is, it can be a deep exploration of the most fundamental challenges, whether these are psychological, physiological, social, cultural, or environmental. At such times, play is not a moving ahead, it is a moving into. Finally, play can manifest itself as "digression," what Erikson (1963 p. 222) called a step "sideward into another reality." Surely, that light, dabbling quality marks many kinds of playful exploration.

Another issue, brought into focus by the modernism-postmodernism split, is the extent to which development moves through a clearly recognized sequence of levels. Once again, modernist theories (such as Piaget's and Erikson's) emphasize a progression of stages, each of which builds on earlier resolutions. Play behaviors both replicate and advance this pattern; increasingly complicated challenges, moral frameworks, and social arrangements are erected and negotiated. Participants "play themselves ahead" with the goal of creating increasingly well-established personal resource-banks of comprehension and skill.

However, and as Sutton-Smith and Kelly-Byrne (1984) emphasized, play features dis-equilibration as much as equilibration. It is disorderly as well as orderly (Henricks, 2009a). It both constructs and deconstructs. This concept or deconstruction or dissimulation is central to postmodernism. In that view, players (as meaning-makers) take apart the officially promoted realities of their societies. Those "texts" (Derrida, 1995) are explored, tweaked, and teased; underlying assumptions are called into question. Players move in unpermitted directions; they resist, rebel, and loiter. That anti-authoritarianism spirit dominates much of Sutton-Smith's writing.

For our purposes here, it is important to see such maneuvers as a legitimate part of development. Play does not establish clearly marked pathways into the future (arguably, work and ritual do this much better). Play does support creaturely existence by expanding repertoires of thought, feeling, and behavior. That cultivation of "variability" (Sutton-Smith, 2008, p. 90) should be seen as more of a lateral (or multilateral) movement than a straight-ahead ascent. To say this is not to deny the profound importance of the play-as-progress rhetoric. But it does mean that tearing down is often a prelude to building up, that strategies of resistance are as important as creative and cooperative ventures, and that determinations of "usefulness" in skill-sets stem as much from the demands of unanticipated situations as from the resolve of the skill-holders themselves.

Two other issues should be mentioned briefly. Both center on questions of "what" is being developed. It is generally acknowledged that development involves many different kinds of capabilities. Reasoning skills are not identical to moral judgments; emotional management and social adaptability are different again. More than that, abilities related to personal assertion and self-regulation are different from those requisite to adjustment and sensitivity. People are said to have many kinds of "intelligence" (Eberle, 2011). The challenge at this point is to understand the links between play and these differing capabilities, not just for play in general as a certain style of thinking and behavior (Bruner, 1986) but for the specific kinds of playful expression.

Finally, there is the matter of the individualistic bias of the development approach. For the most part, development is understood to be the advancement of individual organisms, be these persons or animals. Creatures with wide-ranging skill sets (and abilities to employ these quickly) are thought to have survival advantages. To their credit, some animal behavior scholars (Fagen, 1981; Burghardt, 2005) have expanded this concern to include communities of organisms or even the species as a whole. And postmodern thought tends to emphasize that development is less a solitary pursuit than it is *envelopment,* a pattern of social and cultural embedding.

Whatever the merits of the above arguments, it seems fair to say that more research is needed on the uses of play to develop social groups—and cultures. To be sure, the foundations of this have been established by historians and anthropologists and by classic contributors like Huizinga and Caillois. Furthermore, and as suggested above, affirmative postmodernists, performance theorists, and group therapists are using play to build communities. So are playworkers, the emerging field that promotes play-based interaction among disadvantaged and marginalized persons (Brown, 2003). At one level, the challenge ahead is to understand how play in general builds social alliances and the cultural forms that support these. More difficult is the task of learning which kinds of play promote which kinds of relationships.

The above listing of issues may seem to be only that, a statement of the different directions in which play studies might expand. Instead, it is important also to see how these concerns are related. In the view of this author, the theme that unifies play—and thus play studies—is the commitment to explore and consolidate the different dimensions of self. Doubtless, one version of this is the privatized, entrepreneurial self that is sponsored by modernism. But more socially and culturally engaged versions of personhood, such as those emphasized by traditional societies and by postmodern thinkers, are critical as well. In other words, selfhood should mean not only the individual's sense of location and sphere of capability but also patterns of communal awareness and support that promote feelings of "we" and "us").

Seeing self-development in this expanded sense also means that a purely psychological approach is not sufficient. Psychological matters (how persons encounter and organize their own thoughts, feelings, and actions) are crucial elements. But so also are negotiations of social, cultural, bodily, and environmental patterns. A truly multidisciplinary approach makes clear that play is a special way of recognize and responding to the many settings of personhood.

How stable are these self-formations? As emphasized in the modernist tradition, and following William James (1952), it is surely the case that selves features consistency and continuity. People occupy ongoing patterns; they rely on these to move confidently from one moment to the next. But that theme of continuity must (once again) be counterbalanced by postmodernism's sensitivity to the intense particularity and transience of people's involvement in situations. Who would deny that all of us are engaged not only in narrowly bounded situations but also in the much wider formations that frame the possibilities of living? Understanding how people are committed to both the momentary and the transcendent is critical. Just as much play is a "presenting" (and in the process, refining) of identities we currently hold so other play is a "performing" of roles we have never encountered before.

When we play, we travel along such avenues for self-experience. Sometimes, those routes, and their end-points, are fairly predictable; often they are not. We move in such ways because we are fascinated by what we discover along the way. Unintentionally, we pick up a range of experiences, skills, beliefs, and comrades. In its purest form, play is driven by a curiosity about what humans can be and do. Play studies would do well to envision its quest in similar terms.

REFERENCES

Bertens, H. (1995). *The idea of the postmodern: A history.* New York: Routledge.

Brown, F. (Ed.) (2003). *Playwork: Theory and practice.* Philadelphia, PA: Open University.

Bruner, J. (1986). Play, thought, and language. *Prospects - Quarterly Review of Education, 16* (1), 77–83.

Burghardt, G. (2005). *The genesis of animal play: Testing the limits.* Cambridge, MA: MIT Press.

Caillois, R. (2001b). *Man, play, and games.* Urbana, IL: University of Illinois Press.

Dewey, J. (1910). *How we think.* New York: D. C. Heath.

Derrida, J. (1976). *Of grammatology.* Baltimore, MD: Johns Hopkins University Press.

Derrida, J. (1981). *Positions.* Chicago: University of Chicago Press.

Derrida, J. (1995). The play of substitution. In W. Anderson (Ed.). *The truth about the truth: De-confusing and re-constructing the postmodern world.* Pp. 86–91. New York: Putnam.

Dickens, C. (1991). First published 1850. *The personal history of David Copperfield.* New York: Oxford University Press.

Eberle, S. (2011). Playing with multiple intelligences: How play helps them grow. *American Journal of Play, 4*(1), 19–51.

Edmiston, B. (2008). *Forming ethical identities in childhood play.* New York: Routledge.

Erikson, E. (1963). Eight Ages of Man. In Erikson, *Childhood and society*, 2nd Edition. (pp. 247–274). New York: Norton.

Fagen, R. (1981). *Animal play behavior.* New York: Oxford University Press.

Fagen, R. (2005). Play, five evolutionary gates, and paths to art. In F. McMahon, D. Lytle, and B. Sutton-Smith (Eds.). *Play: An interdisciplinary synthesis. Play and Culture Studies,* 6 (pp. 9–42). Lanham, MD: University Press of America.

Flax, J. (1990). *Thinking fragments: Psychoanalysis, feminism, and postmodernism in the contemporary West.* Berkeley: University of California Press.

Garvey, C. (1990). *Play.* Cambridge, MA: Harvard University Press.

Gergen, K. (1995). The healthy, happy human wears many masks. In W. Anderson, (Ed.). *The truth about the truth: De-confusing and re-constructing the postmodern world.* (pp. 136–144). New York: Putnam.

Gergen, K. (2000). *The saturated self: Dilemmas of identity in contemporary life.* New York: Basic Books.

Groos, K. (1898). First published 1895. *The play of animals.* E. L. Baldwin (Trans.). New York: D. Appleton and Company.

Hans, J. (1981). *The play of the world.* Amherst, MA: University of Massachusetts Press.

Henricks, T. (2006). *Play reconsidered: Sociological perspectives on human expression.* Urbana, IL: University of Illinois.

Henricks, T. (2009a). Orderly and disorderly play: A comparison. *American Journal of Play. 2*(1): 12–40.

Henricks, T. (2009b). Play and the rhetorics of time: Progress, regression, and the meanings of the present. In D. Kuschner (Ed.), *From children to red hatters: Diverse images and issues of play (Play and Culture Studies,* vol. 8) pp. 14–38. New York: University Press of America.

Henricks, T. (2015). *Play and the human condition.* Urbana, IL: University of Illinois Press.

Huizinga, J. (1955). *Homo ludens: A study of the play-element in culture.* Boston: Beacon.

James, W. (1952). *Principles of psychology.* Chicago: Encyclopedia Britannica.

Jameson, F. (1984). Postmodernism: Or the cultural logic of late capitalism. *New Left Review* 146: 53–92.

Johnson, J., Christie, J., & Wardle, F. (2004). *Play, development, and early education.* New York: Pearson.

Kahler, E. (1956). *Man the measure: A new approach to history.* New York: George Braziller.

Kuchler, T. (1994). *Post-modern gaming: Heidegger, Duchamp, Derrida.* New York: Peter Lang.

Lancy, D. (2008). *The anthropology of childhood: Cherubs, chattel, changelings.* Cambridge: Cambridge University Press.

Lobman, C., & O'Neill, B. (Eds.). (2011). *Play and performance: Play and Culture Studies,* 11: New York: University Press.

Lyotard, J. (1986). *The postmodern condition: A report on knowledge.* Manchester: Manchester University Press.

Mead, G.H. (1964). *On social psychology.* A. Strauss (Ed.). Chicago: University of Chicago Press.

Newman, F., & Holzman, L. (2006). *Unscientific psychology: A cultural-performatory approach to understanding human life*, 2nd ed. New York: iUniverse, Inc.

Paley, V. (2005). *A child's work: The importance of fantasy play.* Chicago: University of Chicago Press.

Panksepp, J. (1998). *Affective neuroscience: The foundations of human and animal emotions.* New York: Oxford University Press.

Piaget, J. (1962). *Play, dreams, and imitation in childhood.* New York: W. W. Norton.

Power, T. (2005). *Play and exploration in children and animals.* Mahwah, NJ: Lawrence Erlbaum.

Roopnarine, J., Johnson, J., & Hooper, F. (Eds.). (1994). *Children's play in diverse cultures.* Albany, NY: State University of New York Press.

Rosenau, P. (1992). *Post-modernism and the social sciences: Insights, inroads, intrusions.* Princeton, NJ: Princeton University Press.

Schechner, R. (2002). *Performance studies: An introduction.* New York: Routledge.

Singer, D., & Singer. J.L. (1990). *The House of Make-Believe: Children's Play and the Developing Imagination*. Cambridge, MA: Harvard University Press.

Smith, P. (2010). *Children and play.* Malden, MA: Wiley-Blackwell.

Snow, C.P. (1961). The two cultures. In Snow, *The scientific revolution* (pp. 1–22). New York: Cambridge University Press.

Spariosu, M. (1989). *Dionysus reborn: Play and the aesthetic dimension in modern philosophical and scientific discourse.* Ithaca, NY: Cornell University Press.

Stevens, P. (2014). 40 years at play. Keynote address. The Association for the Study of Play. Rochester, NY. April 25, 2014.

Sutton-Smith, B. (1966). Piaget on play: A critique. *Psychological Review, 73*(1): 104–110.

Sutton-Smith, B. (1997). *The ambiguity of play.* Cambridge, MA: Harvard University Press.

Sutton-Smith, B. (2008). Play theory: A personal journey and new thoughts. *American Journal of Play, 1*(1): 80–123.

Sutton-Smith, B. and Kelly-Byrne, D. (1984). The phenomenon of bipolarity in play theories. In T. Yawkey and A. Pellegrini, (Eds.), *Child's play: Developmental and applied.* (pp. 29–47). Hillsdale, NJ: Lawrence Erlbaum.

Vygotsky, L. (1976). Play and its role in the mental development of the child. In J. Bruner, A Jolly, & K. Silva (Eds.), *Play: Its role in development and evolution* (pp. 537–554). Middlesex, England: Penguin Books.

Wardrip-Fruin, N. (2009). *Expressive Processing: Digital fictions, computer games, and software studies.* Cambridge, MA: MIT Press.

Wolf, M. (Ed) (2008). *The video game explosion: A history from Pong to Playstation and beyond.* Westport, CT: Greenwood.

Contributors

Monirah A. Al-Mansour is an Assistant Professor of Educational Policies and Early Childhood Education at King Saud University, Saudi Arabia. She teaches a range of courses related to play, approaches to early childhood education, and movement education. She has co-authored book chapters, conducted workshops, and presented research papers at national and international conferences on play from a cross-cultural perspective. She is an active member of TASP and NAEYC. Her research interests are open-ended play as a vehicle for creative expression for young children, the use of recycled items and reusable resources to enhance creativity, and children's play in nature. She is currently the Executive Director of the Global Play Conference in Riyadh titled *Children and Electronic and Traditional Games: A Futuristic and Educational Vision.*

Keith R. Alward is a well-known independent Piagetian scholar who received his Ph.D. from UC Berkeley in Educational and Developmental Psychology. He is writer and producer of *The Growing Mind*, a 2-hour video series available through the Jean Piaget Society and author of *Exploring Children's Thinking* and *Working with Children's Concepts.* Dr. Alward is also co-author of *Play at the Center of the Curriculum,* presently in its sixth edition. He is an active member of the Jean Piaget Society and The Association for the Study of Play.

Lynn E. Cohen is a Professor in the Department of Special Education and Literacy at Long Island University, C.W. Post. Dr. Cohen was a kindergarten and reading recovery teacher for the Great Neck Public Schools, and during the past 11 years she has trained more than 100 in-service teachers in early childhood curricula. Her research interests include play from a sociocultural perspective, school readiness, and theories of Mikhail Bakhtin. Dr. Cohen has published over 40 peer reviewed and practitioner articles, as well as book chapters dealing with dual language learners, play, vocabulary, and emergent literacy. She has co-edited with Sandra Waite Stupiansky *Play: A Polyphony of Research, Theories, and Issues, Play & Culture Studies, Volume 12* and *Learning Across the Early Childhood Curriculum, Advances in Early Education and Day Care,* Volume 17. In addition, she is preparing another co-edited book (with Sandra Waite Stupiansky) entitled, *Theories of Early Childhood Education: Developmental, Behaviorist, and Critical*, for Routledge Press.

Walter F. Drew is the founder of the Institute for Self Active Education and creator of Dr. Drew's Discovery Blocks. Since 1975 he has pioneered the development of reusable resource centers as a sustainable community building strategy that provides a wealth of open-ended materials for teachers to enrich play and learning with children and families. He serves as a facilitator for the *Play, Policy, and Practice Interest Forum* of NAEYC and the Reusable Resources Association. Walter is co-author of *From Play to Practice: Connecting Teachers' Play with Children's Learning* published by The National Association for the Education of Young Children.

Ann Marie Guilmette is retired from the Department of Recreation and Leisure Studies, and the Women's Studies Program at Brock University. Ann Marie completed a Ph.D. in social psychology from the University of Windsor in 1980. She studied such adult forms of play as leisure, humor, astrology, and gambling. Her undergraduate and graduate Master degrees were in Physical and Health Education. At Brock, she taught courses in play and culture, foundations of leisure studies, the social psychology of leisure and recreation, therapeutic benefits of humor, leisure education, and leisure research. Dr. Guilmette conducted community-based action research with a focus on adult leisure. Her scholarship resulted in a multitude of academic presentations, publications, and reports on play, games, sport, recreation, gambling, and humor in cultural contexts, especially for socially disadvantaged and de-valued populations, with a special interest in First Nations, immigrants, the poor, people with disabilities, seniors, and women. She served on the Board of Directors for the Ontario Problem Gambling Research Centre, and is a Past-President of the International Society for Humor Studies (ISHS), the Brock University Faculty Association (BUFA), and The Association for the Study of Play (TASP). In 1989 and 2007, she served as TASP President, and organized TASP conferences at Berkley (1988), New Mexico (2005), and at Brock in Canada (2006). She was acknowledged in Phil Stevens' article in the *International Journal of Play* as a founding scholar member of TASP, and in 2009 received TASP's Brian Sutton-Smith Play Scholar Career Achievement Award.

Mia Heikkilä is senior lecturer and researcher in education at the School of Education, Culture, and Communication at Mälardalen University in Västerås, Sweden. Her research interests are gender in preschool, play and learning, and gender equality in society. Her recent publications are *Don't Be Such a Baby! Competence and Age as Intersectional Co-Markers on Children's Gender* and *Lärande Och Jämställdhet I Förskola Och* Skola, a research based textbook on gender equality issues in preschool and compulsory school in Sweeden.

Thomas Henricks is Danieley Professor of Sociology and Distinguished University Professor at Elon University in the United States. Much of his scholarship has focused on the nature of human play, particularly as that activity can be contrasted to other pathways for human expression, including ritual, communitas, and work. More generally, he studies how experience and self-awareness are socially and culturally constructed. He is the author of numerous writings on play, many of which have appeared in *The American Journal of Play* and in *Play and Culture Studies*. His books include *Disputed Pleasures: Sport and Society in Preindustrial England*; *Play Reconsidered: Sociological Perspectives on Human Expression*; and *Selves, Societies, and Emotions: Understanding the Pathways of Experience*. Another book, *Play and the Human Condition,* was published in Spring 2015. He is also a co-editor of the new *Handbook of the Study of Play*. He serves on the editorial boards of the *American Journal of Play* and the *International Journal of Play*.

Olga S. Jarrett is Professor Emerita of Early Childhood Education and Science Education at Georgia State University (GSU). Her teaching/research interests include child development, research methods, science education, science inquiry, teacher/student empowerment, anti-bully strategies, and play. She is a past president of The Association for the Study of Play, past chair of the Peace Education Special Interest Group of the American Educational Research Association, and a past president of the American Association for the Child's Right to Play (IPA/USA), an organization that supports ratification of the Convention on the Rights of the Child. Dr. Jarrett is recipient of The Association for the Study of Play's Brian Sutton-Smith Play Scholar Award (2010) and the GSU Martin Luther King Torch of Peace Award (2014). She is author of *Drawing on the Child's World: Science Made Relevant* (2013) and co-author of *In the Service of Learning and Empowerment: Service-learning, Critical Pedagogy, and the Problem-Solution Project* (2014).

James E. Johnson is professor and program coordinator of early childhood education at the Pennsylvania State University in University Park, PA. He is currently a USA representative on the Scientific Committee of the International Council for Children's Play, and continues to serve on the Board of The Association for the Study of Play as a Past President and Publications Editor. He is recently co-editor of *International Perspectives on Children's Play* and the *Handbook of the Study of Play*. He serves as Interest Forum co-facilitator of Play, Policies, and Practices of the National Association for the Education of Young Children.

Marcia L. Nell is Associate Professor of Education at Millersville University in Millersville, PA, where she teaches graduate and undergraduate early childhood education courses and supervises student teachers. She serves as the Director of Research for the Institute for Self Active Education as well as a facilitator for the *Play, Policy & Practice Interest Forum* of NAEYC. Marcia is co-author of *From Play to Practice: Connecting Teachers' Play with Children's Learning* published by The National Association for the Education of Young Children.

Michael M. Patte is a Professor of Teaching and Learning at Bloomsburg University of Pennsylvania where he prepares undergraduate and graduate students for careers in education. During his 25-year career he developed an interest in the fields of creativity, child development, early childhood education, and play and has shared his scholarship through publications, international and national conference presentations, and advocacy projects. His latest co-authored/edited books include *Beyond the Classroom Walls: Developing Mindful Home, School, and Community Partnerships* (2016) and *International Perspectives on Children's Play* (2015). Dr. Patte is a Distinguished Fulbright Scholar, Co-editor of the International Journal of Play, past president of The Association for the Study of Play, board member of The International Council for Children's Play, and a member of the Pennsylvania Governor's Early Learning Council, responsible for planning the expansion of effective early learning and development services for Pennsylvania's young children and families.

Serap Sevimli-Celik is an Assistant Professor of Early Childhood Education at the Middle East Technical University, Turkey. She teaches a range of courses related to movement, play, creativity, visual arts, and material development. A focus of her research interests have been movement education and play in early years, in-service and pre-service teacher education, and environmental designs for active play. Her recent research investigates pre-service teachers' competence using movement education while working with young children. She is currently working on a book chapter about active designs for movement in early childhood education.

Phillips Stevens, Jr. is Associate Professor of Anthropology at the State University of New York at Buffalo. He received his B.A. in English from Yale in 1963, then went to Nigeria with the Peace Corps. Dr. Stevens received his Ph.D. in anthropology in 1973, with a dissertation based on research in a different area of Nigeria. He has conducted subsequent anthropological research in West Africa and the Caribbean. Dr. Stevens is the author of many publications, and the recipient of two awards for excellence in teaching and an African chieftaincy title. He was a founder of TASP in 1973-74, and President 1977-78.

John A. Sutterby is an Associate Professor in the Department of Interdisciplinary Learning and Teaching at The University of Texas San Antonio. He teaches courses such on play, creativity and learning, and advanced studies in play. He has been active in The Association for the Study of Play for more than a decade, twice serving as president of the organization. He is also the series editor for *Advances in Early Education and Day Care* published by Emerald Publications. His research interests include play environments, play and social justice, and play and language development.

Vicki Thomas wrote an extended essay *A Sociology of Fashion and Design* at the London School of Economics, and then went on to study for her Masters at the Royal College of Art and Victoria & Albert Museum. Her dissertation focused on the commercialization of Marcel Mauss's Gift Exchange process. This then led her to found a specialist gift design consultancy called Vicki Thomas Associates. She is also an alumnus of the Toy Design & Making Course at the London College of Furniture. Her research examines the relationships between social processes and creative design practice. Vicki currently teaches at The University of Northampton, and works with the University's Design Research Group exploring issues about making in the digital era, as well as, continuing to develop an understanding of the creative benefits of play – in theory and in practice.

Sandra Waite-Stupiansky recently retired as Professor of Early Childhood and Reading at Edinboro University. Her research interests include recess in elementary schools, play, and all areas of child development. She was the managing editor of *Play, Policy, and Practice Connections,* an online publication of the *Play, Policy, and Practice Interest Forum* of the National Association for the Education of Young Children from 1995-2013. Recently, she co-edited two books with Lynn Cohen: *Play: A Polyphony of Research, Theories, and Issues, Play & Culture Studies, Volume 12* and *Learning*

Across the Early Childhood Curriculum: Advances in Early Education and Day Care, Volume 17. Another recent project was joining the writing team for the 6th edition of *Play at the Center of the Curriculum* (2015). Dr. Waite-Stupiansky is the co-editor, along with Dr. Lynn Cohen of an upcoming book on early childhood curriculum entitled, *Theories of Early Childhood Education: Developmental, Behaviorist, and Critical*, due to be published in 2016 by Routledge Press.

Index

191